FIFTH EDITION

The Humanistic Tradition

Book 6

Modernism, Globalism, and the
Information Age

FIFTH EDITION

The Humanistic Tradition

Book 6

Modernism, Globalism, and the
Information Age

Gloria K. Fiero

Boston   Burr Ridge, IL   Dubuque, IA   Madison, WI   New York
San Francisco   St. Louis   Bangkok   Bogotá   Caracas   Kuala Lumpur
Lisbon   London   Madrid   Mexico City   Milan   Montreal   New Delhi
Santiago   Seoul   Singapore   Sydney   Taipei   Toronto

Higher Education

THE HUMANISTIC TRADITION, BOOK 6

MODERNISM, GLOBALISM, AND THE INFORMATION AGE

Published by McGraw-Hill, a business unit of The McGraw-Hill Companies, Inc.
1221 Avenue of the Americas, New York, NY, 10020.

This book is printed on acid-free paper.

1 2 3 4 5 6 7 8 9 0 DOW/DOW 0 9 8 7 6 5

Library of Congress Cataloging-in-Publication Data

Fiero, Gloria K.
  The humanistic tradition / Gloria K. Fiero.– 5th ed.
    p. cm.
  Includes bibliographical references and indexes.
  ISBN 0-07-291007-0 – ISBN 0-07-291009-7
  1. Civlization, Western–History–Textbooks. 2. Humanism–History–Textbooks. I.
Title.

CB245.F47 2006
909'.09821–dc22

2005052239

ISBN 0-07-291023-2

Permissions Acknowledgments appear on page 171,
and on this page by reference.

Publisher: *Lyn Uhl*
Director of Development: *Lisa Pinto*
Marketing manager: *Zina Craft*
Media technology producer: *Shannon Gattens*
Editorial Assistant: *Elizabeth Sigal*
Managing Editor: *Jean Dal Porto*
Production supervisor: *Randy Hurst*
Typeface: *10/12 Goudy*
Printer: *RR Donnelley, Willard*

http://www.mhhe.com

This book was designed and produced by
Laurence King Publishing Ltd., London
www.laurenceking.co.uk

Commissioning Editor: *Melanie White*
Picture researcher: *Fiona Kinnear*
Designer: *Ian Hunt*

Front cover
Main image: Cai Guo-Qiang, *Inopportune*,
stage 1, 2005. Mixed media. Location:
Massachusetts Museum of Contemporary
Art Photo: Courtesy Cai Guo Qiang Studio

Inset: Ceremonial mask, from Wobé or
Grebo, Ivory Coast, late nineteenth century.
Painted wood, feathers, and fibers,
height 11 in. Musée de l'Homme, Paris.
Photo: © R.M.N., Paris.

Frontispiece: Detail of Jean-Michel Basquiat,
Horn Players, 1983. Acrylic and mixed
media on canvas, 8 ft. x 6 ft. 3 in. The Broad
Art Foundation, Santa Monica. Photograph
© Douglas M. Parker Studio, Los Angeles.
© ADAFGP, Paris and DACS, London
2005.

Series Contents

Book 6 Contents

MAPS

MUSIC LISTENING SELECTIONS

CD Two Selections 17 to 26

Preface

"It's the most curious thing I ever saw in all my life!" exclaimed Lewis Carroll's Alice in Wonderland, as she watched the Cheshire Cat slowly disappear, leaving only the outline of a broad smile. "I've often seen a cat without a grin, but a grin without a cat!" A student who encounters an ancient Greek epic, a Yoruba mask, or a Mozart opera—lacking any context for these works—might be equally baffled. It may be helpful, therefore, to begin by explaining how the artifacts (the "grin") of the humanistic tradition relate to the larger and more elusive phenomenon (the "cat") of human culture.

The Humanistic Tradition and the Humanities

In its broadest sense, the term *humanistic tradition* refers to humankind's cultural legacy—the sum total of the significant ideas and achievements handed down from generation to generation. This tradition is the product of responses to conditions that have confronted all people throughout history. Since the beginnings of life on earth, human beings have tried to ensure their own survival by achieving harmony with nature. They have attempted to come to terms with the inevitable realities of disease and death. They have endeavored to establish ways of living collectively and communally. And they have persisted in the desire to understand themselves and their place in the universe. In response to these ever-present and universal challenges—*survival, communality,* and *self-knowledge*—human beings have created and transmitted the tools of science and technology, social and cultural institutions, religious and philosophic systems, and various forms of personal expression, the sum total of which we call *culture.*

Even the most ambitious survey cannot assess all manifestations of the humanistic tradition. This book therefore focuses on the creative legacy referred to collectively as *the humanities*: literature, philosophy, history (in its literary dimension), architecture, the visual arts (including photography and film), music, and dance. Selected examples from each of these disciplines constitute our *primary sources*. Primary sources (that is, works original to the age that produced them) provide first-hand evidence of human inventiveness and ingenuity. The primary sources in this text have been chosen on the basis of their authority, their beauty, and their enduring value. They are, simply stated, the great works of their time and, in some cases, of all time. Universal in their appeal, they have been transmitted from generation to generation.

Such works are, as well, the landmark examples of a specific time and place: they offer insight into the ideas and values of the society in which they were produced. *The Humanistic Tradition* joins "the grin" to "the cat" by examining them within their political, economic, and social contexts.

The humanities are the legacy of a given culture's values, ambitions, and beliefs. Poetry, painting, philosophy, and music are not, generally speaking, products of unstructured leisure or indulgent individuality; rather, they are tangible expressions of the human quest for the good (one might even say the "complete") life. Throughout history, these forms of expression have served the domains of the sacred, the ceremonial, and the communal. And even in the early days of the twenty-first century, as many time-honored traditions come under assault, the arts retain their power to awaken our imagination in the quest for survival, communality, and self-knowledge.

The Scope of the Humanistic Tradition

The humanistic tradition is not the exclusive achievement of any one geographic region, race, or class. For that reason, this text assumes a global and multicultural rather than exclusively Western perspective. At the same time, Western contributions are emphasized, first, because the audience for these books is predominantly Western, but also because in recent centuries the West has exercised a dominant influence on the course and character of global history. Since, the humanistic tradition belongs to all of humankind, the best way to understand the Western contribution to that tradition is to examine it in the arena of world culture.

As a survey, *The Humanistic Tradition* cannot provide an exhaustive analysis of our creative legacy. The critical reader will discover many gaps. Some aspects of culture that receive extended examination in traditional Western humanities surveys have been pared down to make room for the too often neglected contributions of Islam, Africa, and Asia. This book is necessarily selective—it omits many major figures and treats others only briefly. Primary sources are arranged, for the most part, chronologically, but they are presented as manifestations of the informing ideas of the age in which they were produced. The intent is to examine the evidence of the humanistic tradition thematically and topically, rather than to compile a series of mini-histories of the individual arts.

Studying the Humanistic Tradition

To study the creative record is to engage in a dialogue with the past, one that brings us face to face with the values of our ancestors, and, ultimately, with our own. This dialogue is (or should be) a source of personal revelation and delight; like Alice in Wonderland, our strange, new encounters will be enriched according to the degree of curiosity and patience we bring to them. Just as lasting friendships with special people are cultivated by extended familiarity, so our appreciation of a painting, a play, or a symphony depends on close attention and repeated contact. There are no shortcuts to the study of the humanistic tradition, but there are some techniques that may be helpful. It is useful, for instance, to approach each primary source from the triple perspective of its text, its context, and its subtext.

TEXT

The *text* of any primary source refers to its *medium* (that is, what it is made of), its *form* (its outward shape), and its *content* (the subject it describes).

LITERATURE   Whether intended to be spoken or lead, literature depends on the medium of words—the American poet Robert Frost once defined literature as "performance in words." Literary form varies according to the manner in which words are arranged. So poetry, which shares with music and dance rhythmic organization, may be distinguished from prose, which normally lacks regular rhythmic pattern. The main purpose of prose is to convey information, to narrate, and to describe; poetry, by its freedom from conventional patterns of grammar, provides unique opportunities for the expression of intense emotions. Philosophy (the search for truth through reasoned analysis) and history (the record of the past) make use of prose to analyze and communicate ideas and information. In literature, as in most kinds of expression, content and form are usually interrelated. The subject matter or the form of a literary work determines its *genre*. For instance, a long narrative poem recounting the adventures of a hero constitutes an *epic*, while a formal, dignified speech in praise of a person or thing constitutes a *eulogy*.

THE VISUAL ARTS   The *visual arts*—painting, sculpture, architecture, and photography—employ a wide variety of media, such as wood, clay, colored pigments, marble, granite, steel, and (more recently) plastic, neon, film, and computers. The form or outward shape of a work of art depends on the manner in which the artist manipulates the formal elements of color, line, texture, and space. Unlike words, these formal elements lack denotative meaning. The artist may manipulate form to describe and interpret the visible world (as in such genres as portraiture and landscape painting); to generate fantastic and imaginative kinds of imagery; or to create imagery that is non-representational—without identifiable subject matter. In general, however, the visual arts are spatial; that is, they operate and are apprehended in space.

MUSIC AND DANCE   The medium of *music* is sound. Like literature, music is durational: it unfolds over the period of time in which it occurs. The formal elements of music are melody, rhythm, harmony, and tone color—elements that also characterize the oral life of literature. As with the visual arts, the formal elements of music are without symbolic content: literature, painting, and sculpture may imitate or describe nature, but music is almost always nonrepresentational—it rarely has meaning beyond the sound itself. For that reason, music is the most difficult of the arts to describe in words. It is also (in the view of some) the most affective of the arts. Dance, the artform that makes the human body itself a medium of expression, resembles music in that it is temporal and performance-oriented. Like music, dance exploits rhythm as a formal tool, but, like painting and sculpture, it unfolds in space as well as time.

In analyzing the text of a work of literature, art, or music, we ask how its formal elements contribute to its meaning and affective power. We examine the ways in which the artist manipulates medium and form to achieve a characteristic manner of execution and expression that we call *style*. And we try to determine the extent to which a style reflects the personal vision of the artist and the spirit of his or her time and place. Comparing the styles of various artworks from a single era, we may discover that they share certain defining features and characteristics. Similarities (both formal and stylistic) between, for instance, golden age Greek temples and Greek tragedies, between Chinese lyric poems and landscape paintings, and between postmodern fiction and pop sculpture, prompt us to seek the unifying moral and aesthetic values of the cultures in which they were produced.

CONTEXT

We use the word *context* to describe the historical and cultural environment. To determine the context, we ask: in what time and place did the artifact originate? How did it function within the society in which it was created? Was the purpose of the piece decorative, didactic, magical, propagandistic? Did it serve the religious or political needs of the community? Sometimes our answers to these questions are mere guesses. Nevertheless, understanding the function of an artifact often serves to clarify the nature of its form (and vice versa). For instance, much of the literature produced prior to the fifteenth century was spoken or sung rather than read; for that reason, such literature tends to feature repetition and rhyme, devices that facilitate memorization. We can assume that literary works embellished with frequent repetitions, such as the *Epic of Gilgamesh* and the Hebrew Bible, were products of an oral tradition. Determining the original function of an artwork also permits us to assess its significance in its own time and place: the paintings on the walls of Paleolithic caves, which are among the most compelling animal illustrations in the history of world art, are not "artworks" in the modern sense of the term but, rather, magical signs that accompanied hunting rituals, the performance of which was essential to the survival of the community. Understanding the relationship between text and context is one of the principal concerns of any inquiry into the humanistic tradition.

SUBTEXT

The *subtext* of the literary or artistic object refers to its secondary and implied meanings. The subtext embraces the emotional or intellectual messages embedded in, or implied by, a work of art. The epic poems of the ancient Greeks, for instance, which glorify prowess and physical courage in battle, suggest that such virtues are exclusively male. The state portraits of the seventeenth-century French ruler Louis XIV carry the subtext of unassailable and absolute power. In our own century, Andy Warhol's serial adaptations of soup cans and Coca-Cola bottles offer wry commentary on the supermarket mentality of postmodern American culture. Identifying the implicit message of an artwork helps us to determine the values and customs of the age in which it was produced and to assess those values against others.

Beyond *The Humanistic Tradition*

This book offers only small, enticing samples from an enormous cultural buffet. To dine more fully, students are encouraged to go beyond the sampling presented at this table; and for the most sumptuous feasting, nothing can substitute for first-hand experience. Students, therefore, should make every effort to supplement this book with visits to art museums and galleries, concert halls, theaters, and libraries. *The Humanistic Tradition* is designed for students who may or may not be able to read music, but who surely are able to cultivate an appreciation of music in performance. The music logos ♪ that appear in the margins of the text refer to the Music Listening Selections found on two accompanying compact discs, available from the publishers. Lists of suggestions for further reading are included at the end of each book, while a selected general bibliography of electronic humanities resources appears in the Online Learning Center at http://www.mhhe.com/fierotht5.

The Fifth Edition

In the fifth edition of *The Humanistic Tradition*, Study Questions follow each primary source readings; thse are desinged to provoke thought and discussion. Chapter 37 has been reorganized and expanded to explore a number of important global themes, such as ethnic identity and ecology. There is a reading selection from the Book of Psalms, a new modern translation of the *Quran*, and excerpts from the writings of Annie Dillard, E.O Wilson, Sandra Cisneros, Mahmoud Darwish, and Yehuda Amichai. Content has been expanded to a number of topics, including the life of Muhammad (Chapter 10), the Columbian Exchange (Chapter 18), artists' optical aids (Chapters 17 and 23), Islam since 1500 (Chapters 21, 35, 37), the training of female artists (Chapters 20 and 23, and the Middle Passage (Chapter 25). Among the new color illustrations for the fifth edition are Zoser's Pyramid, Nok sculpture, London's new Globe Theater, Bernini's *David*, Steen's *Drawing Lesson*, Hick's *Peaceabie Kingdom*, Monet's Japanese Bridge, and Beardon's Empress of the Blues. This edition also updates the contemporary scene to include significant developments in architecture, photography, and film (Chapter 38). Two new Sony Music Listening CDs illustrate the muscial works discussed in the text, and new Music Listening Guides provide helpful analyses of these selections. Revised and expanded Timelines and Glossaries, along with Science and Technology boxes, locator maps, and pedagogical resources provide useful study aids (see the "Guided Tour" on page xii). Updated suggestions for additional reading appear at the end of each book, rather than by chapter.

A Note to Instructors

The key to successful classroom use of *The Humanistic Tradition* is *selectivity*. Although students may be assigned to read whole chapters that focus on a topic or theme, as well as complete works that supplement the abridged readings, the classroom should be the stage for a selective treatment of a single example or a set of examples. The organization of this textbock is designed to emphasize themes that cut across geographic boundaries—themes whose universal significance prompts students to evaluate and compare rather than simply memorize and repeat lists of names and places. To assist readers in achieving global cultural literacy, every effort has been made to resist isolating (or "ghettoizing") individual cultures and to avoid the inevitable biases we bring to our evaluation of relatively unfamiliar cultures.

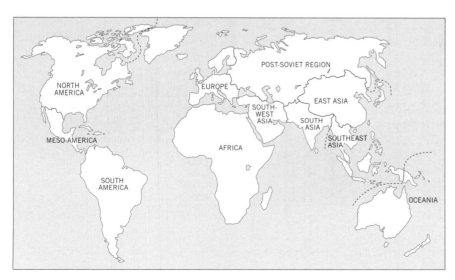

Key Map Indicating Areas Shown as White Highlights on the Locator Maps

Acknowledgments

Writing *The Humanistic Tradition* has been an exercise in humility. Without the assistance of learned friends and colleagues, assembling a book of this breadth would have been an impossible task. James H. Dormon read all parts of the manuscript and made extensive and substantive editorial suggestions; as his colleague, best friend, and wife, I am most deeply indebted to him.

The following colleagues generously shared their knowledge and training in matters of content: in the sciences, Barbara J. Reeves (Virginia Tech); literature, Robert W. Butler, Darrell Bourque (University of Louisiana, Lafayette), and John Lowe (Louisiana State University); in the visual arts, Roy Barineau (Tallahassee Community College); music, Richard Harrison, Stephen Husarik (University of Arkansas), and Jack Jacobs; film, Joseph Warfield (New York University).

In the preparation of the fifth edition, I have also benefited from the suggestions and comments generously offered by Linda A. Austin (Glendale Community College), Edward Bonahue (Santa Fe Community College), Diane Boze (Northeastern State University), Peggy Brown (Collin County Community College), Michael Coste (Front Range Community College), Harry Coverston (University of Central Florida), Jaymes Dudding (Albuquerque Technical Vocational Institute), Scott Earle (Tacoma Community College), Joshua Fausty (New Jersey City University), Luis Samuel Gonzalez (Sinclair Community College), Jeanne McGlinn (University of North Carolina—Asheville), Khadijah O. Miller (Norfolk State University), Yvonne Milspaw (Harrisburg Area Community College), Thomas R. Moore (Maine Maritime Academy), Rachel M. Rumberger (Valencia Community College), Jerome P. Soneson (University of Northern Iowa), Sonia Sorrell (Pepperdine University), Nancy A. Taylor (California State University—Northridge), Mary Tripp (University of Central Florida), and Naomi Yavneh (University of South Florida).

The burden of preparing the fifth edition has been lightened by the assistance of Kristen N. Mellit (McGraw-Hill) and the editors at Laurence King Publishing. I am also indebted to Lyn Uhl, Lisa Pinto, and Elizabeth Sigal (McGraw-Hill) for their support and encouragement, and to Fiona Kinnear for discerning photographic research.

A Guided Tour of *The Humanistic Tradition*, FIFTH EDITION

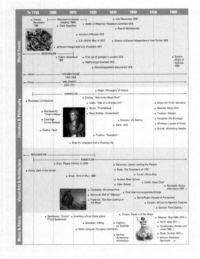

Illustrated part-opening **TIMELINES** provide a chronological overview of major historical events, as well as key works of literature, art, and music featured in each part.

Science and Technology

2650 B.C.E.	Pharaoh Khufu (or Cheops) orders construction of the Great Pyramid of Gizeh†
1500 B.C.E.	Egyptians employ a simple form of the sundial
1450 B.C.E.	the water clock is devised in Egypt
1400 B.C.E.	glass in produced in Egypt and Mesopotamia

†All dates in this chapter are approximate

SCIENCE AND TECHNOLOGY BOXES offer a chronology of key scientific and technological developments.

READING 4.7 From Donne's *Meditation 17* (1623)

All mankind is of one author, and is one volume; when one man   1
dies, one chapter is not torn out of the book, but translated into
a better language; and every chapter must be so translated. God
employs several translators; some pieces are translated by age,
some by sickness, some by war, some by justice; but God's hand   5
is in every translation, and his hand shall bind up all our
scattered leaves again for that library where every book shall lie
open to one another. As therefore the bell that rings to a
sermon calls not upon the preacher only but upon the
congregation to come, so this bell calls us all. . . . No man is an   10
island entire of itself; every man is a piece of the continent, a
part of the main. If a clod be washed away by the sea, Europe is
the less, as well as if a promontory were, as well as if a manor
of thy friend's or of thine own were. Any man's death diminishes
me, because I am involved in mankind, and therefore never send   15
to know for whom the bell tolls; it tolls for thee.

 Q. What three metaphors are invoked in *Meditation 17*?

PRIMARY SOURCE READINGS from a variety of genres provide a wealth of important and influential writings. New to the fifth edition, study questions designed to provoke thought and discussion follow each primary source reading.

GLOSSARY

asceticism strict self-denial and self-discipline

bodhisattva (Sanskrit, "one whose essence is enlightenment") a being who has postponed his or her own entry into *nirvana* in order to assist others in reaching that goal; worshiped as a deity in Mahayana Buddhism

Messiah Anointed One, or Savior; in Greek, *Christos*

rabbi a teacher and master trained in the Jewish law

sutra (Sanskrit, "thread") an instructional chapter or discourse in any of the sacred books of Buddhism

Terms marked in bold are defined in a **GLOSSARY** at the end of each chapter.

 **MUSICAL LOGOS** in the margins refer to the Music Listening Selections found on accompanying compact disks, available separately from the publisher.

LOCATOR MAPS give readers their geographical bearings, alerting them to where events discussed in the section to follow took place.

EXPERIMENTAL FILM

Léger produced one of the earliest and most influential abstract films in the history of motion pictures. Developed in collaboration with the American journalist Dudley Murphy, *Ballet mécanique* (*Mechanical Ballet*, 1923–1924) puts into motion a series of abstract shapes and mundane objects (such as bottles and kitchen utensils), which, interspersed with human elements, convey a playful but dehumanized sense of everyday experience. The rhythms and juxtapositions of the images suggest—without any narrative—the notion of modern life as mechanized, routine, standardized, and impersonal. The repeated image of a laundry woman, for instance, alternating with that of a rotating machine part, plays on the associative qualities of visual motifs in ways that would influence film-makers for decades.

FILM ESSAYS explore various aspects of this important, relatively new medium.

Supplements for the Instructor and the Student

A number of useful supplements are available to instructors and students using *The Humanistic Tradition*. Please contact your sales representative to obtain these resources, or to ask for further details.

ONLINE LEARNING CENTER A complete set of web-based resources for *The Humanistic Tradition* can be found at www.mhhe.com/fierotht5.com. Materials for students include an audio pronunciation guide, self-tests, interactive maps, links to relevant images and complete primary source readings. Instructors will benefit from discussion and lecture suggestions, chapter summaries, music listening guides, and other resources. All resources from the Online Learning Center are also available in cartridges for WebCT and Blackboard course management systems.

INSTRUCTOR'S RESOURCE CD-ROM The Instructor's Resource CD-ROM (IRCD) is designed to assist instructors as they plan and prepare for classes. Chapter summaries emphasize key themes and topics that give focus to the primary source readings. Music listening guides provide instructors with ideas for integrating selections on the Music Listening CDs into their courses. Study questions for each chapter can be used for student discussion or written assignments. A list of suggested videos, DVDs, and recordings is also included. The CD-ROM also offers a Test Bank containing a comprehensive bank of multiple-choice questions for use in constructing student exams.

EZ TEST McGraw-Hill's EZ Test, also included on the IRCD, is a flexible and easy-to-use electronic testing program that allows instructors to create book-specific tests, drawing from a ready-made database and/or designing their own questions. Tests can be exported for use with course management systems such as WebCT, BlackBoard or PageOut. The program is available for use with Windows and Macintosh.

CORE CONCEPTS A groundbreaking *Core Concepts in the Humanities* DVD-ROM may be packaged free with every new copy of *The Humanistic Tradition* (ISBN 0073136433). The DVD-ROM augments students' understanding of the humanities through multimedia presentations on visual art, dance, theater, film, literature, and music. With over eighty interactive exercises, timelines, and extensive video clips, the DVD-ROM allows students to explore these disciplines in an exciting way. Study materials such as outlines,

summaries, and self-correcting quizzes are provided for every chapter of the text. Contact your McGraw-Hill representative at www.mhhe.com/rep for information about packaging this program with the textbook.

MUSIC LISTENING COMPACT DISCS Two audio compact discs have been designed exclusively for use with T*he Humanistic Tradition*. CD One corresponds to the music listening selections discussed in Books 1-3 (Volume I), and CD Two contains the music in Books 4-6 (Volume II). Instructors may obtain copies of the recordings for classroom use and the CDs are also available for individual purchase by students. They can be packaged with any or all of the six books or two-volume versions of the text. Consult your local sales representative for details.

SLIDE SETS A set of book-specific slides is available to qualified adopters of *The Humanistic Tradition*. These slides have been especially selected to include many of the key images in the books. Additional slides are available for purchase directly from Universal Color Slides. For further information, consult our web site at www.mhhe.com/fierotht5.com.

IMAGE VAULT Selected images from *The Humanistic Tradition*'s illustration program are available to adopting instructors in digital format in *The Image Vault*, McGraw-Hill's new web-based program. Instructors can incorporate images from *The Image Vault* in digital presentations that can be used in class offline, burned to CD-ROM, or embedded in course Web pages. See www.mhhe.com/theimage-vault for more details.

Detail from facade, Kandariya Mahadeva temple

PART 1

The Triumph of Modernism

Since the birth of civilization, no age broke with tradition more radically or more self-consciously than the twentieth century. In part, the modernist break with the past represented the willful rejection of former values, but it also registered the revolutionary effects of science and technology on all aspects of life. Among the swelling populations of modern cities, the pace of living became faster and more chaotic than ever before. At the same time, electronic technology began to transform the planet earth into what Canadian sociologist Marshall McLuhan called a "global village." In the global village of the twentieth century, communication between geographically remote parts of the world was almost instantaneous, and every new development—technological, ecological, political, and intellectual—potentially affected every villager. Social and geographic mobility, receptivity to change, and a self-conscious quest for the new, the different, and even the outrageous were the hallmarks of this largely secular and materialistic world community.

The metaphoric "shrinking" of the planet actually began at the end of the nineteenth century, with the invention of the telephone (1876), wireless telegraphy (1891), and the internal combustion engine (1897), which made possible the first automobiles. By 1903, the airplane joined the string of enterprises that ushered in an era of rapid travel and communication. Such technology was as revolutionary for the twentieth century as metallurgy was for

the fourth millennium B.C.E. However, while metallurgy fostered the birth of civilization, modern technology (machine guns, poison gas, and nuclear power) provided the tools for its self-destruction.

The end of the nineteenth century was a time of relative peace and optimistic faith in technological progress and human productivity. Throughout the world, however, sharp contrasts existed between rich and poor, between democratic and totalitarian ideologies, and between technologically backward and technologically advanced nations. As the powerful nations jockeyed for political and economic primacy, and as Europe and the United States continued to build their industrial and military might, few anticipated the possibility of armed conflict. In 1914, that possibility became a reality in the outbreak of the first of two world wars. The "Great War," the first total war in European history, ended forever the so-called "age of innocence." And by the end of World War II, in 1945, nothing would ever seem certain again.

The modern era—roughly the first half of the twentieth century—yielded a rich diversity of ideas and art styles. These are addressed thematically: in chapters that treat the modernist assault on tradition, Sigmund Freud's influential role in the culture of the twentieth century, the brutal impact of totalitarianism and two world wars, and finally, the arts at mid-century, as they reflect the alienation and anxiety that dominated the postwar era.

(opposite) **WILLEM DE KOONING**, *Woman and Bicycle*, 1952–1953. Oil on canvas, 6 ft. 4½ in. × 4 ft. 1 in. Whitney Museum of American Art, New York. Purchase 55.35. Photograph: Geoffrey Clements © 1998 Whitney Museum of American Art, New York. © Willem de Kooning Revocable Trust/ARS, New York and DACS, London 2005.

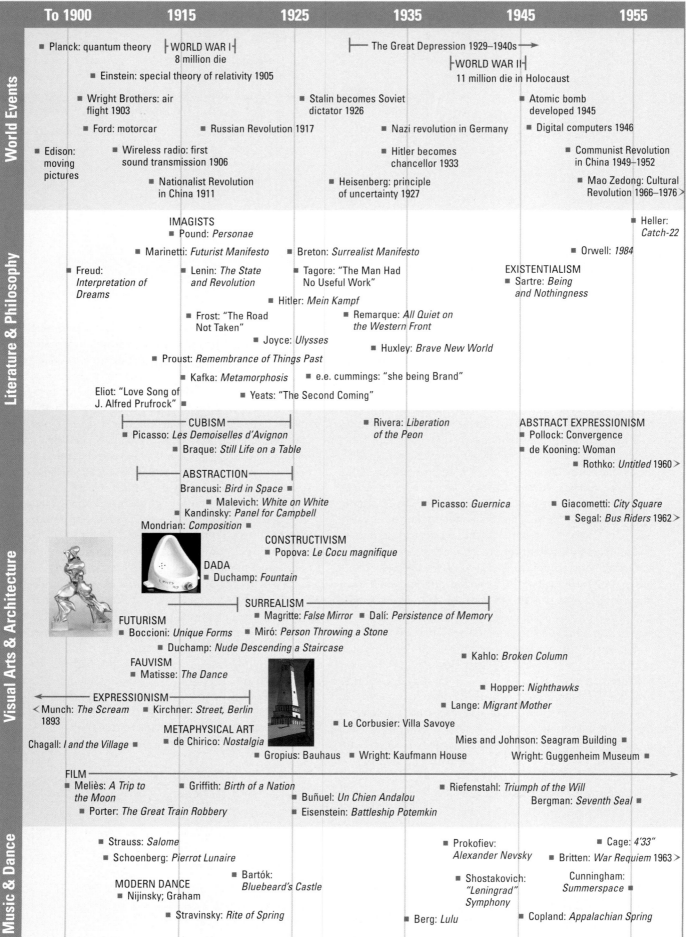

	To 1900	1915	1925	1935	1945	1955

World Events

- Planck: quantum theory
- ⊢WORLD WAR I⊣ 8 million die
- ⊢ The Great Depression 1929–1940s →
- Einstein: special theory of relativity 1905
- ⊢WORLD WAR II⊣ 11 million die in Holocaust
- Wright Brothers: air flight 1903
- Stalin becomes Soviet dictator 1926
- Atomic bomb developed 1945
- Ford: motorcar
- Russian Revolution 1917
- Nazi revolution in Germany
- Digital computers 1946
- Edison: moving pictures
- Wireless radio: first sound transmission 1906
- Hitler becomes chancellor 1933
- Communist Revolution in China 1949–1952
- Nationalist Revolution in China 1911
- Heisenberg: principle of uncertainty 1927
- Mao Zedong: Cultural Revolution 1966–1976 >

Literature & Philosophy

IMAGISTS
- Pound: *Personae*
- Heller: *Catch-22*
- Marinetti: *Futurist Manifesto*
- Breton: *Surrealist Manifesto*
- Orwell: *1984*
- Freud: *Interpretation of Dreams*
- Lenin: *The State and Revolution*
- Tagore: "The Man Had No Useful Work"
- EXISTENTIALISM
- Sartre: *Being and Nothingness*
- Hitler: *Mein Kampf*
- Frost: "The Road Not Taken"
- Remarque: *All Quiet on the Western Front*
- Joyce: *Ulysses*
- Huxley: *Brave New World*
- Proust: *Remembrance of Things Past*
- Kafka: *Metamorphosis*
- e.e. cummings: "she being Brand"
- Eliot: "Love Song of J. Alfred Prufrock"
- Yeats: "The Second Coming"

Visual Arts & Architecture

- ⊢CUBISM⊣
- Rivera: *Liberation of the Peon*
- ABSTRACT EXPRESSIONISM
- Picasso: *Les Demoiselles d'Avignon*
- Pollock: *Convergence*
- Braque: *Still Life on a Table*
- de Kooning: *Woman*
- Rothko: *Untitled* 1960 >
- ⊢ABSTRACTION⊣
- Brancusi: *Bird in Space*
- Malevich: *White on White*
- Picasso: *Guernica*
- Giacometti: *City Square*
- Kandinsky: *Panel for Campbell*
- Segal: *Bus Riders* 1962 >
- Mondrian: *Composition*
- CONSTRUCTIVISM
- Popova: *Le Cocu magnifique*
- DADA
- Duchamp: *Fountain*
- ⊢SURREALISM⊣
- Magritte: *False Mirror*
- Dalí: *Persistence of Memory*
- FUTURISM
- Miró: *Person Throwing a Stone*
- Boccioni: *Unique Forms*
- Duchamp: *Nude Descending a Staircase*
- Kahlo: *Broken Column*
- FAUVISM
- Matisse: *The Dance*
- Hopper: *Nighthawks*
- ← ⊢EXPRESSIONISM⊣
- Lange: *Migrant Mother*
- < Munch: *The Scream* 1893
- Kirchner: *Street, Berlin*
- Le Corbusier: Villa Savoye
- METAPHYSICAL ART
- de Chirico: *Nostalgia*
- Mies and Johnson: Seagram Building
- Chagall: *I and the Village*
- Gropius: Bauhaus
- Wright: Kaufmann House
- Wright: Guggenheim Museum
- FILM →
- Meliès: *A Trip to the Moon*
- Griffith: *Birth of a Nation*
- Riefenstahl: *Triumph of the Will*
- Buñuel: *Un Chien Andalou*
- Bergman: *Seventh Seal*
- Porter: *The Great Train Robbery*
- Eisenstein: *Battleship Potemkin*

Music & Dance

- Strauss: *Salome*
- Prokofiev: *Alexander Nevsky*
- Cage: *4'33"*
- Schoenberg: *Pierrot Lunaire*
- Britten: *War Requiem* 1963 >
- MODERN DANCE
- Bartók: *Bluebeard's Castle*
- Shostakovich: "Leningrad" Symphony
- Cunningham: *Summerspace*
- Nijinsky; Graham
- Stravinsky: *Rite of Spring*
- Berg: *Lulu*
- Copland: *Appalachian Spring*

CHAPTER 32

The Modernist Assault

*"What is real is not the external form,
but the essence of things."*
Constantin Brancusi

The New Physics

At the turn of the twentieth century, atomic physicists advanced a model of the universe that challenged the one Isaac Newton had provided two centuries earlier. Newton's universe operated according to smoothly functioning laws that generally corresponded with the world of sense perception. Modern physicists found, however, that at the physical extremes of nature—the microcosmic (the very small or very fast) realm of atomic particles and the macrocosmic world of heavy astronomical bodies—the laws of Newton's *Principia* did not apply. A more comprehensive model of the universe began to emerge began after 1880 when two American physicists, Albert Michelson and Edward Morley, determined that the speed of light is a universal constant. In 1900, the German physicist Max Planck (1858–1947) suggested that light waves sometimes behaved as *quanta*, that is, as separate and discontinuous bundles of energy. Alongside this and other groundbreaking work in *quantum physics* (as the field came to be called), yet another German physicist, Albert Einstein (1879–1955), made public his *special theory of relativity* (1905), a radically new approach to the new concepts of time, space, motion, and light. While Newton had held that objects preserved properties such as mass and length whether at rest or in motion, Einstein theorized that as an object's speed approached the speed of light, its mass increased and its length contracted; no object could move faster than light, and light did not require any medium to carry it. Time and space intervals (duration and length) could not be described as absolutes (as heretofore conceived), since they were relative to the motion of the observer. Following Einstein, Werner Heisenberg (1901–1976) theorized that since the very act of measuring subatomic phenomena altered them, the position and velocity of a subatomic particle could not be measured simultaneously with absolute accuracy. Heisenberg's *principle of uncertainty* (1927)—the more precisely the position of a particle is determined, the less precisely its momentum can be known—replaced the absolute and rationalist model of the universe with one whose exact mechanisms at the subatomic level are indeterminate.

Quantum physics gave humankind greater insight into the workings of the universe, but it also made the operation of that universe more remote from the average person's understanding. The basic components of nature—subatomic particles—were inaccessible to both the human eye and the camera, hence beyond the realm of the senses. Nevertheless, the practical implications of the new physics were immense: radar technology, computers, and consumer electronics were only three of its numerous long-range consequences. Atomic fission, the splitting of atomic particles (begun only after 1920), and the atomic bomb itself (first tested in 1945) confirmed the validity of Einstein's famous formula, $E=mc^2$, which shows that (in his words) "a very small amount of mass [matter] can be converted into a very large amount of energy." The new physics paved the way for the atomic age, but that age carried with it the possibility and the threat of total annihilation.

While Einstein challenged the established way of viewing the external world, the Austrian physician Sigmund Freud was proposing a new and equally revolutionary way of perceiving the internal, or subconscious, world of the human being (see chapter 33). And, as if to confirm Freud's darkest insights, in 1914 Europe embarked on the first of two wars, both of which used the potentially liberating tools of the new science to annihilate human life. World War I, more devastating than any previously fought on this planet, compounded the prevailing mood of insecurity and convinced many that the death of culture was at hand.

Early Twentieth-Century Poetry

The literature of the early twentieth century mirrored the mood of uncertainty. Unlike the romantics of the nineteenth century, early modern poets found in nature neither a source of ecstasy nor a means of personal redemption. Their poetry did not characterize human beings as heroic or inspired; rather, it described an indifferent cosmos, whose inhabitants might be insecure, questioning, and even perverse. While early twentieth-century poetry was less optimistic than romantic poetry, it was also less effusive and self-indulgent. Indeed, its lyric strains were frequently as discordant as those of early modern music and modern art.

The Imagists

Poets of the early twentieth century cultivated a language of expression that was as conceptual and abstract as that of modern physics. Like the nineteenth-century symbolists (see chapter 31), early twentieth-century poets rejected self-indulgent sentiment. They sought a more concentrated style that involved paring down the subject in order to capture its intrinsic or essential qualities—a process called **abstraction**. They rejected fixed meter and rhyme and wrote instead in a style of free verse that became notorious for its abrupt and discontinuous juxtaposition of lean images. Appropriately, these poets called themselves *imagists*. Led by the Americans Ezra Pound (1885–1972), Amy Lowell (1874–1925), and Hilda Doolittle (1886–1961), who signed her poems simply "H.D.," the imagists took as their goal the search for verbal compression, concentration, and economy of expression.

The American expatriate Ezra Pound was one of the most influential of the imagist poets. By the age of twenty-three, Pound had abandoned his study of language and literature at American universities for a career in writing that led him to Europe, where he wandered from England to France and Italy. A poet, critic, and translator, Pound was thoroughly familiar with the literature of his contemporaries. But he cast his net wide: he studied the prose and poetry of ancient Greece and Rome, China and Japan, medieval France and Renaissance Italy—often reading the work of literature in its original language. As a student of Oriental calligraphy, he drew inspiration from the sparseness and subtlety of Chinese characters. He was particu-

larly fascinated by the fact that the Chinese poetic line, which presented images without grammar or syntax, operated in the same intuitive manner that nature worked upon the human mind. It was this vitality that Pound wished to bring to poetry.

In Chinese and Japanese verse—especially in the Japanese poetic genre known as *haiku* (see chapter 21)—Pound found the key to his search for concentrated expression. Two *haiku*-like poems are to be found in the collection called *Personae*.

READING 6.1 From Pound's *Personae* (1926)

"In a Station of the Metro"
The apparition of these faces in the crowd;
Petals on a wet, black bough.

"The Bathtub"
As a bathtub lined with white porcelain,
When the hot water gives out or goes tepid,
So is the slow cooling of our chivalrous passion,
O my much praised but-not-altogether-satisfactory lady.

 Q In what ways are these poems abstract?
Q What are the key images?

Pound imitated the *haiku*-style succession of images to evoke subtle, metaphoric relationships between things. He conceived what he called the "rhythmical arrangement of words" to produce an emotional "shape." In the *Imagist Manifesto* (1913) and in various interviews, Pound outlined the cardinal points of the imagist doctrine: poets should use "absolutely no word that does not contribute to the presentation"; they should employ free verse rhythms "in sequence of the musical phrase." Ultimately, Pound summoned his contemporaries to cast aside traditional modes of Western versemaking and to "make it new"—a dictum allegedly scrawled on the bathtub of an ancient Chinese emperor. "Day by day," wrote Pound, "make it new/cut underbrush/pile the logs/keep it growing." The injunction to "make it new" became the rallying cry of modernism.

The imagist search for an abstract language of expression, which, as we shall see, loosely paralleled the visual artist's quest for absolute form, stood at the beginning of the modernist revolution in poetry. It also opened the door to a more concealed and elusive style of poetry, one that drew freely on the cornucopia of world literature and history. The poems that Pound wrote after 1920, particularly the *Cantos* (the unfinished opus on which Pound labored for fifty-five years), challenge the reader with foreign language phrases, obscene jokes, and arcane literary and historical allusions juxtaposed without connective tissue. These poems contrast sharply with the terse precision and eloquent purity of Pound's early imagist efforts.

Frost and Lyric Poetry

Not all of Pound's contemporaries heeded the imagist doctrine. Robert Frost (1874–1963), the best known and one of the most popular of American poets, offered an alternative to the highly abstract style of the modernists. While Frost rejected the romantic sentimentality of much nineteenth-century verse, he embraced the older tradition of Western lyric poetry. He wrote in metered verse and jokingly compared the modernist use of free verse to playing tennis without a net. Frost avoided dense allusions and learned references. In plain speech he expressed deep affection for the natural landscape and an abiding sympathy with the frailties of the human condition. He described American rural life as uncertain and enigmatic—at times, notably dark. "My poems," explained Frost, "are all set to trip the reader head foremost into the boundless." Frost's "The Road Not Taken" is written in the rugged and direct language that became the hallmark of his mature style. The poem exalts a profound individualism as well as a sparseness of expression in line with the modernist injunction to "make it new."

READING 6.2   Frost's "The Road Not Taken"
(1916)

Two roads diverged in a yellow wood,	1
And sorry I could not travel both	
And be one traveler, long I stood	
And looked down one as far as I could	
To where it bent in the undergrowth;	5
Then took the other, as just as fair,	
And having perhaps the better claim,	
Because it was grassy and wanted wear,	
Though as for that the passing there	
Had worn them really about the same,	10
And both that morning equally lay	
In leaves no step had trodden black.	
Oh, I kept the first for another day!	
Yet knowing how way leads on to way,	
I doubted if I should ever come back.	15
I shall be telling this with a sigh	
Somewhere ages and ages hence:	
Two roads diverged in a wood, and I—	
I took the one less traveled by,	
And that has made all the difference.	20

Q Why might Frost's choice of roads have made "all the difference"?

Q How does the poem illustrate Frost's fondness for direct language?

Early Twentieth-Century Art

As with modernist poetry, the art of the early twentieth century came to challenge all that preceded it. Liberated by the camera from the necessity of imitating nature, **avant-garde** painters and sculptors turned their backs on the tyranny of representation. They pioneered an authentic, "stripped down" style that, much like imagist poetry, *evoked* rather than *described* experience. Like the imagists, visual artists might abstract the intrinsic qualities and essential meanings of their subject matter to arrive at a concentrated emotional experience. The language of pure form did not, however, rob art of its humanistic dimension; rather, it provided artists with a means by which to move beyond traditional ways of representing the visual world. Abstraction—one of the central tenets of modernism—promised to purify nature so as to come closer to its true reality.

Early modern artists probed the tools and techniques of formal expression more fully than any artists since the Renaissance. They challenged the role of art as illusion and broadened Western conceptions of the meaning and value of art. Exploring unconventional media, they created art that blurred the boundaries between painting and sculpture. And, like the imagists, they found inspiration in the arts of non-Western cultures; primitivism, abstraction, and experimentation were hallmarks of the modernist revolt against convention and tradition.

Picasso and the Birth of Cubism

The giant of twentieth-century art was the Spanish-born Pablo Picasso (1881–1973). During his ninety-two-year life, Picasso worked in almost every major art style of the century, some of which he himself inaugurated. He produced thousands of paintings, drawings, sculptures, and prints—a body of work that in its size, inventiveness, and influence, is nothing short of phenomenal. As a child, he showed an extraordinary gift for drawing, and by the age of twenty his precise and lyrical line style rivaled that of Raphael and Ingres. In 1903, the young painter left his native Spain to settle in Paris. There, in the bustling capital of the Western art world, he came under the influence of impressionist and postimpressionist painting, taking as his subjects café life, beggars, prostitutes, and circus folk. Much like the imagists, Picasso worked to refine form and color in the direction of concentrated expression, reducing the colors of his palette first to various shades of blue and then, after 1904, to tones of rose. By 1906, the artist began to abandon traditional Western modes of pictorial representation. Adopting the credo that art must be subversive—that it must defy all that is conventional, literal, and trite—he initiated a bold new style. That style was shaped by two major forces: Cézanne's paintings, which had been the focus of two large Paris exhibitions; and the arts of Africa, Iberia, and Oceania, examples of which

were appearing regularly in Paris galleries and museums (see chapters 18 and 31). In Cézanne's canvases, with their flattened planes and arbitrary colors (Figure **32.1**), Picasso recognized a rigorous new language of form that seemed to define nature's underlying structure. And in African and Oceanic sculpture he discovered the power of art as fetish—that is, as the palpable embodiment of potent magical forces. As he later explained, "For me the masks were not just sculptures; they were magical objects . . . intercessors against unknown, threatening spirits."

Picasso's foremost assault on tradition was *Les Demoiselles d'Avignon,* a large painting of five nude women —the prostitutes of a Barcelona bordello—in a curtained interior (Figure **32.2**). The subject matter of the work embraced the long, respectable tradition of the female nude group in a landscape setting (see Figure 32.1). However, *Les Demoiselles* violated every shred of tradition, making even Manet's *Olympia* (see Figure 30.18) look comfortably old-fashioned.

The manner in which Picasso "made new" a traditional subject in Western art is worth examining: in the early sketches for the painting, originally called *The Philosophical Brothel,* Picasso included two male figures, one of whom resembled the artist himself. However, in the summer of 1907, Picasso fell deeply under the spell of African art on display at the Musée d'Ethnographie du Trocadéro in Paris. Reworking the canvas, he transformed the five prostitutes into a group of fierce iconic images. For what he would later call his "first exorcism picture," he seems to have taken apart and reassembled the figures as if to test the physics of disjunction and discontinuity. At least three

of the figures are rendered not from a single vantage point but from multiple viewpoints, as if one's eye could travel freely in time and space. The body of the crouching female on the far right is seen from the back, while her face, savagely striated like the scarified surface of an African sculpture (Figure **32.3**), is seen from the front. The noses of the two central females appear in profile, while their eyes are frontal—a convention Picasso may have borrowed from ancient Egyptian frescoes. The relationship between the figures and the shallow space they occupy is equally disjunctive, a condition compounded by brutally fractured planes of color—brick reds and vivid blues—that resemble shards of glass. Picasso stripped the female of all sensuous appeal and made her as forbidding as a tribal fetish. In one disquieting stroke, he banished the alluring female nude from the domain of Western art.

Les Demoiselles was the precursor of an audacious new style known as *cubism,* a bold and distinctive formal language that came to challenge the principles of Renaissance painting as dramatically as Einstein's theory of relativity had challenged Newtonian physics. In the cubist canvas, the comfortable, recognizable world of the senses disappears beneath a scaffold of semitransparent planes and short, angular lines; ordinary objects are made to look as if they have exploded and been reassembled somewhat arbitrarily in bits and pieces (Figure **32.4**). With *analytic cubism,* as the style came to be called, a multiplicity of viewpoints replaced one-point perspective. The cubist image, conceived as if one were moving around, above, and below the subject and even perceiving it from within, appropriated the fourth dimension—time itself. Abrupt

Figure 32.2 PABLO PICASSO, *Les Demoiselles d'Avignon*, Paris, 1907. Oil on canvas, 8 ft. × 7 ft. 8 in. The Museum of Modern Art, New York. Acquired through the Lillie P. Bliss Bequest. © 2005, Digital Image, the Museum of Modern Art, New York/Scala, Florence . © Succession Picasso/DACS, London 2005.

shifts in direction call up the uncertainties of the new physics. As Picasso and his French colleague Georges Braque (1882–1963) collaborated in a search for an ever more pared down language of form, compositions became increasingly abstract and colors became cool and controlled: cubism came to offer a new formal language, one wholly unconcerned with narrative content. Years later, Picasso defended the viability of this new language: "The fact that for a long time cubism has not been understood . . . means nothing. I do not read English, an English book is a blank book to me. This does not mean that the English language does not exist."

Around 1912, a second phase of cubism, namely *synthetic cubism*, emerged, when Braque first included three pieces of wallpaper in a still-life composition. Picasso and Braque, who thought of themselves as space pioneers (much like the Wright brothers), pasted mundane objects such as wine labels, playing cards, and scraps of newspaper onto the surface of the canvas—a technique known as **collage** (from the French *coller*, "to paste"). The result was a kind of art that was neither a painting nor a sculpture, but both at the same time. The two artists filled their canvases with puns, hidden messages, and subtle references to

Figure 32.3 Mask from Etoumbi region, Democratic Republic of the Congo. Wood, height 14 in. Musée Barbier-Müller, Geneva.

Figure 32.4 PABLO PICASSO, *Man with a Violin*, 1911. Oil on canvas, 3 ft. 3½ in. × 29⅝ in. Philadelphia Museum of Art. Louise and Walter arensberg Collection.
© Succession Picasso/DACS 2005.

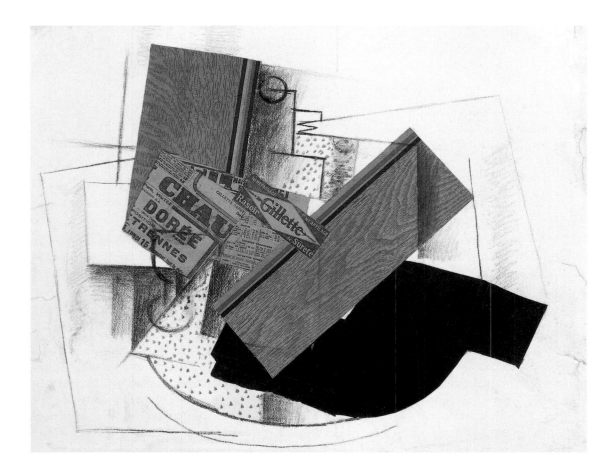

Figure 32.5 (left) **GEORGES BRAQUE**, *Still Life on a Table*, ca. 1914. Collage on paper, 18⅛ × 24⅛ in. Collection of Mr and Mrs Claude Lauren, Paris. Photo: Musée National d'Art Moderne, Centre Georges Pompidou, Paris. © ADAGP, Paris and DACS, London, 2005.

Figure 32.7 (below) **PABLO PICASSO**, *Guitar*, 1912–1913. Construction of sheet metal and wire, 30½ × 13¾ × 7⅞ in. The Museum of Modern Art, New York. Gift of the Artist. © 2003 Digital Image MoMA, New York/Scala, Florence. © Succession Picasso/DACS, London 2005.

contemporary events; but the prevailing strategy in all of these artworks was to test the notion of art as illusion. In Braque's *Still Life on a Table* (Figure **32.5**), strips of imitation wood graining, a razor blade wrapper, and newspaper clippings serve the double function of "presenting" and "representing." Words and images wrenched out of context here play off one another like some cryptographic billboard. Prophetic of twentieth-century art in general, Braque would proclaim, "The subject is not the object of the painting, but a new unity, the lyricism that results from method."

In these same years, Picasso created the first **assemblages**—artworks that were built up, or pieced together, from miscellaneous or commonplace materials. Like the collage, the assemblage depended on the inventive combination of found objects and materials. As such, it constituted a radical alternative to traditional techniques of carving in stone, metal-casting, and modeling in clay or plaster. The art of assemblage drew inspiration from African and Oceanic traditions of combining natural materials (such as cowrie beads and raffia) for masks and costumes; it also took heed of the expressive simplifications that typify fetish figures, reliquaries, and other tribal artforms (Figure **32.6**). Picasso's *Guitar* of 1912–1913 achieves its powerful effect by means of fragmented planes, deliberate spatial inversions

Figure 32.6 (below) Ceremonial mask, from Wobé or Grebo, Ivory Coast, late nineteenth century. Painted wood, feathers, and fibers, height 11 in. Musée de l'Homme, Paris. Photo: © R.M.N., Paris.

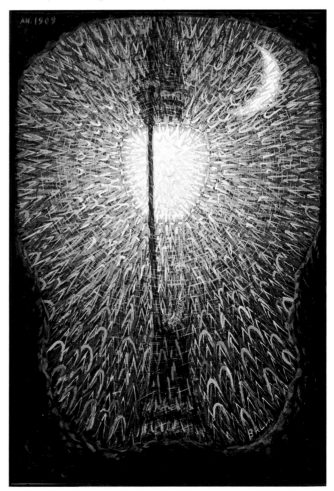

(note the projecting soundhole), and the wedding of sheet-metal and wire (Figure **32.7**).

Within a decade, Western sculptors were employing the strategies of synthetic cubism in ways that reflected abstract models of time and space. The Russian-born cubist Alexander Archipenko (1887–1964) fashioned the female form so that an area of negative space actually constitutes the head (Figure **32.8**). Similar efforts at integrating space and mass characterize the monumental bronze sculptures of the British artist Henry Moore (1898–1986).

Futurism

Technology and art, linked by the modernist mandate to "make it new," sparked the Italian movement known as *futurism*. The poet and iconoclast Filippo Tommaso Marinetti (1876–1944) issued a series of manifestoes that attacked museum art (and all forms of academic culture) and linked contemporary artistic expression to industry, technology, and urban life. Marinetti, who held that "war was the only healthgiver of the world," demanded an art of "burning violence" that would free Italy from its "fetid gangrene of professors, archeologists, antiquarians, and rhetoricians." "We declare," he wrote in his *Futurist Manifesto* of 1909, "that there can be no modern painting except from the starting point of an absolutely modern sensation. ... A roaring motorcar is more beautiful than the winged *Victory of Samothrace*"

Figure 32.8 (left) **ALEXANDER ARCHIPENKO**, *Woman Combing Her Hair*, 1915. Bronze, 13¾ × 3¼ × 3⅛ in. (including base). The Museum of Modern Art, New York. Acquired through the Lillie P. Bliss Bequest. Photograph © 2000 The Museum of Modern Art, New York. © ARS, NY and DACS, London 2000.

(the famous Hellenistic sculpture illustrated as Figure 5.31). "The gesture that we would reproduce on canvas shall no longer be a fixed moment in universal dynamism. It shall simply be the dynamic sensation itself."

The futuristic alternative to static academicism was produced by Umberto Boccioni (1882–1916). His near life-sized bronze sculpture captures the sensation of motion as it pushes forward like a automated robot (Figure **32.9**). The striding figure, which consists of an aggressive series of dynamic, jagged lines, is clearly human in form, despite Boccioni's assertion (in his 1912 *Technical Manifesto of Futurist Sculpture*) that artists should "abolish .. the traditionally exalted place of subject matter."

Figure 32.10 GIACOMO BALLA, *Streetlight*, 1909. Oil on canvas 5 ft. 8½ in. × 3 ft. 8⅝ in. Museum of Modern Art, New York.. © 2004 Digital Image MoMA, New York/Scala, Florence. © ADAGP, Paris and DACS, London 2005

The futurists were enthralled by the speed and dynamism of automobiles, trains, and airplanes, and by such new forms of technology as the machine gun and the electric light. In the painting *Street Light* (Figure **32.10**), the Italian futurist Giacomo Balla (1871–1958) paid homage to the electric Brunt Arc lamps that were installed in the streets of Rome during the first decade of the century. Balla wittily claimed that this painting, in which electric light outshines moonlight, hailed the demise of romantic art in the West. Futurists were also inspired by the time-lapse photography of Eadweard Muybridge (see Figure 31.8), the magical properties of X-rays (not in wide use until 1910), and by pioneer efforts in the new industry of motion pictures, in which "multiple profiles"

gave the appearance of movement in time and space. These modern phenomena shaped the early career of the French artist Marcel Duchamp (1887–1968). When Duchamp's *Nude Descending a Staircase, No. 2* (Figure **32.11**) was exhibited at the International Exhibition of Modern Art (known as the Armory Show) in New York City, one critic mockingly called it "an explosion in a shingle factory." Yet, from the time of its first showing in 1913, the painting (and much of the art in the Armory exhibition) had a formative influence on the rise of American modernism. Futurism did not last beyond the end of World War I, but its impact was felt in both the United States and Russia, where futurist efforts to capture the sense of form in motion would coincide with the first developments in the technology of cinematography (discussed later in this chapter).

Figure 32.9 UMBERTO BOCCIONI, *Unique Forms of Continuity in Space*, 1913. Bronze (cast 1931), 3 ft. 7⅞ in. × 34⅞ in. × 15¾ in. The Museum of Modern Art, New York. Acquired through the Lillie P. Bliss Bequest. © 2004 Digital Image MoMA, New York/Scala, Florence.

Figure 32.11 MARCEL DUCHAMP, *Nude Descending a Staircase, No. 2*, 1912. Oil on canvas, 4 ft. 10 in. × 35 in. Philadelphia Museum of Art. Louise and Walter Arensberg Collection. © Succession Marcel Duchamp/ ADAGP, Paris and DACS, London, 2005.

Matisse and Fauvism

While cubists and futurists were principally concerned with matters of space and motion, other modernists, led by the French artist Henri Matisse (1869–1954), made *color* the principal feature of their canvases. This group, branded as "fauves" (from the French *fauve*, "wild beast") by a critic who saw their work at the 1905 exhibition in Paris, employed flat, bright colors in the arbitrary manner of van Gogh and Gauguin. But whereas the latter had used color to evoke a mood or a symbolic image, the younger artists were concerned with color only as it served pictorial structure; their style featured bold spontaneity and the direct and instinctive application of pigment. Critics who called these artists "wild beasts" were in fact responding to the use of color in ways that seemed both crude and savage. They attacked the art of the fauves as "color madness" and "the sport of a child." For Matisse, however, color was the font of pure and sensuous pleasure. In his portrait of Madame Matisse (which he subtitled *The Green Line*), broad flat swaths of paint give definition to a visage that is

THE BIRTH OF MOTION PICTURES

It is no coincidence that the art of motion pictures was born at a time when artists and scientists were obsessed with matters of space and time. Indeed, as an artform that captures rapidly changing experience, cinema is *the* quintessentially modern medium. The earliest public film presentations took place in Europe and the United States in the mid-1890s: in 1895, Thomas Edison (1867–1931) was the first American to project moving images on a screen publicly, while in France the brothers Auguste and Louis Lumière (1862–1954; 1864–1948) perfected the process by which cellulose film ran smoothly in a commercial projector. They pioneered the first cinematic projection in an auditorium equipped with seats and piano accompaniment. These first experiments delighted audiences with moving pictures of everyday reality.

It was not until 1902, however, that film was used to create a reality all its own: in that year the French filmmaker Georges Méliès (1861–1938) completed a thirteen-minute theatrical sequence called *A Trip to the Moon*, a fantastic reconstruction of reality based on a Jules Verne novel. One year later, the American director Edwin S. Porter (1869–1941) produced the twelve-minute silent film *The Great Train Robbery*, which treated the myth of American frontier life in the story of a sensational holdup, followed by the pursuit and capture of the bandits. These pioneer narrative films established the idiom for two of the most popular genres in cinematic history: the science fiction film and the "western."

Between 1908 and 1912, Hollywood became the center of American cinema. D. W. Griffith (1875–1948), the leading director of his time, made major innovations in cinematic technique. He introduced the use of multiple cameras and camera angles, as well as such new techniques as close-ups, fade-outs, and flashbacks, which, when joined together in an edited sequence, greatly expanded the potential of film narrative. Griffith's three-hour-long silent film, *The Birth of a Nation* (1915), was an epic account of the American Civil War and the Reconstruction Era that followed in the South. Unfortunately, despite the film's technical excellence, its negative portrayal of African-Americans contributed to creating a stereotype of blacks as violent and ignorant savages.

Until the late 1920s, all movies were silent—filmmakers used captions to designate the spoken word wherever appropriate and live musical accompaniment was often provided in the theater. Well before the era of the "talkies," cinematographers used the camera not simply as a disinterested observer, but as a medium for conveying the emotional states of the characters. Indeed, in the absence of sound, filmmakers were forced to develop the affective structure of the film by essentially visual means. According to some film critics, the aesthetics of film as a medium were compromised when sound was added. Nevertheless, by 1925 it was apparent that film was destined to become one of the major artforms of the twentieth (and, indeed, the twenty-first) century.

bisected vertically by an acrid green stripe (Figure **32.12**). Matisse brought new daring to Cézanne's flat color patches, using them to stylize form in the manner of the tribal artworks that he collected. At the same time, he invested the canvas with a thrilling color radiance, that, like smell (as Matisse himself observed), suffuses our senses subtly but intensely. In contrast with Picasso, who held that art was a weapon with which to jar the senses, Matisse sought "an art of balance, of purity and serenity, devoid of troubling or depressing subject matter . . . something like a good armchair in which to rest from physical fatigue."

Matisse was among the first to articulate the modernist scorn for representational art: "Exactitude is not truth," he insisted. In *Notes of a Painter*, published in 1908, he explained that colors and shapes were the equivalents of feelings rather than the counterparts of forms in nature. Gradually, as he came to be influenced by Islamic miniatures and Russian icons, Matisse moved in the direction of schematic simplicity and extraordinary color sensuousness. A quintessential example of his facility for color abstraction

Figure 32.12 (left) **HENRI MATISSE**, *Madame Matisse (The Green Line)*, 1905. Oil on canvas, 16 × 12 ¾ in. Statens Museum for Kunst. Photo: Hans Peterson. © Succession H Matisse and DACS, London, 2005.

Figure 32.13 HENRI MATISSE, *Dance 1*, 1909. Oil on canvas, 8 ft. 6½ in. × 12 ft. 9½ in. The Museum of Modern Art, New York. Gift of Nelson A. Rockefeller in honor of Alfred H. Barr, Jr. © 2004 Digital Image MoMA, New York/Scala, Florence. © Succession H Matisse and DACS, London, 2005.

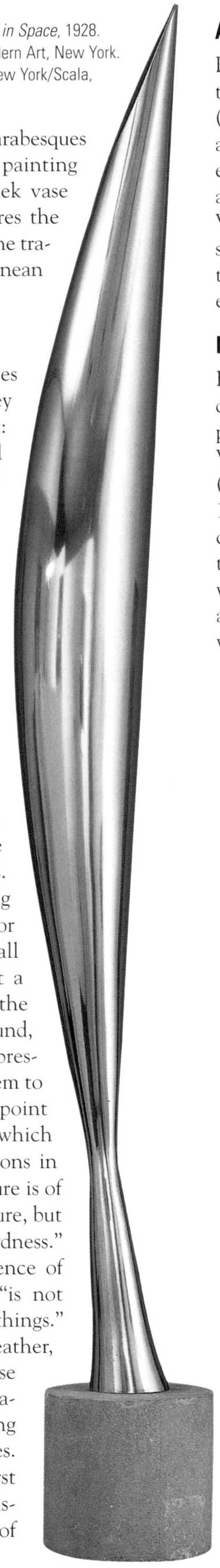

Figure 32.14 (right) **CONSTANTIN BRANCUSI**, *Bird in Space*, 1928. Polished bronze, height 4 ft. 6 in. The Museum of Modern Art, New York. Given anonymously. © 2004 Digital Image MoMA, New York/Scala, Florence. © ADAGP, Paris and DACS, London, 2005.

is *Dance I* (Figure **32.13**). In its lyrical arabesques and unmodeled fields of color, the painting calls to mind the best of ancient Greek vase paintings. At the same time, it captures the exhilaration of the primordial round—the traditional dance of almost all Mediterranean cultures.

Brancusi and Abstraction

Although cubists, futurists, and fauves pursued their individual directions, they all shared the credo of abstract art: the artist must evoke the essential and intrinsic qualities of the subject rather than describe its physical properties. In early modern sculpture, the guardian of this credo was Constantin Brancusi (1876–1957). Born in Romania and trained in Bucharest, Vienna, and Munich, Brancusi came to Paris in 1904. There, after a brief stay in Rodin's studio, he fell under the spell of ancient fertility figures and the sculpture of Africa and Polynesia. Inspired by these objects, whose spiritual power lay in their visual immediacy and their truth to materials, Brancusi proceeded to create an art of radically simple, organic forms. While he began by closely observing the living object—whether human or animal—he progressively eliminated all naturalistic details until he arrived at a form that captured the essence of the subject. Like his good friend Ezra Pound, Brancusi achieved a concentrated expression in forms so elemental that they seem to speak a universal language. A case in point is *Bird in Space* (Figure **32.14**), of which Brancusi made more than thirty versions in various sizes and materials. The sculpture is of no particular species of feathered creature, but it captures perfectly the concept of "birdness." It is, as Brancusi explained, "the essence of flight." "What is real," he insisted, "is not the external form, but the essence of things." The elegant form, curved like a feather, unites birdlike qualities of grace and poise with the dynamic sense of soaring levitation characteristic of mechanical flying machines, such as rockets and airplanes. Indeed, when Brancusi's bronze *Bird* first arrived in America, United States customs officials mistook it for a piece of industrial machinery.

Abstraction and Photography

Photography enthusiastically embraced the modernist aesthetic. The American photographer Edward Weston (1886–1953) was among the pioneers of photographic abstraction. His close-up photograph of two nautilus shells evokes the twin ideas of flower (a magnolia blossom, according to Weston himself) and female (Figure **32.15**). Weston took photography beyond the realm of the representational: he used the camera not simply to record the natural world, but to explore new avenues of visual experience.

Nonobjective Art

Between 1909 and 1914, three artists working independent of one another in different parts of Europe moved to purge art of all recognizable subject matter. The Russians Wassily Kandinsky (1866–1944) and Kasimir Malevich (1878–1935) and the Dutchman Piet Mondrian (1872–1944), pioneers of **nonobjective art**, had all come into contact with the principal art movements of the early twentieth century: cubism, futurism, and fauvism. They were also familiar with the postimpressionist premise that a painting was, first and foremost, a flat surface covered with colors assembled in a particular order. But their

Figure 32.15 EDWARD WESTON, *Two Shells*, 1927. Photograph. Print by Cole Weston. Reproduced by permission of the Center for Creative Photography, University of Tucson Arizona.

research into subjectless form had yet another goal: that of achieving an art whose purity would offer a spiritual remedy for the soullessness of modern life.

Kandinsky, whose career in art only began at the age of forty, was deeply influenced by the fauves, the symbolists (see chapter 31), and by Russian folk art. (He confessed a debt as well to atomic theory and urged young artists to study the new physics.) While he filled his early paintings with intense and vibrant colors, he observed with some dismay that the subject matter in his canvases tended to "dissolve" into his colors. One evening, upon returning to his studio in Munich, Kandinsky experienced a "revelation" that led him to abandon pictorial subject matter. The incident is described in his *Reminiscences* of 1913:

> I saw an indescribably beautiful picture drenched with an inner glowing. At first I hesitated, then I rushed toward this mysterious picture, of which I saw nothing but forms and colors, and whose content was incomprehensible. Immediately I found the key to the puzzle: it was a picture I had painted, leaning against the wall, standing on its side. . . . Now I knew for certain that the [pictorial] object harmed my paintings.*

From this point on, Kandinsky began to assemble colors, lines, and shapes without regard to recognizable objects (Figure **32.16**). He usually called his nonrepresentational paintings "improvisations" or "abstract compositions" and numbered them in series. In his treatise *Concerning the Spiritual in Art* (1910), he argued that form and color generate meaning without reference to the natural world. "Color can exercise enormous influence upon the body," wrote Kandinsky; it functions to influence mood. Such insights anticipated modern research in chromotherapy, that is, the use of colors and colored light to affect body states. According to Kandinsky, painting was a spiritually liberating force akin to music—he himself was an amateur cellist and friend of many avant-garde composers. "Painting," he proclaimed, "is a thundering collision of different worlds, intended to create a new world."

*"Reminiscences," in *Modern Artists on Art*, ed. Robert L. Herbert. Englewood Cliffs, N.J.: Prentice Hall, 1964, 32.

Kandinsky's Russian contemporary Kasimir Malevich arrived at nonrepresentational art not by way of fauvism but through the influence of analytic cubism, a style that asserted the value of line over color. Seeking to "free art from the burden of the object" and to rediscover "pure feeling in creative art," Malevich created an austere style limited to the strict geometry of the square, the circle, and

Figure 32.17 KASIMIR MALEVICH, *Suprematist Composition: White on White*, 1918. Oil on canvas, 31¼ × 31¼ in. The Museum of Modern Art, New York. © 2004 Digital Image MoMA, New York/Scala, Florence.

the rectangle (Figure **32.17**). Malevich called these shapes "suprematist elements" and his style *suprematism*. "To the suprematist," wrote Malevich, "the visual phenomena of the objective world are, in themselves, meaningless; the significant thing is feeling . . . quite apart from

the environment in which it is called forth."* By restricting his art to the arrangement of ideal geometric shapes on the two-dimensional picture plane, Malevich replaced the world of appearance with a language of form as abstract and exacting as that of modern physics.

The early works of the third pioneer of nonobjective art, Piet Mondrian, reveal this Dutch artist's keen sensitivity to his native countryside as well as his inclination to discover geometric order in nature (Figure **32.18**). Mondrian's methodical landscapes reflect his distant kinship to Jan Vermeer (see Figure 23.11). As early as 1910, however, Mondrian began to strip his canvases of references to recognizable subject matter. He limited his visual vocabulary to "pure" forms: rectangles laid out on a grid of horizontal and vertical lines, the three primary colors (red, yellow, and blue), and three values—white, gray, and black (Figure **32.19**). The paring-down process achieved a compositional balance of geometric elements, an "equivalence of opposites" similar to the dynamic equilibrium of an algebraic equation. Although Mondrian would eventually migrate to America, in the Netherlands the movement he initiated was called simply *De Stijl* (The Style). Despite differences of opinion among its members—Mondrian resigned in 1925 in opposition to a colleague's use of diagonals—De Stijl was to have worldwide impact, especially in the areas of architecture and furniture design (Figure **32.20**).

The disappearance of the object in early twentieth-century art is often mistakenly associated with the dehumanization

---

*"Suprematism," in *Modern Artists on Art*, 93.

Figure 32.18 PIET MONDRIAN, *Tree*, 1912. Oil on canvas, 29¼ × 43⅞ in. Munson-Williams-Proctor Institute, Utica, New York. © 2006 Mondrian/Holzman Trust c/o hcr@hcrinternational.com.

Figure 32.19 (right) **PIET MONDRIAN**, *Composition with Large Red Plane, Yellow, Black, Gray, and Blue*, 1921. Oil on canvas, 23⅜ × 23⅜ in. Collection Haags Gemeentemuseum, The Hague. © 2006 Mondrian/Holtzman Trust c/o hcr@hcrinternational.

Figure 32.20 (below) **GERRIT RIETVELD**, *Red Blue Chair*, 1923. Painted wood, 34⅛ × 26 × 33 in; seat height 13 in. The Museum of Modern Art, New York. Gift of Philip Johnson. © 2004 Digital Image MoMA, New York/Scala, Florence. © DACS, London 2005.

of modern life. However, one of the great ironies of the birth of nonobjective art is its indebtedness to the mystical and transcendental philosophies that were current in the early modern era. One of the most influential of these was *theosophy*, a blend of Eastern and Western religions that emphasizes communion with nature by purely spiritual means. Mondrian, a member of the Dutch Theosophical Society, equated spiritual progress with geometric clarity. In his view, the law of equivalence reflected "the true content of reality." "Not only science," wrote Mondrian, "but art also, shows us that reality, at first incomprehensible, gradually reveals itself by the mutual relations that are inherent in things. Pure science and pure art, disinterested and free, can lead the advance in the recognition of the laws which are based on these relationships."* The commitment to pure abstraction as the language of spirituality—a commitment central to the careers of Kandinsky, Malevich, and Mondrian—reflects the utopian humanism of modernists who perceived their art as a wellspring of social harmony and order.

*"Plastic Art and Pure Plastic Art," in *Modern Artists on Art*, 119.

Russian Constructivism

While De Stijl had a formative influence on modern architecture, furniture design, and commercial advertising, the most utilitarian and (at the same time) utopian of the movements for "pure art" flourished in prerevolutionary Russia. *Constructivism*, which had its roots in both futurism and the purist teachings of Malevich, advocated the application of geometric abstraction to all forms of social enterprise. Russian constructivists, who called themselves "artist–engineers," worked to improve the everyday lives of the masses by applying the new abstraction to the industrial arts, theater, film, typography, textile design, and architecture. Liubov Popova (1889–1924), one of the many talented female members of this movement, designed stage sets and costumes for the Russian theater (Figure **32.21**), thus putting into practice the constructivist motto "Art into production." Like other modernists, the constructivists worked to break down the barriers between fine and applied art, but unlike any other modern art movement, constructivism received official state sanction. Following the Russian Revolution, however, the Soviet Union would bring about the demise of one of the most innovative episodes in modern art (see chapter 34).

Early Twentieth-Century Architecture

The revolution in visual abstraction found monumental expression in architecture. Early modern architects made energetic use of two new materials—structural steel and **ferroconcrete**—in combination with cantilever construction. The cantilever, a horizontal beam supported at only one end and projecting well beyond the point of support, had first appeared in the timber buildings of China (see chapter 14); but the manufacture of the structural steel cantilever ushered in a style whose austere simplicity had no precedents. That style was inaugurated by Frank Lloyd Wright (1869–1959), the leading figure in the history of early modern architecture.

The Architecture of Wright

Frank Lloyd Wright, the first American architect of world significance, was the foremost student of the Chicago architect Louis Sullivan (see chapter 30). Wright's style combined the new technology of steel and glass with the aesthetic principles of Asian architecture. Wright visited Japan when he was in his thirties and was impressed by

Figure 32.21 LIUBOV POPOVA, Set design for Fernand Crommelynk, *Le Cocu magnifique*, State Institute of Theatrical Art, Moscow, 1922. Gouache on paper, 19½ × 27 in. State Trekiov Gallery, Moscow. Gift of George Custakis.

Figure 32.22 FRANK LLOYD WRIGHT, Robie House, Chicago, Illinois, 1909. Brick, glass, natural rock. Photo: Wayne Andrews/Esto.

the grace and purity of Japanese art. He especially admired the respect for natural materials and the sensitivity to the relationship between setting and structure that characterized traditional Japanese architecture (see chapter 14). In his earliest domestic commissions, Wright embraced the East Asian principle of horizontality, by which the building might hug the earth. He imitated the low, sweeping ceilings and roofs of Chinese and Japanese pavilions and pagodas. From Japanese interiors, where walls often consist of movable screens, Wright borrowed the idea of interconnecting interior and exterior space. He used the structural steel frame and the cantilever to create large areas of uninterrupted space. In every one of Wright's designs, the exterior of the structure reflects the major divisions of its interior space. Wright refined this formula in a series of innovative homes in the American Midwest, pioneering the so-called "Prairie School" of architecture that lasted from roughly 1900 until World War I.

The classic creation of Wright's early career was the Robie House in Chicago, completed in 1909 (Figure **32.22**). Here, Wright made the fireplace the center of the residential interior. He crossed the long main axis of the house with counteraxes of low cantilevered roofs that push out into space over terraces and verandas. He subordinated decorative details to the overall design, allowing his materials—brick, glass, and natural rock—to assume major roles in establishing the unique character of the structure. As Wright insisted, "To use any material wrongly is to abuse the integrity of the whole design." The result was a style consisting of crisp, interlocking planes, contrasting textures, and interpenetrating solids and voids—a domestic architecture that was as abstract and dynamic as an analytic cubist painting. Wright's use of the cantilever and his integration of landscape and house

reached new imaginative heights in Fallingwater, the residence he designed in 1936 for the American businessman Edgar J. Kaufmann at Bear Run, Pennsylvania (Figure **32.23**). Embracing a natural waterfall, the ferroconcrete and stone structure seems to grow organically out of the natural wooded setting, yet dominate that setting by its pristine equilibrium.

The Bauhaus and the International Style

Wright's synthesis of art and technology melded with the utopian vision of Russian constructivism to pave the way for the establishment of the *Bauhaus*, modernism's most influential school of architecture and applied art. Founded in 1919 by the German architect and visionary Walter Gropius (1883–1969), the Bauhaus pioneered an instructional program that reformed modern industrial society by fusing the technology of the machine age with the purest principles of functional design. Throughout its brief history (1919–1933), and despite its frequent relocation (from Weimar to Dessau, and finally Berlin), the Bauhaus advocated a close relationship between the function of an object and its formal design, whether in furniture, lighting fixtures, typography, photography, industrial products, or architecture. Bauhaus instructors had little regard for traditional academic styles; they eagerly endorsed the new synthetic materials of modern technology, a stark simplicity of design, and the standardization of parts for affordable, mass-produced merchandise, as well as for large-scale housing. Some of Europe's leading artists, including Kandinsky and Mondrian, taught at the Bauhaus. Like Gropius, these artists envisioned a new industrial society liberated by the principle of abstraction. When the Nazis closed down the school in 1933, many of its finest instructors, such as the photographer László Moholy-Nagy,

Figure 32.23 FRANK LLOYD WRIGHT, Fallingwater, Kaufmann House, Bear Run, Pennsylvania, 1936–1939. Reinforced concrete, stone, masonry, steel-framed doors and windows, enclosed area 5,800 sq. ft. Photo: Hedrich-Blessing, courtesy Chicago Historical Society.

architect and designer Marcel Breuer, and artist Josef Albers, went to the United States, where they exercised tremendous influence on the development of American architecture and industrial art. (In 1929, a group of wealthy Americans had already established the first international collection of modern art: New York City's Museum of Modern Art.)

Under the direction of Gropius, the Bauhaus launched the *international style* in architecture, which brought to the marriage of structural steel, ferroconcrete, and sheet glass a formal precision and geometric austerity resembling a Mondrian painting (see Figure 32.19). In the four-story glass building Gropius designed to serve as the Bauhaus craft shops in Dessau, unadorned curtain walls of glass (which meet uninterrupted at the corners of the structure) were freely suspended on structural steel cantilevers (Figure **32.24**). This fusion of functional space and minimal structure produced a purist style that paralleled the abstract trends in poetry, painting, and sculpture discussed earlier in this chapter.

The revolutionary Swiss architect and town planner Charles-Edouard Jeanneret (1887–1965), who called himself Le Corbusier (a pun on the word "raven"), was not directly affiliated with the Bauhaus, but he shared Gropius' fundamental concern for efficiency of design, standardization of building techniques, and promotion of low-cost housing. In 1923, Le Corbusier wrote the treatise *Towards a New Architecture*, in which he proposed that modern architectural principles should imitate the efficiency of the machine. "Machines," he predicted, "will lead to a new order both of work and of leisure." Just as form follows function in the design of airplanes, automobiles, and machinery in general, so it must in modern domestic architecture. Le Corbusier was fond of insisting that "the house is a machine for living." With utopian fervor he urged,

> We must create the mass-production spirit.
> The spirit of constructing mass-production houses.
> The spirit of living in mass-production houses.
> The spirit of conceiving mass-production houses.
>
> If we eliminate from our hearts and minds all dead concepts in regard to the house, and look at the question from a critical and objective point of view, we shall arrive at the "House-Machine," the mass-production house, healthy (and morally so too) and beautiful in the same way that the working tools and instruments that accompany our existence are beautiful.*

In the Villa Savoye, a residence located outside of Paris at Poissy, Le Corbusier put these revolutionary concepts to work (Figure **32.25**). The residence, now considered a "classic" of the international style, consists of simple and

---

*Le Corbusier, *Towards a New Architecture*, translated by Frederick Etchells. New York: Praeger, 1970, 12–13.

Figure 32.24 WALTER GROPIUS, Workshop wing, Bauhaus Building, Dessau, Germany, 1925–1926. Steel and glass. Photograph courtesy The Museum of Modern Art, New York.

Figure 32.25 LE CORBUSIER, Villa Savoye, Poissy, France, 1928–1929. Ferroconcrete and glass.

Figure 32.26 LE CORBUSIER, Unité d'Habitation apartment block, Marseilles, France, 1946–1952. Photo: Lucien Hervé, Paris.

unadorned masses of ferroconcrete punctured by ribbon windows. It is raised above the ground on *pilotis*, pillars that free the ground area of the site. (More recently, architects have abused the *pilotis* principle to create parking space for automobiles.) The Villa Savoye features a number of favorite Le Corbusier devices, such as the roof garden, the open spatial plan that allows one to close off or open up space according to varying needs, and the free façade that consists of large areas of glass—so-called "curtain walls." Le Corbusier's genius for fitting form to function led, during the 1930s, to his creation of the first high-rise urban apartment buildings—structures that housed more than a thousand people and consolidated facilities for shopping, recreation, and child care under a single roof (Figure **32.26**). These "vertical cities," as stripped of decorative details as the sculptures of Brancusi, have become hallmarks of urban modernism.

Early Twentieth-Century Music

As with poetry, painting, and architecture, the music of the early twentieth century represents an assault on tradition, and most dramatically so in the areas of tonality and meter. Until the late nineteenth century, most music was tonal; that is, structured on a single key or tonal center. However, by the second decade of the twentieth century, musical compositions might be **polytonal** (having several tonal centers) or **atonal** (without a tonal center). Further, instead of following a single meter, a modern composition might be **polyrhythmic** (having two or more different meters at the same time), or (as with imagist poems) it might obey no fixed or regular metrical pattern.

Modern composers tended to reject conventional modes of expression, including traditional harmonies and instrumentation. Melody—like recognizable subject matter in painting—became of secondary importance to formal composition. Modernists invented no new forms comparable to the fugue or the sonata; modern composers instead explored innovative effects based on dissonance, the free use of meter, and the unorthodox combination of musical instruments, some of which they borrowed from non-Western cultures. They employed unorthodox sources of sound, such as sirens, bullhorns, and doorbells. Some incorporated silence in their compositions, much as cubist sculptors introduced negative space into mass. The results were as startling to the ear as cubism was to the eye.

Schoenberg

The most radical figure in early twentieth-century music was the Austrian composer Arnold Schoenberg (1874–1951). Schoenberg was born in Vienna, the city of Mozart and Beethoven. He learned to play the violin at the age of eight and began composing music in his late teens. Schoenberg's first compositions were conceived in the romantic tradition, but by 1909 he was writing music punctuated by dissonant and unfamiliar chords. Instead of organizing tones around a home key (the tonal center) in the time-honored tradition of Western musical composition, he treated all twelve notes of the chromatic scale equally. Schoenberg's atonal works use abrupt changes in rhythm, tone color, and dynamics—features evidenced in his expressionistic song cycle *Pierrot Lunaire* (*Moonstruck Pierrot*; see also chapter 33) and in his *Five Pieces for Orchestra*, Opus 16, both written in 1912. In the former work, which one critic described as "incomprehensible as a Tibetan poem," the instruments produce a succession of

_____

♭ See Music Listening Selections at end of chapter.

individual, contrasting tones that, like the nonobjective canvases of his good friend Kandinsky, resist harmony and resolution.

During the 1920s, Schoenberg went on to formulate a unifying system for atonal composition based on **serial technique**. His type of *serialism*, called "**the twelve-tone system**," demanded that the composer use all twelve tones of the chromatic scale either melodically or in chords before any one of the other eleven notes might be repeated. The twelve-tone row might be inverted or played upside down or backwards—there are actually forty-eight possible musical combinations for each tone row. Serialism, like quantum theory or Mondrian's "equivalence of opposites," involved the strategic use of a sparse and elemental language of form. It engaged the composer in the highly controlled (even mathematical) disposition of musical elements. In theory, the serial technique invited creative invention rather than mechanical application. Nevertheless, to the average listener, who could no longer leave the concert hall humming a melody, Schoenberg's atonal compositions seemed forbidding and obscure.

Stravinsky

In 1913, one year after Schoenberg's Opus 16 was first performed—and the same year Ezra Pound issued his *Imagist Manifesto* and Malevich and Kandinsky painted their first nonobjective canvases—a Paris audience witnessed the premiere of the ballet *Le Sacre du printemps* (*The Rite of Spring*). The ballet was performed by the *Ballets Russes*, a company of expatriate Russians led by Sergei Diaghilev (1872–1929), and the music was written by the Russian composer Igor Stravinsky (1882–1971; Figure **32.27**). Shortly after the music began, catcalls, hissing, and booing disrupted the performance, as members of the audience protested the "shocking" sounds that were coming from the orchestra. By the time the police arrived, Stravinsky had disappeared through a backstage window. What offended this otherwise sophisticated audience was Stravinsky's bold combination of throbbing rhythms and dissonant harmonies, which, along with the jarring effects of a new style in choreography, ushered in the birth of modern music.

Stravinsky was one of the most influential figures in the history of twentieth-century music. Like Schoenberg, he began to study music at a young age. His family pressed him to pursue a career in law, but Stravinsky was intent on becoming a composer. At the age of twenty-eight, he left Russia for Paris, where he joined the company of the *Ballets Russes*. Allied with some of the greatest artists of the time, including Picasso, the writer Jean Cocteau, and the choreographer Vaslav Nijinsky (1888–1950), Stravinsky was instrumental in making the *Ballets Russes* a leading force in modern dance theater. His influence on

See Music Listening Selections at end of chapter.

Figure 32.27 PABLO PICASSO, *Igor Stravinsky*, 1920. Drawing. Private collection. © Succession Picasso/DACS, London, 2005.

American music was equally great, especially after 1939, when he moved permanently to the United States.

Russian folk tales and songs provided inspiration for many of Stravinsky's early compositions, including *The Rite of Spring*. Subtitled *Pictures from Pagan Russia*, this landmark piece was based on an ancient Slavonic ceremony that invoked the birth of spring with the ritual sacrifice of a young girl. The themes of death and resurrection associated with traditional pagan celebrations of seasonal change provided the structure of the suite, which was divided into two parts: "The Fertility of the Earth" and "The Sacrifice." Like Picasso and Gauguin, Stravinsky was captivated by primitivism; he shared the fascination with ancient rituals and tribal culture that had gripped late nineteenth-century Europe (see chapter 31). These subjects were popularized by Sir James Frazer in his widely acclaimed book, *The Golden Bough* (1890), which had been reissued in twelve volumes between 1911 and 1915.

The Rite of Spring is a pastoral piece, but its music lacks the calm grace traditionally associated with that genre. Its harsh chordal combination and unexpected shifts of meter set it apart from earlier pastorals, such as Debussy's *Prelude to the Afternoon of a Faun*. While Debussy's tonal shifts are as subtle and nuanced as a Monet seascape, Stravinsky's are as abrupt and disjunctive as Picasso's *Demoiselles* and Pound's imagist poems—so disjunctive, in fact, that critics questioned whether the composer was even capable of writing conventional musical transitions. Although not atonal, portions of the work are polytonal, while other passages are ambiguous in tonality, especially in the opening sections. If the shifting tonalities and pounding rhythms of the piece were "savage," as critics claimed, so too were its orchestral effects: Its unorthodox scoring calls for eighteen woodwind instruments, eighteen brass instruments, and a *quiro* (a Latin American gourd that is scraped with a wooden stick). *The Rite* had an impact on twentieth-century music comparable to that of *Les Demoiselles d'Avignon* on the visual arts. It shattered the syntax of traditional musical language with the same force that this painting had attacked traditional pictorial norms. It rewrote the rules of musical composition as they had been practiced for centuries. No greater assault on tradition could have been imagined at the time.

The Beginnings of Modern Dance

By 1912, the brilliant dancer and choreographer Vaslav Nijinsky had already laid the basis for modern dance with his choreography for the *Prelude to the Afternoon of a Faun*, his debut piece (Figure **32.28**). He had shocked audiences by violating the canon of classical dance with erotic movements that he rightly conceived as appropriate to Mallarmé's poem (see chapter 31). And in Russia, he had scandalized the Saint Petersburg ballet by refusing to wear the traditional pair of floppy shorts over his ballet tights. Nijinsky's choreography for *The Rite of Spring* was even more controversial: his angular movements, interrupted by frozen stillnesses, imitated the flattened appearance of cubist paintings. At the same time (and to Stravinsky's dismay), he took the rhythmic complexity of the music as inspiration for a series of frenzied leaps and wild, wheeling rounds. "They stamp, they stamp, and they stamp," complained one French critic. Like *The Rite* itself, Nijinsky's choreography seemed to express what one critic called "the hidden primitive in man." Tragically, Nijinsky's career came to an end in 1917, when he became incurably insane. In his ten years as the West's first dance superstar, Nijinsky choreographed only four ballets; and not until 1987 was his most famous ballet, *The Rite of Spring*, revived for the American stage.

No less than poets, painters, architects, and composers, choreographers of the early twentieth century found inspiration in non-Western forms of artistic expression. They drew freely on the dance traditions of Asia, Africa, and Native America, among others. The eclectic and innovative character of early modern dance is best illustrated in the work of the pioneer American choreographer Martha Graham (1894–1991). Graham once defined dance as "making visible the interior landscape." Following Isadora Duncan and Nijinsky, she rejected the conventional positions of classical ballet and explored the expressive power of natural movements of the body. But Graham went even further—she sought in dance a direct correspondence between body movement and human emotion. Just as Pound tried to capture the ideal "rhythmical arrangement of words" to convey an emotional "shape," so Graham attempted to find definitive gestures for feeling states. Dramatic abstraction, along with a fierce, earthy expressiveness, was a major feature of Graham's style and of early modern dance in general. While classical dancers were trained to conceal any display of the physical effort that goes into dance, modern dancers exposed the process and the techniques of dancing, thus making new the art of dance.

SUMMARY

During the first decades of the twentieth century, quantum physicists provided a model of the universe that was both more dynamic and more complex than any previously conceived. Matter, they explained, is a form of energy; time and space are relative to the position of the individual observer and the operations of the universe can not be measured with absolute certainty. Not surprisingly, artists

Figure 32.28 Vaslav Nijinsky, "Afternoon of a Faun," 1912. Photo: L. Roosen. Courtesy of the New York Public Library. Dance Collection, Astor, Lennox, and Tilden Foundations.

of this era began to challenge the established ways of viewing the cosmos they occupied. The fragmentation of form and the disjunctive juxtaposition of motifs in the poetry, art, music, and dance of this period seem to mirror the modern physicist's image of an atomic universe, whose laws are relative and whose operations lack smooth and predictable transitions.

Abstraction and formalism characterize the modernist aesthetic. In the poems of the imagists, as in the cubist paintings of Picasso and the sculpture of Brancusi, a concentrated reduction of form overtook naturalism and realistic representation. With Kandinsky, Malevich, and Mondrian, painting freed itself entirely of recognizable objects. These artists shared a utopian faith in the reforming power of the arts. In architecture, Frank Lloyd Wright combined the tools of glass and steel technology with the aesthetics of Asian art to invent a style of unprecedented simplicity. Gropius, founder of the Bauhaus, and Le Corbusier, pioneer of the vertical city, developed the international style, which proclaimed the credo of functional design. The austere formalism of the international style would come to dominate much of the urban architecture of the twentieth century. In music and dance, the modernist assault was equally evident. Arnold Schoenberg and Igor Stravinsky introduced atonality, polytonality, and polyrhythm as formal alternatives to the time-honored Western traditions of pleasing harmonies and uniform meter. Vaslav Nijinsky and Martha Graham liberated dance from academic strictures.

Armed with up-to-date theories of time and space, modernists rallied to "make it new." Pound's poems, Picasso's cubist compositions, and Stravinsky's early scores remain exemplary of the modernist search for powerful new kinds of expression. And while such works may have seemed as strange and forbidding as modern physics, they were equally effective in challenging the time-honored principles and values of the humanistic tradition.

MUSIC LISTENING SELECTIONS

CD Two Selection 17 Schoenberg, *Pierrot Lunaire*, Op. 21, Part 3, No. 15, "Heimweh," 1912.

CD Two Selection 18 Stravinsky, *The Rite of Spring*, "Sacrificial Dance," 1913, excerpt.

GLOSSARY

abstraction the process by which subject matter is pared down or simplified in order to capture intrinsic or essential qualities; also, any work of art that reflects this process

assemblage an artwork composed of three-dimensional objects, either natural or manufactured; the sculptural counterpart of collage

atonality in music, the absence of a tonal center or definite key

avant-garde (French, "vanguard") those who create or produce styles and ideas ahead of their time; also, an unconventional movement or style

collage (French, *coller*, "to paste") a composition created by pasting materials such as newspaper, wallpaper, photographs, or cloth on a flat surface or canvas

ferroconcrete a cement building material reinforced by embedding wire or iron rods; also called "reinforced concrete"

haiku a Japanese light verse form consisting of seventeen syllables (three lines of five, seven, and five)

nonobjective art art that lacks recognizable subject matter; also called "nonrepresentational art"

polyrhythm in music, the device of using two or more different rhythms at the same time; also known as "polymeter"

polytonality in music, the simultaneous use of multiple tonal centers or keys; for compositions using only two tonal centers, the word "bitonality" applies

serial technique in music, a technique that involves the use of a particular series of notes, rhythms, and other elements that are repeated over and over throughout the piece

twelve-tone system a kind of serial music that demands the use of all twelve notes of the chromatic scale (all twelve half-tones in an octave) in a particular order or series; no one note can be used again until all eleven have appeared

The Freudian Revolution

"Only children, madmen, and savages truly understand the 'in-between' world of spiritual truth."
Paul Klee

Freud and the Psyche

No figure in modern Western history has had more influence on our perception of ourselves than Sigmund Freud (1856–1939). Freud, a Jewish intellectual who graduated in medicine from the University of Vienna, Austria, in 1880, was the first to map the geography of the human psyche (or mind). His early work with severely disturbed patients, followed by a period of intensive self-analysis, led him to develop a systematic procedure for treating emotional illnesses. Freud was the founder of *psychoanalysis*, a therapeutic method by which repressed desires are brought to the conscious level to reveal the sources of emotional disturbance. Freud pioneered the principal tools of this method—dream analysis and "free association" (the spontaneous verbalization of thoughts)—and favored these techniques over hypnosis, the procedure preferred by notable physicians with whom he had studied.

Freud theorized that instinctual drives, especially the libido, or sex drive, governed human behavior. According to Freud, guilt from the repression of instinctual urges dominates the unconscious life of human beings and manifests itself in emotional illness. Most psychic disorders, he argued, were the result of sexual traumas stemming from the child's unconscious attachment to the parent of the opposite sex and jealousy of the parent of the same sex, a phenomenon Freud called the Oedipus complex (in reference to the ancient Greek legend in which Oedipus, king of Thebes, unwittingly kills his father and marries his mother). Freud shocked the world with his analysis of infant sexuality and, more generally, with his proclamation that the psychic lives of human beings were formed by the time they were five years old.

Of all his discoveries, Freud considered his research on dream analysis most important. In 1900 he published *The Interpretation of Dreams*, in which he defended the significance of dreams in deciphering the unconscious life of the individual. In *Totem and Taboo* (1913), he examined the function of the unconscious in the evolution of the earliest forms of religion and morality. And in "The Sexual Life of Human Beings," a lecture presented to medical students at the University of Vienna in 1916, he examined the psychological roots of sadism, homosexuality, fetishism, and voyeurism—subjects still considered taboo in some social circles. Freud's theories opened the door to the clinical appraisal of previously guarded types of human behavior; and, by bringing attention to the central place of erotic desire in human life, they irrevocably altered popular attitudes toward human sexuality. His controversial writings also had a major impact on the treatment of the mentally ill. Until at least the eighteenth century, people generally regarded psychotic behavior as evidence of possession by demonic or evil spirits, and the mentally ill were often locked up like animals. Freud's studies argued that neuroses and psychoses were illnesses that required medical treatment.

In describing the activities of the human psyche, Freud proposed a theoretical model, the terms of which (though often oversimplified and misunderstood) have become basic to *psychology* (the study of mind and behavior) and fundamental to our everyday vocabulary. This model pictures the psyche as consisting of three parts: the *id*, the *ego*, and the *superego*. The id, according to Freud, is the seat of human instincts and the source of all physical desires, including nourishment and sexual satisfaction. Seeking fulfillment in accordance with the pleasure principle, the id (and in particular the *libido*, or sex drive) is the compelling force of the unconscious realm. Freud perceived the second part of the psyche, the ego, as the administrator of the id: the ego is the "manager" that attempts to adapt the needs of the id to the real world. Whether by dreams or by **sublimation** (the positive modification and redirection of primal urges), the ego mediates between potentially destructive desires and social necessities. In Freud's view, civilization was the product of the ego's effort to modify the primal urges of the id. The third agent in the psychic life of the human being, the superego, is the moral monitor commonly called the "conscience." The superego monitors human behavior according to principles inculcated by parents, teachers, and other authority figures.

Freud's tripartite psyche constituted a radical model of human behavior. Copernicus had dislodged human beings from their central location in the cosmos, and Darwin had deposed *Homo sapiens* as unique among the earth's creatures; now Freud—in revealing the dark undersoul of humankind—refuted the precept that human reason governs human behavior. Ironically, while Freud himself believed as firmly as any Enlightenment rationalist in the reforming power of science, his theories challenged the centuries-old belief in the supremacy of human reason.

As is the case with many great thinkers, Freud made some questionable judgments and was likely wrong in some of his formulations. Late twentieth-century revisionists criticized Freud's theories on repression (arguing that they are inherently untestable), his analysis of female sexuality (especially the sexist notion of "penis envy" as a female affliction), and the methodology of psychoanalysis itself (the effectiveness of which has been challenged by proponents of biomedical psychiatry and behavioral psychology). A hotly debated question—yet to be resolved—is whether mental illnesses are biological dysfunctions (best treated pharmacologically) or psychosocial dysfunctions related to infant trauma, early childhood problems, and the like (best treated by some form of psychoanalysis), or both. While Freud may be valued today less as a scientist than as a visionary, it is noteworthy that he anticipated many late twentieth-century developments in neuropsychiatry, the branch of medicine that deals with diseases of the mind and nervous system. In the long run, however, Freud's most significant contributions were to the development of modern intellectual history, specifically in his insistence that the inner recesses of the mind were valid and meaningful parts of the personality, and that dreams and fantasies were as vital to human life as reason itself.

In challenging reason as the governor of human action, Freud questioned the very nature of human morality. He described benevolent action and altruistic conduct as mere masks for self-gratification, and religion as a form of mass delusion. Such views were central to the essay *Civilization and Its Discontents*, in which Freud explored at length the relationship between psychic activity and human society. Enumerating the various ways in which all human beings attempt to escape the "pain and unpleasure" of life, Freud argued that civilization itself was the collective product of sublimated instincts. The greatest impediment to civilization, he claimed, was human aggression, which he defined as "an original, self-subsisting instinctual disposition in man." The following excerpts offer some idea of Freud's incisive analysis of the psychic life of human beings.

READING 6.3 From Freud's *Civilization and Its Discontents* (1930)

We will . . . turn to the less ambitious question of what men themselves show by their behavior to be the purpose and intention of their lives. What do they demand of life and wish **1**

to achieve in it? The answer to this can hardly be in doubt. They strive after happiness; they want to become happy and to remain so. This endeavor has two sides, a positive and a negative aim. It aims, on the one hand, at an absence of pain and unpleasure, and, on the other, at the experiencing of strong feelings of pleasure. In its narrower sense the word "happiness" only relates to the last. In conformity with this **10** dichotomy in his aims, man's activity develops in two directions, according as it seeks to realize—in the main, or even exclusively—the one or the other of these aims.

As we see, what decides the purpose of life is simply the programme of the pleasure principle. This principle dominates the operation of the mental apparatus from the start. There can be no doubt about its efficacy, and yet its programme is at loggerheads with the whole world, with the macrocosm as much as with the microcosm. There is no possibility at all of its being carried through; all the regulations of the universe **20** run counter to it. One feels inclined to say that the intention that man should be "happy" is not included in the plan of "Creation." What we call happiness in the strictest sense comes from the (preferably sudden) satisfaction of needs which have been dammed up to a high degree, and it is from its nature only possible as an episodic phenomenon. When any situation that is desired by the pleasure principle is prolonged, it only produces a feeling of mild contentment. We are so made that we can derive intense enjoyment only from a contrast and very little from a state of things. Thus our **30** possibilities of happiness are already restricted by our constitution. Unhappiness is much less difficult to experience. We are threatened with suffering from three directions: from our own body, which is doomed to decay and dissolution and which cannot even do without pain and anxiety as warning signals; from the external world, which may rage against us with overwhelming and merciless forces of destruction; and finally from our relations to other men. The suffering which comes from this last source is perhaps more painful to us than any other. We tend to regard it as a kind of gratuitous **40** addition, although it cannot be any less fatefully inevitable than the suffering which comes from elsewhere. . . .

An unrestricted satisfaction of every need presents itself as the most enticing method of conducting one's life, but it means putting enjoyment before caution, and soon brings its own punishment. The other methods, in which avoidance of unpleasure is the main purpose, are differentiated according to the source of unpleasure to which their attention is chiefly turned. Some of these methods are extreme and some moderate; some are one-sided and some attack the problem **50** simultaneously at several points. Against the suffering which may come upon one from human relationships the readiest safeguard is voluntary isolation, keeping oneself aloof from other people. The happiness which can be achieved along this path is, as we see, the happiness of quietness. Against the dreaded external world one can only defend oneself by some kind of turning away from it, if one intends to solve the task by oneself. There is, indeed, another and better path: that of becoming a member of the human community, and, with the help of a technique guided by science, going over to the attack **60** against nature and subjecting her to the human will. Then one is working with all for the good of all. But the most interesting methods of averting suffering are those which seek to influence our own organism. In the last analysis, all suffering is nothing else than sensation; it only exists in so far as we feel it, and we only feel it in consequence of certain ways in which our organism is regulated.

The crudest, but also the most effective among these methods of influence is the chemical one—intoxication. I do not think that anyone completely understands its mechanism, **70** but it is a fact that there are foreign substances which, when present in the blood or tissues, directly cause us pleasurable sensations; and they also so alter the conditions governing our sensibility that we become incapable of receiving unpleasurable impulses. The two effects not only occur simultaneously, but seem to be intimately bound up with each other. But there must be substances in the chemistry of our own bodies which have similar effects, for we know at least one pathological state, mania, in which a condition similar to intoxication arises without the administration of any **80** intoxicating drug. Besides this, our normal mental life exhibits oscillations between a comparatively easy liberation of pleasure and a comparatively difficult one, parallel with which there goes a diminished or an increased receptivity to unpleasure. It is greatly to be regretted that this toxic side of mental processes has so far escaped scientific examination. The service rendered by intoxicating media in the struggle for happiness and in keeping misery at a distance is so highly prized as a benefit that individuals and people alike have given them an established place in the economics of their **90** libido.[1] We owe to such media not merely the immediate yield of pleasure, but also a greatly desired degree of independence from the external world. For one knows that, with the help of this "drowner of cares," one can at any time withdraw from the pressure of reality and find refuge in a world of one's own with better conditions of sensibility. As is well known, it is precisely this property of intoxicants which also determines their danger and their injuriousness. They are responsible, in certain circumstances, for the useless waste of a large quota of energy which might have been employed for the **100** improvement of the human lot. . . .

Another technique for fending off suffering is the employment of the displacements of libido which our mental apparatus permits of and through which its function gains so much in flexibility. The task here is that of shifting the instinctual aims in such a way that they cannot come up against frustration from the external world. In this, sublimation of the instincts lends its assistance. One gains the most if one can sufficiently heighten the yield of pleasure from the sources of psychical and intellectual work. When that is so, **110** fate can do little against one. A satisfaction of this kind, such as an artist's joy in creating, in giving his phantasies body, or a scientist's in solving problems or discovering truths, has a special quality which we shall certainly one day be able to characterize in metapsychological terms. At present we can only say figuratively that such satisfactions seem "finer and higher." But their intensity is mild as compared with that derived from the sating of crude and primary instinctual impulses; it does not convulse our physical being. And the

weak point of this method is that it is not applicable generally: **120** it is accessible to only a few people. It presupposes the possession of special dispositions and gifts which are far from being common to any practical degree. And even to the few who do possess them, this method cannot give complete protection from suffering. It creates no impenetrable armor against the arrows of fortune, and it habitually fails when the source of suffering is a person's own body. . . .

Another procedure operates more energetically and more thoroughly. It regards reality as the sole enemy and as the source of all suffering, with which it is impossible to live, so **130** that one must break off all relations with it if one is to be in any way happy. The hermit turns his back on the world and will have no truck with it. But one can do more than that; one can try to re-create the world, to build up in its stead another world in which its most unbearable features are eliminated and replaced by others that are in conformity with one's own wishes. But whoever, in desperate defiance, sets out upon this path to happiness will as a rule attain nothing. Reality is too strong for him. He becomes a madman, who for the most part finds no one to help him in carrying through his delusion. It is **140** asserted, however, that each one of us behaves in some one respect like a paranoiac, corrects some aspect of the world which is unbearable to him by the construction of a wish and introduces this delusion into reality. A special importance attaches to the case in which this attempt to procure a certainty of happiness and a protection against suffering through a delusional remoulding of reality is made by a considerable number of people in common. The religions of mankind must be classed among the mass-delusions of this kind. No one, needless to say, who shares a delusion ever **150** recognizes it as such. . . .

Religion restricts this play of choice and adaptation, since it imposes equally on everyone its own path to the acquisition of happiness and protection from suffering. Its technique consists in depressing the value of life and distorting the picture of the real world in a delusional manner—which presupposes an intimidation of the intelligence. At this price, by forcibly fixing them in a state of psychical infantilism and by drawing them into a mass-delusion, religion succeeds in sparing many people an individual neurosis. But hardly anything more. . . . **160** During the last few generations mankind has made an extraordinary advance in the natural sciences and in their technical application and has established his control over nature in a way never before imagined. The single steps of this advance are common knowledge and it is unnecessary to enumerate them. Men are proud of those achievements, and have a right to be. But they seem to have observed that this newly-won power over space and time, this subjugation of the forces of nature, which is the fulfillment of a longing that goes back thousands of years, has not increased the amount of **170** pleasurable satisfaction which they may expect from life and has not made them feel happier. From the recognition of this fact we ought to be content to conclude that power over nature is not the *only* precondition of human happiness, just as it is not the *only* goal of cultural endeavor; we ought not to infer from it that technical progress is without value for the economics of our happiness. One would like to ask: is there, then, no positive gain in pleasure, no unequivocal increase in

---

[1] The instinctual desires of the id, most specifically, the sexual urge.

my feeling of happiness, if I can, as often as I please, hear the voice of a child of mine who is living hundreds of miles away 180 or if I can learn in the shortest possible time after a friend has reached his destination that he has come through the long and difficult voyage unharmed? Does it mean nothing that medicine has succeeded in enormously reducing infant mortality and the danger of infection for women in childbirth and, indeed, in considerably lengthening the average life of a civilized man? And there is a long list that might be added to benefits of this kind which we owe to the much-despised era of scientific and technical advances. But here the voice of pessimistic criticism makes itself heard and warns us that 190 most of these satisfactions follow the model of the "cheap enjoyment" extolled in the anecdote—the enjoyment obtained by putting a bare leg from under the bedclothes on a cold winter night and drawing it in again. If there had been no railway to conquer distances, my child would never have left his native town and I should need no telephone to hear his voice; if travelling across the ocean by ship had not been introduced, my friend would not have embarked on his sea-voyage and I should not need a cable to relieve my anxiety about him. What is the use of reducing infantile mortality 200 when it is precisely that reduction which imposes the greatest restraint on us in the begetting of children, so that, taken all round, we nevertheless rear no more children than in the days before the reign of hygiene, while at the same time we have created difficult conditions for our sexual life in marriage, and have probably worked against the beneficial effects of natural selection? And, finally, what good to us is a long life if it is difficult and barren of joys, and if it is so full of misery that we can only welcome death as a deliverer? . . .

. . . men are not gentle creatures who want to be loved, and 210 who at the most can defend themselves if they are attacked; they are, on the contrary, creatures among whose instinctual endowments is to be reckoned a powerful share of aggressiveness. As a result, their neighbor is for them not only a potential helper or sexual object, but also someone who tempts them to satisfy their aggressiveness on him, to exploit his capacity for work without compensation, to use him sexually without his consent, to seize his possessions, to humiliate him, to cause him pain, to torture and to kill him. . . .

The existence of this inclination to aggression, which we 220 can detect in ourselves and justly assume to be present in others, is the factor which disturbs our relations with our neighbor and which forces civilization into such a high expenditure [of energy]. In consequence of this primary mutual hostility of human beings, civilized society is perpetually threatened with disintegration. The interest of work in common would not hold it together; instinctual passions are stronger than reasonable interests. Civilization has to use its utmost efforts in order to set limits to man's aggressive instincts and to hold the manifestations of them in check by 230 psychical reaction-formations. Hence, therefore, the use of methods intended to incite people into identifications and aim-inhibited relationships of love, hence the restriction upon sexual life, and hence too the [idealist] commandment to love one's neighbor as oneself—a commandment which is really justified by the fact that nothing else runs so strongly counter to the original nature of man. In spite of every effort, these endeavors of civilization have not so far achieved very much. It hopes to prevent the crudest excesses of brutal violence by itself assuming the right to use violence against criminals, but 240 the law is not able to lay hold of the more cautious and refined manifestations of human aggressiveness. The time comes when each one of us has to give up as illusions the expectations which, in his youth, he pinned upon his fellowmen, and when he may learn how much difficulty and pain has been added to his life by their ill-will. . . .

Q What, according to Freud, are the three main sources of human suffering? By what means does one fend off suffering?

Q What does Freud see as the greatest threat to civilized society?

Freud's Followers

Freud's writings explored so many aspects of human experience that, inevitably, his theories would be tested and laid open to assault. In the second half of the twentieth century, for instance, some physicians questioned the scientific validity of psychoanalysis and its usefulness as a form of treatment. At the same time, feminists, whose movement for women's liberation (see chapter 36) clearly owes much to Freud's critique of sexual morality, have attacked Freud's patriarchal image of the female as passive, weak, and dependent. Nevertheless, Freud's immediate followers recognized that they stood in the shadow of an intellectual giant. Although some theorists disagreed with Freud's dogmatic assertion that all neuroses stemmed from the traumas of the id, most took his discoveries as the starting point for their own inquiries into human behavior. For instance, Freud's Viennese associate Alfred Adler (1870–1937), who pioneered the field of individual psychology, sought to explain the ego's efforts to adapt to its environment. Coining the term "inferiority complex," Adler concentrated on analyzing problems related to the ego's failure to achieve its operational goals in everyday life.

Another of Freud's colleagues, the Swiss physician Carl Gustav Jung (1875–1961), found Freud's view of the psyche too narrow and overly deterministic. Jung argued that the personal, unconscious life of the individual rested on a deeper and more universal layer of the human psyche, which he called the **collective unconscious**. According to Jung, the collective unconscious belongs to humankind at large, that is, to the human family. It manifests itself throughout history in the form of dreams, myths, and fairy tales. The **archetypes** (primal patterns) of that realm reflect the deep psychic needs of humankind as a species. They reveal themselves as familiar motifs and characters, such as "the child-god," "the hero," and "the wise old man." Jung's investigations into the cultural history of humankind disclosed similarities between the symbols and myths of different religions and bodies of folklore. These he took to support his theory that the archetypes were the innate, inherited contents of the human mind.

Some of Jung's most convincing observations concerning the life of the collective unconscious appear in his essay "Psychological Aspects of the Mother Archetype" (1938). In this essay, Jung discusses the manifestations of the female archetype in personal life, as mother, grandmother, stepmother, nurse, or governess; in religion, as the redemptive Mother of God, the Virgin, Holy Wisdom, and the various nature deities of ancient myth and religion; and in the universal symbolism of things and places associated with fertility and fruitfulness, such as the cornucopia, the garden, the fountain, the cave, the rose, the lotus, the magic circle, and the uterus. The negative aspect of the female archetype, observed Jung, usually manifests itself as the witch in traditional fairy tales and legends. Jung emphasized the role of the collective unconscious in reflecting the "psychic unity" of all cultures. He treated the personal psyche as part of the larger human family, and, unlike Freud, he insisted on the positive value of religion in satisfying humankind's deepest psychic desires.

The New Psychology and Literature

The impact of the new psychology was felt throughout Europe. Freud's theories, and particularly his pessimistic view of human nature, intensified the mood of uncertainty produced by the startling revelations of atomic physics and the outbreak of World War I. The Freudian revolution affected all aspects of artistic expression, not the least of which was literature. A great many figures in early twentieth-century fiction were profoundly influenced by Freud; three of the most famous of these are Marcel Proust, Franz Kafka, and James Joyce. In the works of these novelists, the most significant events are those that take place in the psychic life of dreams and memory. The narrative line of the story may be interrupted by unexpected leaps of thought, intrusive recollections, self-reflections, and sudden dead ends. Fantasy may alternate freely with rational thought. The lives of the heroes—or, more exactly, antiheroes—in these stories are often inconsequential, while their concerns, though commonplace or trivial, may be obsessive, bizarre, and charged with passion.

Proust's Quest for Lost Time

Born in Paris, Marcel Proust (1871–1922) spent his youth troubled by severe attacks of asthma and recurring insecurities over his sexual orientation. Devastated by the death of his mother in 1905, Proust withdrew completely from Parisian society. He retreated into the semidarkness of a cork-lined room, where, shielded from noise, light, and frivolous society, he pursued a life of introspection and literary endeavor. Between 1913 and 1927 Proust produced a sixteen-volume novel entitled *A la recherche du temps perdu* (literally, "In Search of Lost Time," but usually translated as *Remembrance of Things Past*). This lengthy masterpiece provides a reflection of the society of turn-of-the-century France, but its perception of reality is wholly internal. Its central theme is the role of memory in retrieving past experience and in shaping the private life of the individual. Proust's mission was to rediscover a sense of the past by reviving sensory

experiences buried deep within his psyche, that is, to bring the unconscious life to the conscious level. "For me," explained Proust, "the novel is . . . psychology in space and time."

In the first volume of *A la recherche du temps perdu*, entitled *Swann's Way*, Proust employs the Freudian technique of "free association" to recapture from the recesses of memory the intense moment of pleasure occasioned by the taste of a piece of cake soaked in tea. The following excerpt illustrates Proust's ability to free experience from the rigid order of mechanical time and to invade the richly textured storehouse of the psyche. It also illustrates the modern notion of the mental process as a "stream of thought," a concept that had appeared as early as 1884 in the writings of the American psychologist William James (1842–1910) and in the works of Henri Bergson (1859–1941), who argued that reality is best understood as a perpetual flux in which past and present are inseparable (see chapter 31).

READING 6.4 From Proust's *Swann's Way* (1913)

The past is hidden somewhere outside the realm, beyond the   1
reach of intellect, in some material object (in the sensation
which that material object will give us) which we do not
suspect. And as for that object, it depends on chance whether
we come upon it or not before we ourselves must die.

Many years had elapsed during which nothing of Combray,
save what was comprised in the theatre and the drama of my
going to bed there, had any existence for me, when one day in
winter, as I came home, my mother, seeing that I was cold,
offered me some tea, a thing I did not ordinarily take. I   10
declined at first, and then, for no particular reason, changed
my mind. She sent out for one of those short, plump little
cakes called "petites madeleines," which look as though they
had been moulded in the fluted scallop of a pilgrim's shell.
And soon, mechanically, weary after a dull day with the
prospect of a depressing morrow, I raised to my lips a spoonful
of the tea in which I had soaked a morsel of the cake. No
sooner had the warm liquid, and the crumbs with it, touched
my palate than a shudder ran through my whole body, and I
stopped, intent upon the extraordinary changes that were   20
taking place. An exquisite pleasure had invaded my senses,
but individual, detached, with no suggestion of its origin. And
at once the vicissitudes of life had become indifferent to me,
its disasters innocuous, its brevity illusory—this new
sensation having had on me the effect which love has of filling
me with a precious essence; or rather this essence was not in
me, it was myself. I had ceased now to feel mediocre,
accidental, mortal. Whence could it have come to me, this all-
powerful joy? I was conscious that it was connected with the
taste of tea and cake, but that it infinitely transcended those   30
savours, could not, indeed, be of the same nature as theirs.
Whence did it come? What did it signify? How could I seize
upon and define it?

I drink a second mouthful, in which I find nothing more than
in the first, a third, which gives me rather less than the
second. It is time to stop; the potion is losing its magic. It is
plain that the object of my quest, the truth, lies not in the cup
but in myself. The tea has called up in me, but does not itself

understand, and can only repeat indefinitely with a gradual loss of strength, the same testimony; which I, too, cannot interpret, though I hope at least to be able to call upon the tea for it again and to find it there presently, intact and at my disposal, for my final enlightenment. I put down my cup and examine my own mind. It is for it to discover the truth. But how? What an abyss of uncertainty whenever the mind feels that some part of it has strayed beyond its own borders; when it, the seeker, is at once the dark region through which it must go seeking, where all its equipment will avail it nothing. Seek? More than that: create. It is face to face with something which does not so far exist, to which it alone can give reality and substance, which it alone can bring into the light of day.

And I begin again to ask myself what it could have been, this unremembered state which brought with it no logical proof of its existence, but only the sense that it was a happy, that it was a real state in whose presence other states of consciousness melted and vanished. I decide to attempt to make it reappear. I retrace my thoughts to the moment at which I drank the first spoonful of tea. I find again the same state, illumined by no fresh light. I compel my mind to make one further effort, to follow and recapture once again the fleeting sensation. And that nothing may interrupt it in its course I shut out every obstacle, every extraneous idea, I stop my ears and inhibit all attention to the sounds which come from the next room. And then, feeling that my mind is growing fatigued without having any success to report, I compel it for a change to enjoy that distraction which I have just denied it, to think of other things, to rest and refresh itself before the supreme attempt. And then for the second time I clear an empty space in front of it. I place in position before my mind's eye the still recent taste of that first mouthful, and I feel something start within me, something that leaves its resting-place and attempts to rise, something that has been embedded like an anchor at a great depth; I do not know yet what it is, but I can feel it mounting slowly; I can measure the resistance, I can hear the echo of great spaces traversed.

Undoubtedly what is thus palpitating in the depths of my being must be the image, the visual memory which, being linked to that taste, has tried to follow it into my conscious mind. But its struggles are too far off, too much confused; scarcely can I perceive the colorless reflection in which are blended the uncapturable whirling medley of radiant hues, and I cannot distinguish its form, cannot invite it, as the one possible interpreter, to translate to me the evidence of its contemporary, its inseparable paramour, the taste of cake soaked in tea; cannot ask it to inform me what special circumstance is in question, of what period in my past life.

Will it ultimately reach the clear surface of my consciousness, this memory, this old, dead moment which the magnetism of an identical moment has travelled so far to importune, to disturb, to raise up out of the very depths of my being? I cannot tell. Now that I feel nothing, it has stopped, has perhaps gone down again into its darkness, from which who can say whether it will ever rise? Ten times over I must essay the task, must lean down over the abyss. And each time the natural laziness which deters us from every difficult enterprise, every work of importance, has urged me to leave the thing alone, to drink my tea and to think merely of the worries of to-day and

of my hopes for tomorrow, which let themselves be pondered over without effort or distress of mind.

And suddenly the memory returns. The taste was that of the little crumb of madeleine which on Sunday mornings at Combray (because on those mornings I did not go out before church-time), when I went to say good day to her in her bedroom, my aunt Léonie used to give me, dipping it first in her own cup of real or of lime-flower tea. The sight of the little madeleine had recalled nothing to my mind before I tasted it; perhaps because I had so often seen such things in the interval, without tasting them, on the trays in pastry-cooks' windows, that their image had dissociated itself from those Combray days to take its place among others more recent; perhaps because of those memories, so long abandoned and put out of mind, nothing now survived, everything was scattered; the forms of things, including that of the little scallop-shell of pastry, so richly sensual under its severe, religious folds, were either obliterated or had been so long dormant as to have lost the power of expansion which would have allowed them to resume their place in my consciousness. But when from a long-distant past nothing subsists, after the people are dead, after the things are broken and scattered, still, alone, more fragile, but with more vitality, more unsubstantial, more persistent, more faithful, the smell and taste of things remain poised a long time, like souls, ready to remind us, waiting and hoping for their moment, amid the ruins of all the rest; and bear unfaltering, in the tiny and a most impalpable drop of their essence, the vast structure of recollection.

And once I had recognized the taste of the crumb of madeleine soaked in her decoction of lime-flowers which my aunt used to give me (although I did not yet know and must long postpone the discovery of why this memory made me so happy) immediately the old grey house upon the street, where her room was, rose up like the scenery of a theatre to attach itself to the little pavilion, opening on to the garden, which had been built out behind it for my parents (the isolated panel which until that moment had been all that I could see); and with the house the town, from morning to night and in all weathers, the Square where I was sent before luncheon, the streets along which I used to run errands, the country roads we took when it was fine. And just as the Japanese amuse themselves by filling a porcelain bowl with water and steeping in it little crumbs of paper which until then are without character or form, but, the moment they become wet, stretch themselves and bend, take on color and distinctive shape, become flowers or houses or people, permanent and recognisable, so in that moment all the flowers in our garden and in M. Swann's park, and the water-lilies on the Vivonne and the good folk of the village and their little dwellings and the parish church and the whole of Combray and of its surroundings, taking their proper shapes and growing solid, sprang into being, towns and gardens alike, from my cup of tea. . . .

Q What links does Proust draw between his unconscious and his conscience self? What role does the madeleine play in these relationships?

The Nightmare Reality of Kafka

For Proust, memory was a life-enriching phenomenon, but for the German-Jewish novelist Franz Kafka (1883–1924), the subconscious life gave conscious experience bizarre and threatening gravity. Written in German, Kafka's novels and short stories take on the reality of dreams in which characters are nameless, details are precise but grotesque, and events lack logical consistency. In the nightmarish world of his novels, the central characters become victims of unknown or imprecisely understood forces. They may be caught in absurd but commonplace circumstances involving guilt and frustration, or they may be threatened by menacing events that appear to have neither meaning nor purpose. In *The Trial* (1925), for instance, the protagonist is arrested, convicted, and executed, without ever knowing the nature of his crime. In "The Metamorphosis," one of the most disquieting short stories of the twentieth century, the central character, Gregor Samsa, wakes one morning to discover that he has turned into a large insect. The themes of insecurity and vulnerability that recur in Kafka's novels reflect the mood that prevailed during the early decades of the century. Kafka himself was afflicted with this insecurity: shortly before he died in 1924, he asked a close friend to burn all of his manuscripts; the friend disregarded the request and saw to it that Kafka's works, even some that were unfinished, were published. Consequently, Kafka's style, which builds on deliberate ambiguity and fearful contradiction, has had a major influence on modern fiction. Although "The Metamorphosis" is too long to reproduce here in full, the excerpt that follows conveys some idea of Kafka's surreal narrative style.

READING 6.5 From Kafka's "The Metamorphosis" (1915)

As Gregor Samsa awoke one morning from uneasy dreams he **1** found himself transformed in his bed into a gigantic insect. He was lying on his hard, as it were armor-plated, back and when he lifted his head a little he could see his dome-like brown belly divided into stiff arched segments on top of which the bed quilt could hardly keep in position and was about to slide off completely. His numerous legs, which were pitifully thin compared to the rest of his bulk, waved helplessly before his eyes.

What has happened to me? he thought. It was no dream. **10** His room, a regular human bedroom, only rather too small, lay quiet between the four familiar walls. Above the table on which a collection of cloth samples was unpacked and spread out—Samsa was a commercial traveler—hung the picture, which he had recently cut out of an illustrated magazine and put into a pretty gilt frame. It showed a lady, with a fur cap on and a fur stole, sitting upright and holding out to the spectator a huge fur muff into which the whole of her forearm had vanished!

Gregor's eyes turned next to the window, and the overcast **20** sky—one could hear raindrops beating on the window gutter—made him quite melancholy. What about sleeping a little longer and forgetting all this nonsense, he thought, but it could not be done, for he was accustomed to sleep on his right side and in his present condition he could not turn himself over. However violently he forced himself towards his right side he always rolled on to his back again. He tried it at least a hundred times, shutting his eyes to keep from seeing his struggling legs, and only desisted when he began to feel in his side a faint dull ache he had never experienced before. **30**

Oh God, he thought, what an exhausting job I've picked on! Traveling about day in, day out. It's much more irritating work than doing the actual business in the office, and on top of that there's the trouble of constant traveling, of worrying about train connections, the bed and irregular meals, casual acquaintances that are always new and never become intimate friends. The devil take it all! He felt a slight itching upon his belly; slowly pushed himself on his back nearer to the top of the bed so that he could lift his head more easily; identified the itching place which was surrounded by many **40** small white spots the nature of which he could not understand and made to touch it with a leg, but drew the leg back immediately, for the contact made a cold shiver run through him. . . .

He looked at the alarm clock ticking on the chest. Heavenly Father! he thought. It was half-past six o'clock and the hands were quietly moving on, it was even past the half-hour, it was getting on toward a quarter to seven. Had the alarm clock not gone off? From the bed one could see that it had been properly set for four o'clock; of course it must have gone off. Yes, but **50** was it possible to sleep quietly through that ear-splitting noise? Well, he had not slept quietly, yet apparently all the more soundly for that. But what was he to do now? The next train went at seven o'clock; to catch that he would need to hurry like mad and his samples weren't even packed up, and he himself wasn't feeling particularly fresh and active. And even if he did catch the train he wouldn't avoid a row with the chief, since the firm's porter would have been waiting for the five o'clock train and would have long since reported his failure to turn up. . . . **60**

As all this was running through his mind at top speed without his being able to decide to leave his bed—the alarm clock had just struck a quarter to seven—there came a cautious tap at the door behind the head of his bed. "Gregor," said a voice—it was his mother's—"it's a quarter to seven. Hadn't you a train to catch?" That gentle voice! Gregor had a shock as he heard his own voice answering hers, unmistakably his own voice, it was true, but with a persistent horrible twittering squeak behind it like an undertone, that left the words in their clear shape only for the first moment and then **70** rose up reverberating round them to destroy their sense, so that one could not be sure one had heard them rightly. Gregor wanted to answer at length and explain everything, but in the circumstances he confined himself to saying: "Yes, yes, thank you, Mother, I'm getting up now." The wooden door between them must have kept the change in his voice from being noticeable outside, for his mother contented herself with this statement and shuffled away. Yet this brief exchange of words had made the other members of the family aware that Gregor was still in the house, as they had not expected, and at one of **80** the side doors his father was already knocking, gently, yet with his fist. "Gregor, Gregor," he called, "what's the matter with you?" And after a little while he called again in a deeper voice: "Gregor! Gregor!" At the other side door his sister was saying in a low, plaintive tone: "Gregor? Aren't you well? Are you needing anything?" He answered them both at once: "I'm just ready," and did his best to make his voice sound as normal as possible by enunciating the words very clearly and leaving long pauses between them. So his father went back to his breakfast, but his sister whispered: "Gregor, open the door, do.". . . 90 [Unexpectedly, the chief clerk arrives to find out why Gregor is not at work. He demands to see him.]

Slowly Gregor pushed the chair towards the door, then let go of it, caught hold of the door for support—the soles at the end of his little legs were somewhat sticky—and rested against it for a moment after his efforts. Then he set himself to turning the key in the lock with his mouth. It seemed, unhappily, that he hadn't really any teeth—what could he grip the key with?—but on the other hand his jaws were certainly very strong; with their help he did manage to set the key in 100 motion, heedless of the fact that he was undoubtedly damaging them somewhere, since a brown fluid issued from his mouth, flowed over the key and dripped on the floor. "Just listen to that," said the chief clerk next door; "he's turning the key." That was a great encouragement to Gregor; but they should all have shouted encouragement to him, his father and mother too: "Go on Gregor," they should have called out, "keep going, hold on to that key!" And in the belief that they were all following his efforts intently, he clenched his jaws recklessly on the key with all the force at his command. As 110 the turning of the key progressed he circled round the lock, holding on now only with his mouth, pushing on the key, as required, or pulling it down again with all the weight of his body. The louder click of the finally yielding lock literally quickened Gregor. With a deep breath of relief he said to himself: "So I didn't need the locksmith," and laid his head on the handle to open the door wide.

Since he had to pull the door towards him, he was still invisible when it was really wide open. He had to edge himself slowly round the near half of the double door, and to 120 do it very carefully if he was not to fall plump upon his back just on the threshold. He was still carrying out this difficult manoeuvre, with no time to observe anything else, when he heard the chief clerk utter a loud "Oh!"—it sounded like a gust of wind—and now he could see the man, standing as he was nearest to the door, clapping one hand before his open mouth and slowly backing away as if driven by some invisible steady pressure. His mother—in spite of the chief clerk's directions—first clasped her hands and looked at his father, then took two steps towards Gregor and fell on the floor 130 among her outspread skirts, her face quite hidden on her breast. His father knotted his fist with a fierce expression on his face as if he meant to knock Gregor back into his room, then looked uncertainly round the living room, covered his eyes with his hands and wept till his great chest heaved. . . .

Q How would you describe Gregor Samsa's personality?

Q What details in this story establish a sense of reality? Of unreality? Of fear?

Joyce and Stream of Consciousness Prose

One of the most influential writers of the early twentieth century, and also one of the most challenging, was the Irish expatriate James Joyce (1882–1941). Born in Dublin and educated in Jesuit schools, Joyce abandoned Ireland in 1905 to live abroad. In Paris, he studied medicine and music but made his livelihood there and elsewhere by teaching foreign languages and writing short stories. Joyce's prose reflects his genius as a linguist and his keen sensitivity to the musical potential of words. His treatment of plot and character is deeply indebted to Freud, whose earliest publications Joyce had consumed with interest. From Freud's works, he drew inspiration from the **interior monologue**, a literary device consisting of the private musings of a character in the form of a "stream of consciousness"—a succession of images and ideas connected by free association rather than by logical argument or narrative sequence. The stream of consciousness device recalls the free association technique used by Freud in psychotherapy; it also recalls the discontinuous verse style of the imagist poets (see chapter 32). In a stream of consciousness novel, the action is developed through the mind of the principal character as he or she responds to the dual play of conscious and subconscious stimuli. The following passage from Joyce's 600-page novel *Ulysses* (1922) provides a brief example:

He crossed to the bright side, avoiding the loose cellarflap of number seventy-five. The sun was nearing the steeple of George's church. Be a warm day I fancy, Specially in these black clothes feel it more. Black conducts, reflects (refracts is it?), the heat. But I couldn't go in that light suit. Make a picnic of it. His Boland's breadvan delivering with trays our daily but she prefers yesterday's loaves turnovers crisp crowns hot. Makes you feel young. Somewhere in the east: early morning: set off at dawn, travel round in front of the sun, steal a day's march on him. Keep it up for ever never grow a day older technically. . . . Wander along all day. Meet a robber or two. Well, meet him. Getting on to sundown. The shadows of the mosques along the pillars: priest with a scroll rolled up. A shiver of the trees, signal, the evening wind. I pass on. Fading gold sky. A mother watches from her doorway. She calls her children home in their dark language. High wall: beyond strings twanged. Night sky moon, violet, colour of Molly's new garters. Strings. Listen. A girl playing one of these instruments what do you call them: dulcimers. I pass. . . .*

Joyce modeled his sprawling novel on the Homeric epic, the *Odyssey*. But Joyce's modern version differs profoundly from Homer's. Leopold Bloom, the main character of *Ulysses*, is as ordinary as Homer's Odysseus was heroic; his adventures seem trivial and insignificant by comparison

---

*James Joyce, *Ulysses*. New York: Vintage Books edition, Knopf, 1966, 57.

with those of his classical counterpart. Bloom's common-place experiences, as he wanders from home to office, pub, and brothel, and then home again—a one-day "voyage" through the streets of Dublin—constitute the plot of the novel. The real "action" of *Ulysses* takes place in the minds of its principal characters: Bloom, his acquaintances, and his wife Molly. Their collective ruminations produce an overwhelming sense of desolation and a startling aware-ness that the human psyche can never extricate itself from the timeless blur of experience. Joyce's stream of consciousness technique and his dense accumulation of unfamiliar and oddly compounded words make this monu-mental novel difficult to grasp—yet it remains more acces-sible than his experimental, baffling prose work, *Finnegans Wake* (1939). Initially, however, it was censorship that made *Ulysses* inaccessible to the public: since Joyce treated sexual matters as freely as all other aspects of human expe-rience, critics judged his language obscene. The novel was banned in the United States until 1933.

The combined influence of Freud and Joyce was visible in much of the first-ranking literature of the twentieth cen-tury. Writers such as Gertrude Stein (1874–1946) and the Nobel laureates Thomas Mann (1875–1955) and William Faulkner (1897–1962) extended the use of the stream of consciousness technique. In theater the American play-wright Eugene O'Neill (1888–1953) fused Greek myth with Freudian concepts of guilt and repression in the dra-matic trilogy *Mourning Becomes Electra* (1931). He devised dramatic techniques that revealed the characters' buried emotions, such as two actors playing different aspects of a single individual, the use of masks, and the embellishment of dialogue with accompanying asides. The new psychology extended its influence to performance style as well: Freud's emphasis on the interior life inspired the development of **method acting**, a style of modern theatrical performance that tried to harness "true emotion" and "affective memory" from childhood experience in the interpretation of dra-matic roles. The pioneer in method acting was the Russian director and actor Konstantin Stanislavsky (1863–1938), whose innovative techniques as head of the Moscow Art Theater spread to the United States in the early 1930s. There, his method inspired some of America's finest screen and stage actors, such as James Dean (1931–1955) and Marlon Brando (1924–2004).

The New Freedom in Poetry

Modern poets avidly seized upon stream of consciousness techniques to emancipate poetry from syntactical and grammatical bonds—a mission that had been initiated by the symbolists and refined by the imagists. The French writer Guillaume Apollinaire (1880–1918), a close friend of Picasso and an admirer of cubism, wrote poems that not only liberated words from their traditional placement in the sentence but also freed sentences from their traditional arrangement on the page. Inspired by the designs of ordi-nary handbills, billboards, and signs, Apollinaire created **concrete poems**, that is, poems produced in the shape of external objects, such as watches, neckties, and pigeons. He arranged the words in the poem "Il Pleut" ("It Rains"),

for instance, as if they had fallen onto the page like raindrops from the heavens. Such word-pictures, which Apollinaire called "lyrical ideograms," inspired the poet to exult, "I too am a painter!"

The American poet e.e.cummings (1894–1962) arrived in France in 1917 as a volunteer ambulance driver for the Red Cross. Like Apollinaire, cummings wrote poems that violated the traditional rules of verse composition. To sharpen the focus of a poem, he subjected typography and syntax to acrobatic distortions that challenged the eye as well as the ear. cummings poked fun at modern society by packing his verse with slang, jargon, and sexual innuendo. As the following poem suggests, his lyrics are often infused with large doses of playful humor.

READING 6.6 cummings' [she being Brand]
(1926)

she being Brand	1
-new;and you	
know consequently a	
little stiff i was	
careful of her and(having	5
thoroughly oiled the universal	
joint tested my gas felt of	
her radiator made sure her springs were O.	
K.)i went right to it flooded-the-carburetor cranked her	
up, slipped the	10
clutch(and then somehow got into reverse she	
kicked what	
the hell)next	
minute i was back in neutral tried and	
again slo-wly;bare,ly nudg. ing(my	15
lev-er Right-	
oh and her gears being in	
A 1 shape passed	
from low through	
second-in-to-high like	20
greasedlightning) just as we turned the corner of Divinity	
avenue i touched the accelerator and give	
her the juice,good	
(it	
was the first ride and believe i we was	25
happy to see how nice she acted right up to	
the last minute coming back down by the Public	
Gardens i slammed on	
the	
internalexpanding	30
&	
externalcontracting	
brakes Bothatonce and	
brought allofher tremB	

Q Who is the "she" in this poem?
Q What liberties does the poet take with form? With subject matter?

The New Psychology and the Visual Arts

It was in the visual arts that the new psychology made its most dramatic and long-lasting impact. As artists brought to their work their hidden emotions, repressed desires, and their dreams and fantasies, art became the pursuit of the subconscious. The irrational and antirational forces of the id became the subject and the inspiration for an assortment of styles. These include expressionism, metaphysical art, dada, and surrealism. Expressionism and surrealism had

particularly important effects on photography and film, as well as on the fields of commercial and applied arts that flourished in the second half of the century. Indeed, in every aspect of our daily experience now, from fashion designs to magazine and television advertisements, the evidence of the Freudian revolution is still visible.

Expressionism

The pioneer expressionist painter of the twentieth century was the Norwegian Edvard Munch (1863–1944). Munch was a great admirer of Henrik Ibsen, his contemporary, whose plays (see chapter 30) examine the inner conflicts and repressed desires of their characters. Obsessed with the traumas of puberty and frustrated sexuality, Munch was also deeply troubled by personal associations with illness and death—tuberculosis had killed both his mother and sister. Such subjects provided the imagery for his paintings and woodcuts; but it was actually in his style—a haunting synthesis of violently distorted forms and savage colors—that Munch captured the anguished intensity of the neurosis that caused his mental collapse in 1908. *The Scream* (Figure **33.1**), a painting that has become a universal

Figure 33.1 EDVARD MUNCH, *The Scream*, 1893. Oil, pastel, and casein on cardboard, 35¾ × 29 in. National Gallery Oslo. © The Munch Museum/The Munch-Ellingsen Group. BONO, Oslo/DACS, London 2005.

symbol of the modern condition, takes its mood of urgency and alarm from the combined effects of sinuous clouds, writhing blue-black waters, and a dramatically receding pier (a popular meeting spot near Munch's summer cottage). These visual rhythms suggest the resonating sound of the voiceless cry described by Munch in the notes to a preliminary drawing for the painting: "I walked with two friends. Then the sun sank. Suddenly the sky turned red as blood. . . . My friends walked on, and I was left alone, trembling with fear. I felt as if all nature were filled with one mighty unending shriek." The ghostly foreground figure—Munch himself—may have been inspired by an Inka mummy the artist had seen in the Paris Exhibition of 1889. The blood-red sky may owe something to the eruption of an Indonesian volcano, whose fiery effects reached Munch's hometown in Norway in August of 1883.

Munch's impassioned style foreshadowed *German expressionism*. Like the cubists and fauves in France and the futurists in Italy, young artists in Germany rebelled against the "old-established forces" of academic art. Influenced by Freud and by the arts of Africa and Oceania, two modernist groups emerged: in Dresden, *Die Brücke* (The Bridge) was founded in 1905; the second, established in Munich in 1911, called itself *Der Blaue Reiter* (The Blue

Rider). Though marked by strong personal differences, the artists of these two groups pursued a style marked by free distortions of form and color that evoke pathos, violence, and emotional intensity. The German expressionists inherited the brooding, romantic sensibility of Goethe, Nietzsche, Wagner, and van Gogh. They favored macabre and intimate subjects, which they rendered by means of distorted forms, harsh colors, and the bold and haunting use of black.

Led by Ernst Ludwig Kirchner (1880–1938), members of *Die Brücke* included Erich Heckel (1883–1970), Karl Schmidt-Rottluff (1884–1976), and Emil Nolde (1867–1956). These artists, who envisioned their movement as a "bridge" to modernism, embraced art as an outpouring of "inner necessity," emotion, and ecstasy. Seized by the prewar tensions of urban Germany, they produced probing self-portraits, tempestuous landscapes, and ominous cityscapes. In the painting *Street, Berlin* (Figure **33.2**), Kirchner's jagged lines and dissonant colors, accented by aggressive areas of black, evoke the image of urban life as crowded, impersonal, and threatening. His convulsive distortions of figural form reveal the influence of African sculpture, while the nervous intensity of his line style reflects his indebtedness to the German graphic tradition

Figure 33.2 ERNST LUDWIG KIRCHNER, *Street, Berlin*, 1913. Oil on canvas, 3 ft. 11½ in. × 35⅞ in. The Museum of Modern Art, New York. Purchase. © 2003 Digital Image MoMA, New York/Scala, Florence.

pioneered by Albrecht Dürer in the sixteenth century (see chapter 19). Like Dürer, Kirchner rendered many of his subjects (including portraits and cityscapes) in woodcut—the favorite medium of German expressionism.

Metaphysical Art and Fantasy

While the German expressionists brought a new degree of subjective intensity to depicting the visible world, other artists explored the life that lay beyond sensory experience. One of these artists was Giorgio de Chirico (1888–1978). Born in Greece, de Chirico moved to Italy in 1909. Rejecting the tenets of Italian futurism (see chapter 32), he pioneered a style that he called "metaphysical," that is, "beyond physical reality." In canvases executed between 1910 and 1920, he brought the world of the subconscious into the realm of art. Combining sharply delineated images, contradictory perspectives, unnatural colors, and illogically cast shadows, he produced disturbing, dreamlike effects similar to those achieved by Kafka in prose. In his painting *The Nostalgia of the Infinite* (Figure **33.3**), two figures, dwarfed by eerie shadows, stand in the empty courtyard; five flags flutter mysteriously in an airless, acid-green sky. The vanishing point established by the orthogonal lines of the portico on the right contradicts the low placement of the distant horizon. About his disquieting cityscapes, de Chirico explained, "There are more enigmas in the shadow of a man who walks in the sun than in all the religions of past, present, and future." De Chirico anticipated a mode of representation known as *magic realism*, in which commonplace objects and events are exaggerated or juxtaposed in unexpected ways to evoke a mood of mystery or fantasy.

Equally fantastic in spirit but more indebted in style to the lessons of cubism and fauvism were the paintings of the Russian-born Marc Chagall (1887–1985). Chagall arrived in Paris in 1910 and, like his countryman and fellow expatriate Igor Stravinsky, he infused his first compositions with the folk tales and customs of his native land. In Chagall's nostalgic recollection of rural Russia called *I and the Village* (Figure **33.4**), the disjunctive sizes and positions of the figures and the variety of arbitrary colors obey the whimsy of the unconscious rather than the laws of physical reality. Chagall freely superimposed images upon one another or showed them floating in space, defying the laws of gravity. Autobiographical motifs, such as fiddle players and levitating lovers, became Chagall's hallmarks in the richly colored canvases, murals, and stained glass windows of his long and productive career.

Figure 33.3 GIORGIO DE CHIRICO, *The Nostalgia of the Infinite*, 1914; dated on painting 1911. Oil on canvas, 4 ft. 5¼ in.× 25½ in. The Museum of Modern Art, New York. Purchase. © 2004 Digital Image MoMA, New York/Scala, Florence. © DACS, London, 2005.

Figure 33.4 MARC CHAGALL, *I and the Village*, 1911. Oil on canvas, 6 ft. 3⅝ in. × 4 ft. 11⅝ in. The Museum of Modern Art, New York. Mrs Simon Guggenheim Fund.

The Dada Movement

Although expressionism and fantasy played major roles in modern art, neither broke with tradition as aggressively as the movement known as *dada*, whose proponents would undertake to challenge the very nature of art. Founded in 1916 in Zürich, Switzerland, the dada movement consisted of a loosely knit group of European painters and poets who, perceiving World War I as evidence of a world gone mad, dedicated themselves to spreading the gospel of irrationality. The nonsensical name of the movement, "dada" ("hobbyhorse"), which was chosen by inserting a penknife at random into the pages of a dictionary, symbolized their irreverent stance. If the world had gone mad, should not its art be equally mad? Dada answered with art that was the product of chance, accident, or outrageous behavior. Such art deliberately violated "good taste," middle-class values, and artistic convention. The dadaists met regularly at the Café Voltaire in Zürich, where they orchestrated "noise concerts" and recited poetry created by way of **improvisation** and free association. The Romanian poet Tristan Tzara (1896–1963) produced poems from words cut out of newspapers and randomly scattered on a table, while the French sculptor and poet Jean Arp (1887–1966) constructed collages and relief sculptures from shapes arranged "according to the laws of chance." Such attacks on rationalist tradition and on modern technocracy in general reflected the spirit of **nihilism** (the denial of traditional and religious and moral principles) that flowered in the ashes of the war. In his "Lecture on Dada" in 1922, Tzara declared, "The acts of life have no beginning or end. Everything happens in a completely idiotic way. Simplicity is called dada. . . . Like everything in life, dada is useless."

Figure 33.5 MARCEL DUCHAMP, *Fountain (Urinal)*, 1917.
Ready-made, height 24 in. Photo courtesy of Sidney Janis Gallery, New York.
© Succession Marcel Duchamp/ADAGP, Paris/DACS, London, 2005.

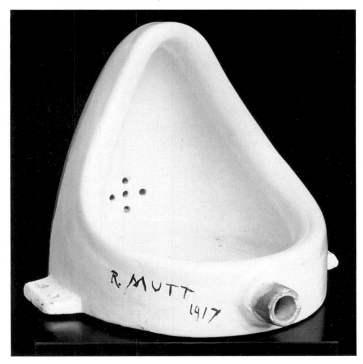

Figure 33.6 MARCEL DUCHAMP, *L.H.O O.Q.*, 1919. Rectified ready-made, pencil on a reproduction of the *Mona Lisa*. 7¾ × 4⅞ in. Collection of Mrs Mary Sisler. © Succession Marcel Duchamp/ADAGP, Paris/DACS, London, 2005.

As with poetry and painting, dada theater paid homage to Freud by liberating "everything obscure in the mind, buried deep, unrevealed," as one French playwright explained. Narrative realism and traditional characterization gave way to improvisation and the performance of random and bizarre incidents. One form of dada theater, the *theater of cruelty*, known for its violent and scatological themes, anticipated the theater of the absurd plays written during the 1950s and 1960s (see chapter 35).

The spirit of the dadaists was most vividly realized in the work of the French artist Marcel Duchamp (1887–1968). Early in his career, Duchamp had flirted with cubism and futurism, producing the influential *Nude Descending a Staircase, No. 2* (see Figure 32.11); but after 1912, he abandoned professional painting and turned to making—or remaking—art objects. In 1913 he mounted a bicycle wheel atop a barstool, thus producing the first "ready-made," as well as the first **mobile** (a sculpture with moving parts). Four years later, Duchamp would launch the landmark ready-made of the century: he placed a common urinal on a pedestal, signed the piece with the fictitious name, "R. Mutt," and submitted it for an exhibition held by the American Society of Independent Artists (Figure **33.5**). The piece, which he called *Fountain*, was rejected, but its long-term impact was enormous. By calling the "found object" a work of art, Duchamp mocked conventional techniques of making art. Further, by wrenching the object out of its preordained context, Duchamp suggested that the image obeyed a logic of its own, a logic whose "rules" flouted traditional aesthetic norms. *Fountain* not only attacked the barriers between art and life, but called forth art that exalted the nonsensical, the accidental, and the absurd. Perhaps most important, however, *Fountain* introduced to modern art the revolutionary notion that a work of art was first and foremost about an artist's *idea*. *Fountain* was not art because Duchamp had "made" it, but because he had removed it from the context of everyday life and had given it a whole new identity (as art). Pursuing this logic, the artist might also alter (or "remake") existing art, as for example, when Duchamp drew a mustache on a reproduction of Leonardo da Vinci's venerable *Mona Lisa*, adding a series of letters at the bottom that, when recited rapidly (in French), describe the sitter in lusty street slang (Figure **33.6**). This "corrected readymade," as Duchamp called the piece, expressed the artist's disdain for Western high art. It established the modern artist as maverick—the self-appointed prophet and defiler of tradition.

Moving to New York City in 1918, Duchamp labored for ten years on his *magnum opus*, a large glass and wire assemblage filled with esoteric sexual symbolism. He called it *The Bride Stripped Bare by Her Bachelors, Even*. After 1920, Duchamp went "underground," spending as much time perfecting his chess game (his favorite pastime) as making art. Nevertheless, his small, pioneering body of work and his irreverent view that art "has absolutely no existence as . . . truth" have had a powerful influence on scores of poets, painters, and composers even into the twenty-first century.

Surrealism and Abstract Surrealists: Picasso, Miró, and Klee

The word *surrealism*, coined by Guillaume Apollinaire in 1917, came to describe one of the century's most intriguing literary and artistic movements—a movement devoted to expressing in conscious life the workings of the unconscious mind. The French critic André Breton (1896–1966) inaugurated surrealism in the first "Surrealist Manifesto" (1924), in which he proclaimed the artist's liberation from reason and the demands of conventional society. The surrealists paid explicit homage to Freud and his writings, especially those on free association and dream analysis. Indeed, Breton himself visited Freud in Vienna in 1921. In describing the surrealist's commitment to glorifying the irrational aspect of the human psyche, Breton proclaimed,

> We are still living under the reign of logic. . . . But in this day and age logical methods are applicable only to solving problems of secondary interest. The absolute rationalism that is still in vogue allows us to consider only facts relating directly to our experience. . . . [Experience] is protected by the sentinels of common sense. Under the pretense of

Figure 33.7 PABLO PICASSO, *Seated Woman*, Paris, 1927. Oil on wood, 4 ft. 3⅛ in. × 3 ft. 2¼ in. The Museum of Modern Art, New York. Gift of James Thrall Soby. © 2004 Digital Image MoMA, New York/Scala, London. © Successsion Picasso/DACS, London 2005.

civilization and progress, we have managed to banish from the mind everything that may rightly or wrongly be termed superstition, or fancy; forbidden is any kind of search for truth which is not in conformance with accepted practices. It was, apparently, by pure chance, that a part of our mental world which we pretended not to be concerned with any longer—and, in my opinion, by far the most important part—has been brought back to light. For this we must give thanks to the discoveries of Sigmund Freud. . . . The imagination is perhaps on the point of reasserting itself, of reclaiming its rights.*

Breton defined surrealism as "psychic automatism, in its pure state," that is, creative effort guided by thought functions free of rational control and "exempt from any aesthetic or

*André Breton, "Manifesto of Surrealism" (1924). From *Manifestoes of Surrealism* by André Breton, translated by Richard Seaver and Helen R. Lane. Ann Arbor, Mich.: University of Michigan Press, 1969, 9.

moral concern." He emphasized the omnipotence of the dream state in guiding the surrealist enterprise.

Just as writers developed new literary techniques to achieve a new freedom from rational control, so visual artists devised a variety of liberating methods and processes. Some explored psychic automatism, allowing the hand to move spontaneously and at random, as if casually doodling or improvising. Others tried to recover a sense of childlike spontaneity by filling their paintings with free-spirited, biomorphic shapes. Fundamentally, however, the paradox of surrealist art rested on the artist's *conscious* effort to capture *unconscious* experience.

Breton recognized Picasso as one of the pioneers of surrealist art. As early as 1907, in *Les Demoiselles d'Avignon* (see Figure 32.2), Picasso had begun to radicalize the image of the human figure; by the mid-1920s, brutal dissection and savage distortion dominated his art. In 1927, Picasso painted the *Seated Woman* (Figure **33.7**), the image of a "split personality" that seemed to symbolize Freud's three-part psyche. The head of the female consists of a frontal view, as well as at least two profile views, each of which reveals a different aspect of her personality. The "split personality" motif continued to preoccupy Picasso throughout his long artistic career. In scores of paintings and sculptures, as well as in the stream of consciousness prose he wrote during the 1930s, Picasso pursued double meanings and visual puns, thus securing his reputation as the master of metamorphosis in twentieth-century art.

In the paintings of the Spanish artist Joan Miró (1893–1983), the surrealist's search for subconscious experience kindled the artist's personal mythology. Employing a style that suggests a child's representation, Miró made biomorphic creatures and spiny, abstract organisms the denizens of a fantastic universe. The "person" in Miró's *Person Throwing a Stone at a Bird* (Figure **33.8**) resembles a large, white, one-footed ameba; the bird is a stick figure with a flaming cockscomb; and the stone is an egglike object whose trajectory is traced by means of a dotted line. Superficially the depiction of a playful act, the painting conjures up a dreamlike ritual that unfolds ominously against a darkened sea and sky.

The Swiss-born painter Paul Klee (1879–1940) stood on the fringes of surrealism. One of the most sophisticated artists of the century, Klee was a brilliant draftsman who

Figure 33.8 JOAN MIRÓ, *Person Throwing a Stone at a Bird*, 1926. Oil on canvas, 29 × 3 ft. ¼ in. The Museum of Modern Art, New York. Purchase. © 2004 Digital Image MoMA, New York/Scala, Florence. © ADAGP, Paris and DACS, London, 2005.

Figure 33.9 PAUL KLEE, *Fish Magic*, 1925. Oil on canvas, mounted on board, 30⅜ × 3 ft. 2½ in. Philadelphia Museum of Art. The Louise and Walter Arensberg Collection ('50–134–112). © DACS, London, 2005.

created physically small artworks that resemble hiero-glyphic puzzles. His abstractions, like the entries in his personal diaries, are characterized by gentle humor and exquisite finesse; they belong to the substratum of the mind—the subconscious repository of mysterious symbols. "Art does not represent the visible," Klee insisted, "rather, it renders visible [the invisible]." Klee's *Fish Magic* (Figure **33.9**), painted during his tenure as a teacher at the Bauhaus, consists of a group of carefully arranged organic motifs that resemble sacred signs. Flowers, fish, and human figure, all executed with pictographic simplicity, share the ambient space of planets whose rhythms are measured by a mysteriously suspended clock. The painting validates Klee's claim that art is "a parable of Creation," the product of imagination guided by instinctual stimuli. Klee was among the first artists to recognize the art of the untutored and the mentally ill. "Only children, madmen, and sav-ages," he wrote, "truly understand the 'in-between' world of spiritual truth."

Visionary Surrealists: Magritte and Dali

While Picasso, Miró, and Klee favored abstract and bio-morphic images, other surrealists juxtaposed meticulously

painted objects in ways that were often shocking or unex-pected. The most notable of these visionary surrealists were René Magritte and Salvador Dali. Both were superb draftsmen whose *trompe l'oeil* skills elicited a disquieting dream reality. Profoundly influenced by de Chirico, the Belgian artist Magritte (1898–1967) combined realisti-cally detailed objects in startling and irrational ways. In one of Magritte's paintings, a coffin takes the place of a reclining figure; in another, a birdcage is substituted for the head of the sitter; and in still another, human toes appear on a pair of leather shoes. In a small piece entitled *The Betrayal of Images* (1928), Magritte portrays with crisp and faultless accuracy a briar pipe, beneath which appears the legend "This is not a pipe." The painting addresses the age-old distinction between the real world—the world of the *actual* pipe—and the painted image, whose reality is the virtual *illusion* of a pipe. At the same time, it antici-pates modern efforts to determine how words and images differ in conveying information. Questions of reality ver-sus illusion are also brought to bear in Magritte's *The False Mirror*, which consists of a single large eye whose iris is the very cloud-filled sky that it perceives (Figure **33.10**). Magritte's magic realism tests assumptions about the real

Figure 33.10 (above) RENÉ MAGRITTE, *The False Mirror* (*Le Faux Miroir*), 1928. Oil on canvas, 21¼ × 31⅞ in. The Museum of Modern Art, New York. Purchase. © 2004 Digital Image MoMA, New York/Scala, Florence. © ADAGP, Paris and DACS, London, 2005.

world, while it asserts with deadpan humor its own bizarre laws. Modern advertising, which owes much to Magritte, has transformed some of his images into contemporary icons—the "false mirror" serves, ironically enough, as the trademark of CBS television.

The Spanish painter and impresario Salvador Dali (1904–1989) was as much a showman as an artist. Cultivating the bizarre as a lifestyle, Dali exhibited a perverse desire to shock his audiences. Drawing motifs from his own erotic dreams and fantasies, he executed both natural and unnatural images with meticulous precision, combining them in unusual settings or giving them grotesque attributes. Dali's infamous *The Persistence of Memory* (Figure 33.11) consists of a broad and barren landscape occupied by a leafless tree, three limp watches, and a watchcase crawling with ants. One the timepieces

Figure 33.11 (left) SALVADOR DALI, *The Persistence of Memory* (*Persistance de la Mémoire*), 1931. Oil on canvas, 9½ × 13 in. The Museum of Modern Art, New York. Given anonymously. © 2004 Digital Image MoMA, New York/Scala, Florence. © Kingdom of Spain, Universal heir of Salvador Dali/DACS, London, 2005.

plays host to a fly, while another rests upon a mass of brain matter resembling a profiled self-portrait—a motif that the artist frequently featured in his works. To seek an explicit message in this painting—even one addressing modern notions of time—would be to miss the point, for, as Dali himself warned, his "hand-painted dream photographs" were designed to "stamp themselves indelibly upon the mind."

The Women of Surrealism

Perhaps more than any other movement in the history of early modernism, surrealism—which encouraged the free and uninhibited exploration of the interior life—attracted women artists. Arguably the most celebrated female painter of the early twentieth century was Mexico's Frida Kahlo (1907–1954). Kahlo's paintings, of which more than one third are self-portraits, reflect the determined effort (shared by many modern feminists) to present the female image as something other than the object of male desire. Her art bears testimony to what she called the "two great accidents" of her life: a bus crash that at the age of eighteen left her disabled, and her stormy marriage to the notorious Mexican mural painter Diego Rivera (see chapter 34). Like Rivera, Kahlo was a fervent Marxist and a nationalist who supported the revolutionary government that took control of Mexico in 1921. But the principal subject matter of Kahlo's art is Frida herself: "I am the subject I know best," she explained. Her paintings bring to life the experience of chronic pain, both physical (her accident required some thirty surgeries and ultimately involved the amputation of her right leg) and psychic (repeated miscarriages, for example, left her incapable of bearing a child). Kahlo's canvases betray her close identification with Mexican folk culture and folk art, which traditionally features visceral and diabolical details. At the same time, her taste for realistically conceived but shockingly juxtaposed images reflects her debt to de Chirico and the magic realist style. In *The Broken Column* (Figure **33.12**), Kahlo pictures herself as sufferer and savior, an emblematic figure that recalls the devotional icons of Mexico's religious shrines.

A pioneer modernist on the American scene, Georgia O'Keeffe (1887–1986) is often classified with America's regional painters. However, her treatment of haunting, biomorphic shapes abstracted from greatly enlarged flowers and bleached animal bones gives her early paintings a menacing presence (Figure 33.13). In a fluid line style that distills the essence of the subject, the so-called "high priestess" of early modernism brought a visionary clarity to the most ordinary ingredients of the American landscape.

Enlarging or combining commonplace objects in ways that were unexpected and shocking—the hallmark of the visionary surrealists—was a particularly effective strategy for surrealist sculptors; and in this domain as well, women made notable contributions. The fur-lined cup and saucer (Figure **33.14**) conceived by the Swiss-German sculptor Meret Oppenheim (1913–1985) is shocking in its irreverent combination of familiar but disparate elements. Conceived in the irreverent spirit of Duchamp's modified ready-mades, Oppenheim's *Object: Breakfast in Fur* provokes a sequence of discomfiting and threatening narrative associations.

Figure 33.12 FRIDA KAHLO, *The Broken Column*, 1944. Oil on canvas, 15¾ × 12¼ in. Museo Frida Kahlo, Mexico City. Collection Lola Olmedo.

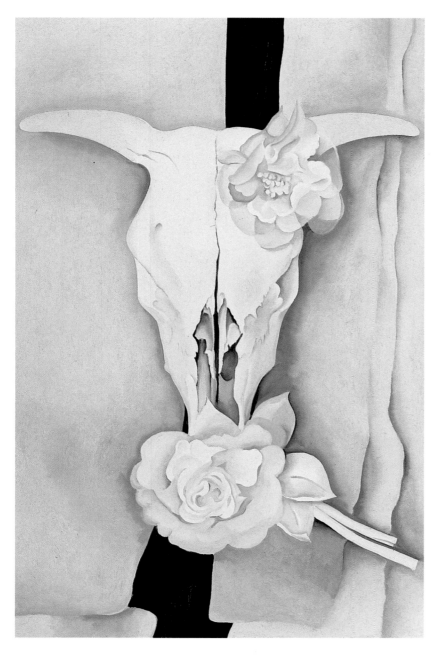

Dada and Surrealist Photography

Photography was an ideal medium with which to explore the layers of the unconscious mind. Photographers experimented with double exposure and unorthodox darkroom techniques to create unusual new effects similar to those of visionary surrealist painters and sculptors. Liberating photography from traditional pictorialism, a group of Berlin Dadaists invented a new kind of collage consisting of "found" images—usually printed materials taken from books, magazines, and newspapers—pasted on a flat surface, a technique called **photomontage**. One champion of the technique, Raoul Hausmann (1886–1971), called photomontage "the 'alienation' of photography"; he defined its importance as "a visually and conceptually new image of the chaos of an age of war and revolution." The only female member of the group, Hannah Höch (1889–1979), who had prepared advertising brochures for a Berlin newspaper, redirected her skills (and feminist concerns) to the creation of intriguing, disorienting compositions such as *Cut with the Kitchen Knife* (Figure 33.15). Bits and pieces of mass-media images are punctuated with the word "dada," inviting interpretation and, at the same time, subverting our visual and conceptual expectations. The series of "quick cuts" between the images anticipated experiments in cinematic photomontage that were to transform the history of film (see chapter 34).

Figure 33.13 (above) **GEORGIA O'KEEFFE**, *Cow's Skull: with Calico Roses*, 1931. Oil on canvas, 3 ft. ⁵⁄₁₆ in. × 24⅛ in. Art Institute of Chicago. Gift of Georgia O'Keeffe. © ARS, New York and DACS, London, 2005.

Figure 33.14 (right) **MERET OPPENHEIM**, *Object: Breakfast in Fur (Object: Le Déjeuner en fourrure)*, 1936. Fur-covered cup, saucer, and spoon; cup 4⅜ in. diameter; saucer 9⅜ in. diameter; spoon 8 in. long; overall height 2⅜ in. The Museum of Modern Art, New York. Purchase. © 2004 Digital Image MoMA, New York/Scala, Florence. © DACS, London, 2005.

Figure 33.15 HANNAH HÖCH, *Cut with the Kitchen Knife*, 1919. Collage of pasted papers, 3 ft. 8⅞ in. × 35½ in. Nationalgalerie, Staatliche Museen Preussischer Kulturbesitz, Berlin. Photo © BPK, Berlin. © DACS, London, 2005.

DADA AND SURREALIST FILM

The pranksters of dada looked to film as a vehicle of the nonsensical. Duchamp and the American photographer Man Ray (1890–1976) matched wits in New York City to make one of the earliest dada films, the entire action of which showed a courtesan, who called herself the baroness Elsa von Freytag-Loringhoven, shaving her pubic hair. In 1928, Salvador Dali teamed up with the Spanish filmmaker Luis Euñuel (1900–1983) to create the pioneer surrealist film, *Un Chien Andalou*. Violence and eroticism are the dominant motifs of this film, whose more famous scenes include ants crawling out of a hole in a man's palm (an oblique reference to Christ's stigmata), a man bleeding from the mouth as he fondles a woman, a woman poking a stick at an amputated hand that lies on the street, an eyeball being sliced with a razor blade, and two pianos filled with the mutilated carcasses of donkeys. Such special techniques as slow motion, close-up, and quick cuts from scene to scene work to create jolting, dreamlike effects. It is no surprise that surrealist film had a formative influence on some of the twentieth century's most imaginative filmmakers, including Jean Cocteau, Jean Renoir, Ingmar Bergman, and Federico Fellini.

The New Psychology and Music

During the 1920s, composers moved beyond the exotic instrumental forays of Stravinsky's *Rite of Spring* to explore even more unorthodox experiments in sound. A group of six artists that included the French composer Eric Satie (1866–1925) incorporated into their music such "instruments" as doorbells, typewriters, and roulette wheels. Satie's style, which is typically sparse, rhythmic, and witty, has much in common with the poetry of Apollinaire and e. e. cummings. His compositions, to which he gave such titles as *Flabby Preludes*, *Desiccated Embryos*, and *Three Pieces in the Form of a Pear*, were, however, less eccentric than was his lifestyle—he ate nothing but white foods and wore only gray suits.

The Freudian impact on music was most evident in the medium of musical drama, which, by the second decade of the century, featured themes of sexuality, eroticism, female hysteria, and the life of dreams. In the opera *Salome* (1905), a modern interpretation of the martyrdom of John the Baptist, the German composer Richard Strauss (1864–1949) dramatized the obsessive erotic attachment of King Herod's beautiful niece to the Christian prophet. Revolutionary in sound (in some places the meter changes in every bar) and in its frank treatment of a biblical subject, the opera shocked critics so deeply that a performance slated for Vienna in 1905 was cancelled; in America, the opera was banned for almost thirty years after its New York performance in 1907. *Bluebeard's Castle* (1918), a one-act opera by the leading Hungarian composer of the twentieth century, Béla Bartók (1881–1945), did not suffer so harsh a fate, despite the fact that the composer had boldly recast a popular fairy tale into a parable of repressed tensions and jealousy between the sexes.

The mood of anxiety and apprehension that characterized expressionist and surrealist art was, however, most powerfully realized in the song cycles of Arnold Schoenberg, whose experiments in atonality were introduced in chapter 32. Schoenberg's song cycles, or **monodramas**, were dramatic pieces written for a single (usually deeply disturbed) character. In the monodrama *Erwartung* (*Expectation*), Schoenberg took as his subject a woman's frenzied search for the lover who has deserted her. In *Pierrot Lunaire* (*Moonstruck Pierrot*) of 1912, a cycle of twenty-one songs for female voice and small instrumental ensemble, Schoenberg brought to life the dreamworld of a mad clown. The texts of his atonal and harshly dissonant song cycles resemble stream of consciousness monologues. They are performed in **Sprechstimme** (or "speech-song"), a style in which words are spoken at different pitches. Neither exclusively song nor speech, *Sprechstimme* is a kind of operatic recitation in which pitches are approximated and the voice may glide in a wailing manner from note to note. Yet despite the fact that his disquieting music stirred up great controversy among audiences and critics, Schoenberg attracted a large following. Even after he moved to the United States in 1933, young composers—including many associated with Hollywood film—flocked to study with him. And while critics found the music of *Pierrot Lunaire* "depraved" and "ugly," movie audiences were quick to accept the jolting dissonances of scores that worked to lend emotional expressiveness to the cinematic narrative.

Schoenberg's foremost student, Alban Berg (1885–1935), produced two of the most powerful operas of the twentieth century. Though less strictly atonal than Schoenberg's song cycles, Berg's operas *Wozzeck* (1921) and *Lulu* (1935) make use of serial techniques and the *Sprechstimme* style. Thematically, they feature the highly charged motifs of sexual frustration, murder, and suicide. The unfinished *Lulu* is the story of a sexually dominated woman who both destroys and is destroyed by her lovers. *Lulu* has been called "sordid," "psychotic," and "shocking." It explores such Freudian subjects as female hysteria and repressed sexuality, while at the same time it exploits the age-old image of woman-as-serpent. Both the music and the story of *Lulu* evoke a nightmarelike atmosphere, which, in modern multimedia productions, has been enhanced by the use of onstage film and slide projections.

_____

♪ See Music Listening Selection at end of chapter.

SUMMARY

Sigmund Freud's theories concerning the nature of the human psyche, the significance of dreams, and the dominating role of human sexuality had a revolutionary effect on modern society and on the arts. Proust, Kafka, and Joyce are representative of the modern novelist's preoccupation with the unconscious mind and with the role of memory in shaping reality. Their fiction reflects a fascination with the methods and principles of Freudian psychoanalysis. Stream of consciousness narrative and the interior monologue are among the modern literary techniques used to develop plot and character. The poetry of e. e. cummings reveals the influence of free association in liberating words from the bounds of syntax and conventional transcription.

In the visual arts, Freud's impact generated styles that gave free play to fantasy and dreams: the expressionism of Munch and Kirchner, the metaphysical art of de Chirico, and the fantasies of Chagall. Duchamp, the most outrageous of the dada cultists, championed a nihilistic, antibourgeois, antiart spirit that had far-reaching effects in the second half of the century. In 1924, André Breton launched surrealism, an international movement to liberate the life of the mind from the bonds of reason. Strongly influenced by Freud, the surrealists viewed the unconscious realm as a battleground of conflicting forces dominated by the instincts. Picasso, Miró, and Klee explored the terrain of the interior life in abstract paintings filled with both playful and ominous images. Dali, Magritte, Kahlo, and O'Keeffe manipulated the stuff of the real world in ways that evoked the visionary incoherence of the dream life.

In music, Satie embraced mundane sounds with the same enthusiasm that e. e. cummings showed for slang and Duchamp exercised for "found objects." In the expressionistic monodramas of Schoenberg and the sexually charged operas of Strauss, Bartók, and Berg, Freud's impact was most powerfully realized. As the events of two world wars would confirm Freud's pessimistic analysis of human nature, so the arts of the twentieth century acknowledged his view that human reason was not the "keeper of the castle"; the castle itself was perilously vulnerable to the dark forces of the human mind.

MUSIC LISTENING SELECTION

CD Two Selection 17   Schoenberg, *Pierrot Lunaire*, Op. 21, Part 3, No. 15, "Heimweh," 1912.

GLOSSARY

archetype the primal patterns of the collective unconscious, which Carl Jung described as "mental forms whose presence cannot be explained by anything in the individual's own life and which seem to be aboriginal, innate, and inherited shapes of the human mind"

collective unconscious according to Jung, the universal realm of the unconscious life, which contains the archetypes

concrete poetry poetry produced in the shape of ordinary, external objects

improvisation the invention of the work of art as it is being performed

interior monologue a literary device by which the stream of consciousness of a character is presented; it records the internal, emotional experience of the character on one or more levels of consciousness

method acting a modern style of theatrical performance that tries to harness childhood emotions and memories in the service of interpreting a dramatic role

mobile a sculpture constructed so that its parts move by natural or mechanical means

monodrama in music, a dramatic piece written for only one character

nihilism a viewpoint that denies objective moral truths and traditional religious and moral principles

photomontage the combination of freely juxtaposed and usually heterogeneous photographic images (see also Glossary, chapter 34, "montage")

Sprechstimme (German, "speech-song") a style of operatic recitation in which words are spoken at different pitches

sublimation the positive modification and redirection of primal urges that Freud identified as the work of the ego

CHAPTER 34

Total War, Totalitarianism, and the Arts

"Where is God now?"
Elie Wiesel

Two fundamentally related calamities afflicted the twentieth century: total war and totalitarian dictatorship. The consequences of both were so great that the world has still not recovered from them. Total war and totalitarianism, facilitated by sophisticated military technology and electronic forms of mass communication, caused the twentieth century to be the bloodiest in world history. Unlike natural disasters—the Black Death or the Lisbon earthquake, for example—the wars and totalitarian regimes of the modern era were disasters perpetrated *on* human beings *by* human beings. Such human-made evils not only challenged the belief that technology would improve the quality of human life, they seemed to validate Freud's theory that mortals are driven by base instincts and the dark forces of self-destruction.

The Great War of 1914, as World War I was called, and World War II, which followed in 1939, were the first *total* wars in European history. They are called total not only because they involved more nations than had ever before been engaged in armed combat, but also because they killed—along with military personnel—large numbers of civilians. Moreover, the wars were total in the sense that they were fought with a "no holds barred" attitude—all methods of destruction were utilized in the name of conquest. The weapons of advanced technology made modern wars more impersonal and more devastating than any previously fought. World War I combatants used machine guns, heavy artillery, hand grenades, poison gas, flame throwers, armored tanks, submarines, dirigibles (airships), and airplanes. From their open cockpits, pilots fired on enemy aircraft, while on land soldiers fought from lines of trenches dug deep into the ground. The rapid-firing, fully automatic machine gun alone caused almost eighty percent of the casualties. The cost of four years of war was approximately $350 billion, and the death tolls were staggering. In all, 70 million armed men fought in World War I, and more than 8 million of them died. In World War II, airplanes and aerial bombs (including, ultimately, the atomic bomb) played major roles; war costs tripled those of

World War I, and casualties among the allied forces alone rose to over 18 million people.

The underlying causes of these wars were aggressive rivalries between European powers. During the nineteenth century, nationalism and industrialism had facilitated militant competition for colonies throughout the world (see chapter 30); the armed forces became the embodiment of a nation's sovereign spirit and the primary tool for imperialism. National leaders fiercely defended the notion that military might was the best safeguard of peace: "*Si vis pacem, para bellum*"—"if you want peace, prepare for war," they argued. Nations believed their safety lay in defensive alliances. They joined with their ideological or geographic neighbors to create a system of alliances that, by the early twentieth century, divided Europe into two potentially hostile camps, each equipped to mobilize their armies if threatened.

The circumstances that led to World War I involved the increasingly visible efforts of Austria-Hungary and Germany to dominate vast portions of Eastern Europe. Germany, having risen to power during the nineteenth century, rivaled all other European nations in industrial might. By the early twentieth century, German efforts to colonize markets for trade took the form of militant imperialism in Eastern Europe. In July of 1914, Austria-Hungary, seeking to expand Austrian territory to the south, used the political assassination of Archduke Francis Ferdinand (heir to the throne of Austria-Hungary) as a pretext to declare war on Serbia. Almost immediately, two opposing alliances came into confrontation: the Central Powers of Austria-Hungary, Germany, and the Ottoman Empire versus the Allied forces of Serbia, Belgium, France, Great Britain, and Russia. Clearly, the policy of peace through military strength had not prevented war but actually encouraged it.

At the beginning of the war, the Central Powers won early victories in Belgium and Poland, but the Allies stopped the German advance at the First Battle of the Marne in September of 1914 (Map **34.1**). The opposing

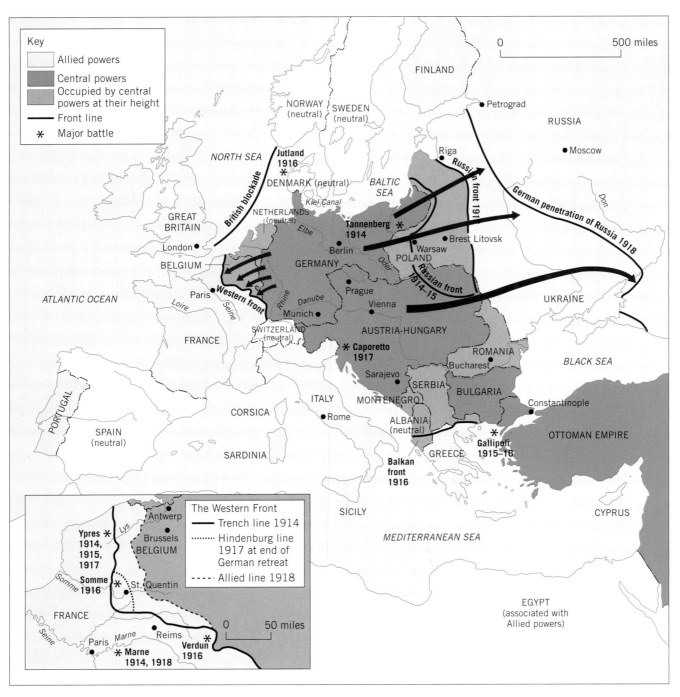

Map 34.1 World War I, 1914–1918.

armies settled down to warfare along the Western front—a solid line of two opposing trenches that stretched 500 miles from the English Channel to the Swiss border. At the same time, on the Eastern front, Russian armies lost over a million men in combat against the combined German and Austrian forces. In the early years of the war, the United States remained neutral, but when German submarines began sinking unarmed passenger ships in 1917, the American president Woodrow Wilson opted to aid the Allies in order to "make the world safe for democracy." Fortified by American supplies and troops, the Allies moved toward victory. In November 1918, the fighting ended with an armistice.

World War I Literature

World War I Poetry

Writers responded to the war with sentiments ranging from buoyant idealism and militant patriotism to frustration and despair. The most enduring literature of the era, however, expressed the bitter anguish of the war experience itself. The poetry of the young British officer Wilfred Owen (1893–1918) reflects the sense of cynicism and futility that was voiced toward the end of the war. Owen viewed war as a senseless waste of human resources and a barbaric form of human behavior. His poems, which question the meaning of wartime heroism, unmask "the old

Lie" that it is "fitting and proper to die for one's country." The poet was killed in combat at the age of twenty-five, just one week before the armistice was signed.

Other poets viewed the war as symbolic of a dying Western civilization. The poet T. S. Eliot, who is discussed in chapter 35, summed up this view in his classic poem *The Waste Land* (1922), a requiem for a dry and sterile culture. Eliot's contemporary and one of the greatest lyricists of the century, William Butler Yeats (1865–1939), responded to the violence of World War I and to the prevailing mood of unrest in his native Ireland with the apocalyptic poem "The Second Coming." The title of the poem alludes both to the long-awaited Second Coming of Jesus and to the nameless force that, in Yeats' view, threatened to enthrall the world in darkness.

READING 6.7 Poems Of World War I

Owen's "Dulce Et Decorum Est"[1] (1918)

Bent double, like old beggars under sacks,	1
Knock-kneed, coughing like hags, we cursed through sludge,	
Till on the haunting flares we turned our backs,	
And towards our distant rest began to trudge.	
Men marched asleep. Many had lost their boots,	5
But limped on, blood-shod. All went lame, all blind;	
Drunk with fatigue; deaf even to the hoots	
Of tired, outstripped Five-Nines[2] that drop behind.	
Gas! GAS! Quick, boys!—An ecstasy of fumbling	
Fitting the clumsy helmets just in time,	10
But someone still was yelling out and stumbling	
And flound'ring like a man in fire or lime.—	
Dim through the misty panes and thick green light,	
As under a green sea, I saw him drowning.	
In all my dreams before my helpless sight	15
He plunges at me, guttering, choking, drowning.	
If in some smothering dreams, you too could pace	
Behind the wagon that we flung him in,	
And watch the white eyes writhing in his face,	
His hanging face, like a devil's sick of sin,	20
If you could hear, at every jolt, the blood	
Come gargling from the froth-corrupted lungs	
Bitter as the cud	
Of vile, incurable sores on innocent tongues,—	
My friend, you would not tell with such high zest	25
To children ardent for some desperate glory,	
The old Lie: *Dulce et decorum est*	
Pro patria mori.	

Yeats' "The Second Coming" (1921)

Turning and turning in the widening gyre[3]	1

The falcon cannot hear the falconer;	
Things fall apart; the center cannot hold;	
Mere anarchy is loosed upon the world,	
The blood-dimmed tide is loosed, and everywhere	5
The ceremony of innocence is drowned;	
The best lack all conviction, while the worst	
Are full of passionate intensity.	
Surely some revelation is at hand;	
Surely the Second Coming is at hand.	10
The Second Coming! Hardly are those words out	
When a vast image out of Spiritus Mundi[4]	
Troubles my sight: somewhere in sands of the desert	
A shape with lion body and the head of a man,	
A gaze blank and pitiless as the sun,	15
Is moving its slow thighs, while all about it	
Reel shadows of the indignant desert birds.	
The darkness drops again; but now I know	
That twenty centuries of stony sleep	
Were vexed to nightmare by a rocking cradle,	20
And what rough beast, its hour come round at last,	
Slouches towards Bethlehem to be born?	

Q What images (descriptive and symbolic) are used in these poems?

Q What sentiments are conveyed by each poet?

World War I Fiction

World War I also inspired some of this century's most outstanding fiction—much of it written by men who had engaged in field combat. The American Ernest Hemingway (1899–1961) immortalized the Allied offensive in Italy in *A Farewell to Arms* (1929). The novel, whose title reflects the desperate hope that World War I would be "the war to end all wars," is a study in disillusionment and a testament to the futility of armed combat. Hemingway's prose, characterized by understatement and journalistic succinctness, and his profound respect for physical and emotional courage were forged on the battlefields of the war, which he observed firsthand.

Armed conflict had a similar influence on the life and work of the novelist Erich Maria Remarque (1898–1970). Remarque, a German soldier who was wounded in combat several times, brought firsthand experience of World War I to his book *All Quiet on the Western Front*—perhaps the finest war novel of the twentieth century. It portrays with horrifying clarity the brutal realities of trench warfare and poison gas, two of the most chilling features of the war. Remarque renders the story in first-person, present-tense narrative, a style that compels the reader to share the apprehension of the protagonist. Over one million copies of Remarque's novel were sold in Germany during the year of its publication, and similar success greeted it in translation and in its three movie versions. In 1939, however,

---

[1]"It is fitting and proper to die for one's country." A line from "Ode III" by the Roman poet Horace (see chapter 6).

[2]Gas-shells.

[3]A circular course traced by the upward sweep of a falcon. The image reflects Yeats' cyclical view of history.

[4]World Spirit, similar to the Jungian Great Memory of shared archetypal images.

the Nazi regime in Germany condemned Remarque's outspoken antimilitarism by publicly burning his books and depriving him of German citizenship. Shortly thereafter, Remarque moved to the United States, where he became an American citizen.

READING 6.8 From Remarque's *All Quiet On The Western Front* (1929)

An indigent looking wood receives us. We pass by the soup-kitchens. Under cover of the wood we climb out. The lorries turn back. They are to collect us again in the morning, before dawn.

Mist and the smoke of guns lie breast-high over the fields. The moon is shining. Along the road troops file. Their helmets gleam softly in the moonlight. The heads and the rifles stand out above the white mist, nodding heads, rocking carriers of guns.

Farther on the mist ends. Here the heads become figures; coats, trousers, and boots appear out of the mist as from a milky pool. They become a column. The column marches on, straight ahead, the figures resolve themselves into a block, individuals are no longer recognizable, the dark wedge presses onward, fantastically topped by the heads and weapons floating off on the milky pool. A column—not men at all.

Guns and munition wagons are moving along a crossroad. The backs of the horses shine in the moonlight, their movements are beautiful, they toss their heads, and their eyes gleam. The guns and the wagons float before the dim background of the moonlit landscape, the riders in their steel helmets resemble knights of a forgotten time; it is strangely beautiful and arresting.

We push on to the pioneer dump. Some of us load our shoulders with pointed and twisted iron stakes; others thrust smooth iron rods through rolls of wire and go off with them. The burdens are awkward and heavy.

The ground becomes more broken. From ahead come warnings: "Look out, deep shell-holes on the left"—"Mind, trenches"— — —

Our eyes peer out, our feet and our sticks feel in front of us before they take the weight of the body. Suddenly the line halts; I bump my face against the roll of wire carried by the man in front and curse.

There are some shell-smashed lorries in the road. Another order: "Cigarettes and pipes out." We are getting near the line.

In the meantime it has become pitch dark. We skirt a small wood and then have the front-line immediately before us.

An uncertain, red glow spreads along the skyline from one end to the other. It is in perpetual movement, punctuated with the bursts of flame from the muzzles of the batteries. Balls of light rise up high above it, silver and red spheres which explode and rain down in showers of red, white, and green stars. French rockets go up, which unfold a silk parachute to the air and drift slowly down. They light up everything as bright as day, their light shines on us and we see our shadows sharply outlined on the ground. They hover for the space of a minute before they burn out. Immediately fresh ones shoot up to the sky, and again, green, red, and blue stars.

"Bombardment," says Kat.

The thunder of the guns swells to a single heavy roar and then breaks up again into separate explosions. The dry bursts of the machine-guns rattle. Above us the air teems with invisible swift movements, with howls, piping, and hisses. They are the smaller shells;—and amongst them, booming through the night like an organ, go the great coal-boxes and the heavies. They have a hoarse, distant bellow like a rutting stag and make their way high above the howl and whistle of the smaller shells. It reminds me of flocks of wild geese when I hear them. Last autumn the wild geese flew day after day across the path of the shells.

The searchlights begin to sweep the dark sky. They slide along it like gigantic tapering rulers. One of them pauses, and quivers a little. Immediately a second is beside him, a black insect is caught between them and tries to escape—the airman. He hesitates, is blinded and falls. . . .

We go back. It is time we returned to the lorries. The sky is become a bit brighter. Three o'clock in the morning. The breeze is fresh and cool, the pale hour makes our faces look grey.

We trudge onward in single file through the trenches and shell-holes and come again to the zone of mist. Katczinsky is restive, that's a bad sign.

"What's up, Kat?" says Kropp.

"I wish I were back home." Home—he means the huts.

"It won't last much longer, Kat."

He is nervous. "I don't know, I don't know— — —"

We come to the communication-trench and then to the open fields. The little wood reappears; we know every foot of ground here. There's the cemetery with the mounds and the black crosses.

That moment it breaks out behind us, swells, roars, and thunders. We duck down—a cloud of flame shoots up a hundred yards ahead of us.

The next minute under a second explosion part of the wood rises slowly in the air, three or four trees sail up and then crash to pieces. The shells begin to hiss like safety-valves—heavy fire— — —

"Take cover!" yells somebody—"Cover!"

The fields are flat, the wood is too distant and dangerous—the only cover is the graveyard and the mounds. We stumble across in the dark and as though spirited away every man lies glued behind a mound.

Not a moment too soon. The dark goes mad. It heaves and raves. Darkness blacker than the night rushes on us with giant strides, over us and away. The flames of the explosions light up the graveyard.

There is no escape anywhere. By the light of the shells I try to get a view of the fields. They are a surging sea, daggers of flame from the explosions leap up like fountains. It is impossible for anyone to break through it.

The wood vanishes, it is pounded, crushed, torn to pieces. We must stay here in the graveyard.

The earth bursts before us. It rains clods. I feel a smack. My sleeve is torn away by a splinter. I shut my fist. No pain. Still that does not reassure me: wounds don't hurt till afterwards. I feel the arm all over. It is grazed but sound. Now a crack on the skull, I begin to lose consciousness. Like lightning the thought comes to me: Don't faint, sink down in the black broth and immediately come up the top again. A splinter slashes into my helmet, but has travelled so far that it does not go through. I wipe the mud out of my eyes. A hole is torn up in front of me. Shells hardly ever land in the same hole twice, I'll get into it. With one bound I fling myself down and lie on the earth as flat as a fish; there it whistles again, quickly I crouch together, claw for cover, feel something on the left, shove in beside it, it gives way, I groan, the earth leaps, the blast thunders in my ears, I creep under the yielding thing, cover myself with it, draw it over me, it is wood, cloth, cover, cover, miserable cover against the whizzing splinters. **110**

I open my eyes—my fingers grasp a sleeve, an arm. A wounded man? I yell to him—no answer—a dead man. My hand gropes farther, splinters of wood—now I remember again that we are lying in the graveyard. **120**

But the shelling is stronger than everything. It wipes out the sensibilities, I merely crawl still deeper into the coffin, it should protect me, and especially as Death himself lies in it too.

Before me gapes the shell-hole. I grasp it with my eyes as with fists. With one leap I must be in it. There, I get a smack in the face, a hand clamps on to my shoulder—has the dead man waked up?—The hand shakes me, I turn my head, in the second of light I stare into the face of Katczinsky, he has his mouth wide open and is yelling. I hear nothing, he rattles me, comes nearer, in a momentary lull his voice reaches me: "Gas—Gaas—Gaaas—Pass it on." **130**

I grab for my gas-mask. Some distance from me there lies someone. I think of nothing but this: That fellow there must know: Gaaas—Gaaas— — —

I call, I lean toward him, I swipe at him with the satchel, he doesn't see—once again, again—he merely ducks—it's a recruit—I look at Kat desperately, he has his mask ready—I pull out mine too, my helmet falls to one side, it slips over my face, I reach the man, his satchel is on the side nearest me, I seize the mask, pull it over his head, he understands, I let go and with a jump drop back into the shell-hole. **140**

The dull thud of the gas-shells mingles with the crashes of the high explosives. A bell sounds between the explosions, gongs, and metal clappers warning everyone—Gas—Gas—Gaas.

Someone plumps down behind me, another. I wipe the goggles of my mask clear of the moist breath. It is Kat, Kropp, and someone else. All four of us lie there in heavy, watchful suspense and breathe as lightly as possible. **150**

These first minutes with the mask decide between life and death: is it tightly woven? I remember the awful sights in the hospital: the gas patients who in day-long suffocation cough their burnt lungs up in clots.

Cautiously, the mouth applied to the valve, I breathe. The gas still creeps over the ground and sinks into all hollows. Like a big, soft jelly-fish it floats into our shell-hole and lolls there obscenely. I nudge Kat, it is better to crawl out and lie on top than to stay here where the gas collects most. But we don't get as far as that; a second bombardment begins. It is no longer as though the shells roared; it is the earth itself raging. **160**

With a crash something black bears down on us. It lands close beside us; a coffin thrown up.

I see Kat move and crawl across. The coffin has hit the fourth man in our hole on his outstretched arm. He tries to tear off his gas-mask with the other hand. Kropp seizes him just in time, twists the hand sharply behind his back and holds it fast.

Kat and I proceed to free the wounded arm. The coffin lid is loose and bursts open, we are easily able to pull it off, we toss the corpse out, it slides to the bottom of the shell-hole, then we try to loosen the under-part. **170**

Fortunately the man swoons and Kropp is able to help us. We no longer have to be careful, but work away till the coffin gives with a sigh before the spade that we have dug in under it.

It has grown lighter. Kat takes a piece of the lid, places it under the shattered arm, and we wrap all our bandages round it. For the moment we can do no more.

Inside the gas-mask my head booms and roars—it is nigh bursting. My lungs are tight, they breathe always the same hot, used-up air, the veins on my temples are swollen, I feel I am suffocating. **180**

A grey light filters through to us. I climb out over the edge of the shell-hole. In the dirty twilight lies a leg torn clean off; the boot is quite whole, I take that all in at a glance. Now someone stands up a few yards distant. I polish the windows, in my excitement they are immediately dimmed again, I peer through them, the man there no longer wears his mask.

I wait some seconds—he has not collapsed—he looks around and makes a few paces—rattling in my throat I tear my mask off too and fall down, the air streams into me like cold water, my eyes are bursting, the wave sweeps over me and extinguishes me. . . . **190**

Q What elements contribute to a sense of the macabre in this piece?

Q How does Remarque achieve cinematic momentum?

World War I Art

In Germany, World War I brought impassioned protests from many visual artists. One of the most outspoken was Max Ernst (1891–1976), whose career flowered in the dada and surrealist movements. Shortly after the war, Ernst began to create unsettling visual fantasies assembled from bits of photographs and prints that he cut from magazines, books, and newspapers. In the collage-painting *Two Ambiguous Figures* (Figure **34.1**), he combined the paraphernalia of modern warfare with the equipment of the scientist's laboratory. Ernst's machinelike monsters are suspiciously reminiscent of the gas-masked soldiers that he encountered during his four-year stint in the German infantry. Sadly enough, Ernst's demons have become prophetic icons of modern warfare. Poison gas, used by the Iraqis in the 1980s war with Iran, received renewed international attention during the widely televised Gulf War of 1991, when images of both soldiers and civilians donning gas masks were a common, if appalling, sight.

The art of George Grosz (1893–1959) was unique in its imaginative blend of social criticism and biting satire. Discharged from the army in 1916 after a brief experience at the front, Grosz mocked the German military and its corrupt and mindless bureaucracy in sketchy, brittle compositions filled with pungent caricatures. For example, the wartime pen and ink drawing, *Fit for Active Service* (Figure **34.2**), shows a fat German army doctor pronouncing a skeletal cadaver "O.K.," hence, fit to serve in combat. Here, Grosz makes pointed reference to the prevailing military practice of drafting old (and even ill) men. In a trenchant line style, he evokes a sense of the macabre similar to that captured by Remarque in the novel *All Quiet on the Western Front*. Like Remarque (and hundreds of other European artists and writers), Grosz fled Nazi Germany for the United States in the 1930s, where he eventually became an American citizen.

Fernand Léger's art (1881–1955) is usually classed with that of the cubists, but it was Léger's wartime experience that actually shaped the artist's long and productive career. During his four years on the front, Léger came to appreciate both the visual eloquence of modern machinery and the common humanity of the working-class soldiers with whom he shared the trenches. "Dazzled" (as he put it) by the breech of a 75-millimetre gun as it stood in the sunlight, Léger discovered similar kinds of beauty in ordinary human beings and in everyday objects—"the pots and pans on the white wall of your kitchen." "I invent images

Figure 34.1 MAX ERNST, *Two Ambiguous Figures*, 1919. Collage with gouache and pencil, 9½ × 6½ in. © ADAGP, Paris and DACS, London, 2005.

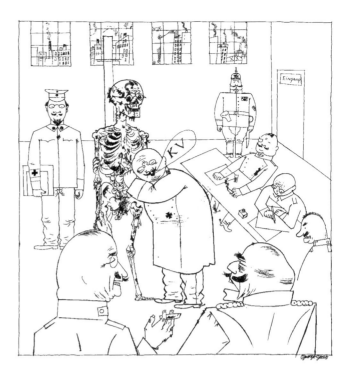

Figure 34.2 (above) **GEORGE GROSZ**, *Fit for Active Service*, 1916–1917. Pen and brush and ink on paper, 20 × 14⅜ in. The Museum of Modern Art, New York. A. Conger Goodyear Fund. © 2003 Digital Image MoMA, New York/Scala, Florence. © DACS, London, 2005.

from machines," he claimed. The anonymity of urban life and the cold monumentality of the city—gray, hard, and sleek—became major themes for Léger in the postwar years. This "mechanical" aesthetic is visible in his painting, *Three Women* (Figure **34.3**). Robust and robotic, the near-identical nudes (and their cat) share a common, austere geometry.

The Russian Revolution

One of the last of the European powers to become industrialized, Russia entered World War I in 1914 under the leadership of Tzar Nicholas II (1868–1918). Within a single year, the Russian army lost over one million men; a million more soldiers deserted. Russian involvement in the war, compounded by problems of government corruption and a weak and essentially agrarian economy, reduced the nation to desperate straits. Food and fuel shortages threatened the entire civilian population. By 1917, a full-scale revolution was under way: strikes and riots broke out in the cities, while in the countryside peasants seized the land of their aristocratic landlords. The Revolution of 1917 forced the abdication of the Tzar and ushered in a new regime, which, in turn, was seized by members of the Russian Socialist party under the leadership of the Marxist revolutionary Vladimir Ilyich Lenin (1870–1924).

Between 1917 and 1921, by means of shrewd political manipulation and a reign of terror conducted by the Red Army and the secret police, Lenin installed the left-wing faction of the Marxist Socialists—the Bolsheviks—as the party that would govern a nation of more than 150 million people. Tailoring Marxist ideas to the needs

Figure 34.3
FERNAND LÉGER,
Three Women, 1921,
Oil on canvas, 6 ft. ½in.
× 8 ft. 3 in. The
Museum of Modern
Art, New York. Mrs
Simon Guggenheim
Fund. © ADAGP, Paris
and DACS, London
2000.

of revolutionary Russia, Lenin became the architect of Soviet communism.

In his treatise *Imperialism, the Highest Stage of Capitalism* (1916), Lenin followed Marx in describing imperialism as an expression of the capitalist effort to monopolize raw materials and markets throughout the world. He agreed with Marx that a "dictatorship of the proletariat" was the first step in liberating the workers from bourgeois suppression. While condemning the state as "the organ of class domination," he projected the transition to a classless society in a series of phases, which he outlined in the influential pamphlet "The State and Revolution" (1917). According to Lenin, in the first phase of communist society (generally called socialism), private property would be converted into property held in common and the means of production and distribution would belong to the whole of society. Every member of society would perform a type of labor and each would be entitled to a "quantity of products" (drawn from public warehouses) that corresponded to his or her "quantity of work." (A favorite Lenin slogan ran, "He who does not work does not eat.") Accordingly, as Lenin explained, "a form of state is still necessary, which, while maintaining public ownership of the means of production, would preserve the equality of labor and equality in the distribution of products." In the first phase of communism, then, the socialist state prevailed.

In the second phase of communism, however, the state would disappear altogether. As Lenin explained,

> The state will be able to wither away completely when society has realized the rule: "From each according to his ability; to each according to his needs," *i.e.*, when people have become accustomed to observe the fundamental rules of social life, and their labor is so productive that they voluntarily work *according to their ability.* . . . There will then be no need for any exact calculation by society of the quantity of products to be distributed to each of its members; each will take freely according to his needs.[*]

EXPERIMENTAL FILM

Fernand Léger produced one of the earliest and most influential abstract films in the history of motion pictures. Developed in collaboration with the American journalist Dudley Murphy, *Ballet mécanique* (*Mechanical Ballet*, 1923– 1924) puts into motion a series of abstract shapes and mundane objects (such as bottles and kitchen utensils), which, interspersed with human elements, convey a playful but dehumanized sense of everyday experience. The rhythms and juxtapositions of the images suggest—without any narrative—the notion of modern life as mechanized, routine, standardized, and impersonal. The repeated image of a laundry woman, for instance, alternating with that of a rotating machine part, plays on the associative qualities of visual motifs in ways that would influence filmmakers for decades.

---

[*] *The State and Revolution.* New York: International Publishers, 1932, 1943, 71–80.

The Communist Party established the first **totalitarian** regime of the twentieth century. Totalitarianism subordinated the life of the individual to the needs of the state. Through strict control of political, economic, and cultural life, and by means of coercive measures such as censorship and terrorism, Soviet communists persecuted those whose activities they deemed threatening to the state. Using educational propaganda and the state-run media, they worked tirelessly to indoctrinate Soviet citizens to the virtues of communism. Under the rule of Joseph Stalin (1879–1953), who took control of the communist bureaucracy in 1926, the Soviets launched vast programs of industrialization and agricultural collectivization (the transformation of private farms into government-run units) that demanded heroic sacrifice among the Soviet people. Peasants worked long hours on state-controlled farms, earning a bare subsistence wage. Stalin crushed all opposition: his secret police "purged" the state of dissidents, who were either imprisoned, exiled to *gulags* (labor camps), or executed. Between 1928 and 1938, the combination of severe famine and Stalin's inhuman policies (later known as "the great terror") took the lives of 15 to 20 million Russians.

Lenin was aware that such a social order might be deemed "a pure Utopia"; yet, idealistically, he anticipated the victory of communist ideals throughout the world. The reality was otherwise. In early twentieth-century Russia, the Bolsheviks created a dictatorship *over* rather than *of* the proletariat. In 1918, when the Constituent Assembly refused to approve Bolshevik power, Lenin dissolved the Assembly. (In free elections Lenin's party received less than a quarter of one percent of the vote.) He then eliminated all other parties and consolidated the Communist Party in the hands of five men—an elite committee called the Politburo, which Lenin himself chaired. Russia was renamed the Union of Soviet Socialist Republics (U.S.S.R.) in 1922, and in 1924 the constitution established a sovereign Congress of Soviets. But this body was actually governed by the leadership of the Communist Party, which maintained absolute authority well after Lenin's death.[1]

Communism enforced totalitarian control over all aspects of cultural expression. In 1934, the First All-Union Congress of Soviet Writers officially approved the style of *socialist realism* in the arts. At the same time, it condemned all expressions of "modernism" (from cubist painting to hot jazz) as "bourgeois decadence." The congress called upon Soviet artists to create "a true, historically concrete portrayal of reality in its revolutionary development." Artists—including Malevich and the pioneer Russian constructivists—were instructed to communicate simply and directly, to shun all forms of decadent (that is, modern) Western art, and to describe only the positive aspects of socialist society. In realistically conceived posters, the new Soviet man and woman were portrayed earnestly operating tractors or running factory machinery (Figure **34.4**). Thus the arts served to reinforce in the public mind the ideological benefits of communism. Socialist realism and the philosophy of art as mass propaganda lent support to almost every totalitarian regime of the twentieth century.

---

[1]The Communist Party ceased to rule upon the collapse of the Soviet Union in 1991.

The Great Depression and the American Scene

World War I left Europe devastated, and massive economic problems burdened both the Central Powers and the Allied nations. In the three years following the war, world industrial production declined by more than a third, prices dropped sharply, and over 30 million people lost their jobs. The United States emerged from the war as the great creditor nation, but its economy was inextricably tied to world conditions. Following the inevitable crash of inflated stock prices in 1929, a growing paralysis swept through the American economy that developed into the Great Depression—a world crisis that lasted until the 1940s.

The Great Depression inspired literary descriptions of economic oppression and misery that were often as much social documents as fictional narratives. The most memorable of these is the American novel *The Grapes of Wrath*, written in 1939 by John Steinbeck (1902–1968). The story recounts the odyssey of a family of Oklahoma migrant farmers who make their way to California in search of a living. In straightforward and photographically detailed prose, Steinbeck describes courageous encounters with starvation, injustice, and sheer evil. Like the soldiers in Remarque's regiment, the members of the Joad family (and especially the matriarch, Ma Joad) display heroism in sheer survival. *The Grapes of Wrath* is an example of *social realism*, a style that presents socially significant subject matter in an objective and lifelike manner. Not to be confused with socialist realism, which operated to glorify the socialist state, social realism was a vehicle of social criticism and political protest. A writer, declared Steinbeck, is "the watchdog of society"; he must "set down his time as nearly as he can understand it."

During the depression, social realism also dominated America's visual arts. In opposition to modernists who sacrificed subject matter to formal abstraction (Picasso, Kandinsky, and Mondrian, for instance), American social realists painted recognizable imagery that communicated the concerns of the masses. The Missouri-born Thomas Hart Benton (1889–1975) devoted his career to depicting scenes that called into question the political and economic

Figure 34.5 THOMAS HART BENTON, *City Activities with Dance Hall*, from the mural series "America Today," 1930. Distemper and egg tempera on gessoed linen with oil glaze, 7 ft. 8 in. × 11 ft. 2½ in. Collection, AXA Financial Inc. through its subsidiary The Equitable Life Assurance Society of the U.S., New York. Photo: Dorothy Zeidman 2000. © T. H. Benton and R. P. Benton Testamentary Trusts/VAGA, New York/DACS, London 2000.

policies leading to the Great Depression. Benton aimed to commemorate "true" American values by immortalizing the lives of common men and women, whom he pictured as rugged and energetic. In three sets of public murals completed between 1930 and 1933, he created an extraordinary pictorial history of the United States. He portrayed steelworking, mining, farming, and other working-class activities, as well as bootlegging, gospel singing, crapshooting, and a wide variety of essentially common pastimes. Benton's *City Activities*, one section from a set of murals depicting American life during the Prohibition era, is a montage of "clips" from such popular urban entertainments as the circus, the movie theater, and the dancehall (Figure **34.5**). A ticker-tape machine—the symbol of Wall Street commercialism and American greed—appears in the upper part of the mural; it is balanced in the lower foreground by another instrument of commercialism—bootlegging equipment. Benton, who appears with paintbrush in hand in the lower-right of the painting, admired the purity of Midwestern rural life. His assessment of America's urban centers as "nothing but coffins for living and thinking" is powerfully conveyed in *City Activities*.

In Benton's hands the mural was not mere decoration. It was a major form of public art, one that revealed ordinary American life as vividly as Renaissance murals mirrored the elitist world of sixteenth-century Italy. Benton drew inspiration from the work of two great Mexican muralists: José Clemente Orozco (1883–1949) and Diego

Science and Technology

1927 the first television transmission is viewed in America
1930 the British invent a workable jet engine
1938 the Germans split the atom to achieve nuclear fission
1939 British scientists produce pure penicillin
1945 the first experimental atomic bomb is exploded at Alamogordo, New Mexico

Rivera (1886–1957). Their paintings, characterized by simple yet powerful forms and bold colors, capture the vitality and the futility of the Mexican Revolution—one of many militant efforts at reforming economic and social conditions in Central and South America during the first half of the twentieth century (Figure **34.6**). The Mexican revolution was particularly significant as the first social revolution of the century to engage the active participation of great masses of peasants and urban workers. Rivera championed their cause by featuring (in his richly populated murals) sympathetic depictions of peasants, often intermingled with the imagery of their Mayan and Aztec forebears. By emphasizing the Amerindian aspect of Mexico's history, Rivera's art—like the revolution itself—helped to effect a change in Mexico's self-image.

During the Great Depression, photography was pressed into political service. United States federal agencies

Figure 34.6 DIEGO RIVERA, *Liberation of the Peon*, 1931. Fresco, 6 ft. 2 in. × 7 ft. 11 in. Philadelphia Museum of Art. Given by Mr. and Mrs. Herbert Cameron Morris ('43–46–1).

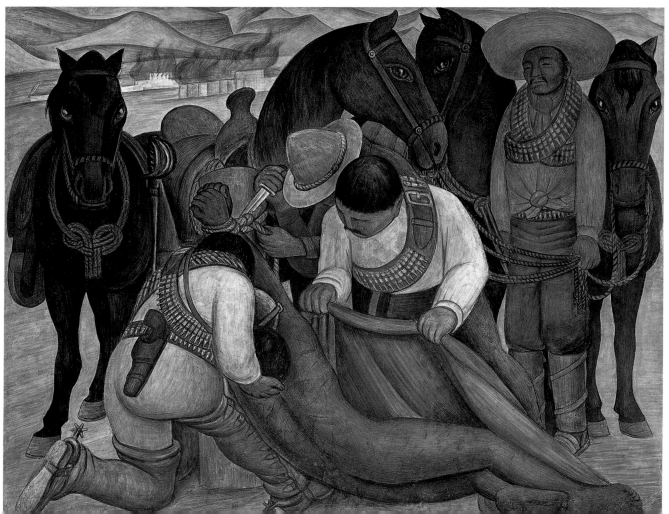

Figure 34.7 DOROTHEA LANGE, *Migrant Mother, Nipomo, California*, 1936. Gelatin-silver print. Library of Congress, Washington, D.C.

sponsored a program to provide a permanent record of economic and social conditions in rural America. Migration and rural poverty—bread-lines, beggars, and the shanty-towns of America's impoverished classes—became part of the straightforward style of *documentary photography*. The New York photographer Dorothea Lange (1895–1965) traveled across the country to record the conditions of destitute farmers who had fled the Midwestern Dust Bowl for the fields of California. *Migrant Mother* (Figure **34.7**), which Lange photographed at a farm camp in Nipomo, California, is the portrait of a gaunt thirty-two-year-old woman who had become the sole supporter of her six children. Forced to sell her last possessions for food, the anxious but unconquerable heroine in this photograph might have stepped out of the pages of Steinbeck's *Grapes of Wrath*. Lange's moving image reaches beyond a specific time and place to universalize the twin evils of poverty and oppression.

Totalitarianism and World War II

In Germany, widespread discontent and turmoil followed the combined effects of the Great Depression and the humiliating peace terms dictated by the victorious Allies. Crippling debts forced German banks to close in 1931, and at the height of the depression only one-third of all Germany's workers were fully employed. In the wake of these conditions, the

young ideologue Adolf Hitler (1889–1945) rose to power. By 1933, Hitler was chancellor of Germany and the leader (in German, *Führer*) of the National Socialist German Workers' party (the *Nazi* party), which would lead Germany again into world war.

A fanatic racist, Hitler shaped the Nazi platform. He blamed Germany's ills on the nation's internal "enemies," whom he identified as Jews, Marxists, bourgeois liberals, and "social deviates." Hitler promised to "purify" the German state of its "threatening" minorities and rebuild the country into a mighty empire. He manipulated public opinion by using all available means of propaganda—especially the radio, which brought his voice into every German home. In his autobiographical work *Mein Kampf* (*My Struggle*), published in 1925, Hitler set forth a fanatical theory of "Aryan racial superiority" that would inspire some of the most malevolent episodes in the history of humankind, including genocide: the systematic extermination of millions of Jews, along with thousands of Roman Catholics, gypsies, homosexuals, and other minorities. Justifying his racist ideology, he wrote:

> What we must fight for is to safeguard the existence and reproduction of our race and our people, the sustenance of our children and the purity of our blood, the freedom and independence of the fatherland so that our people may mature for the fulfillment of the mission allotted to it by the creator of the universe.*

Mein Kampf exalted the totalitarian state as "the guardian of a millennial future in the face of which the wishes and the selfishness of the individual must appear as nothing and submit." "The state is a means to an end," insisted Hitler. "Its end lies in the preservation and advancement of physically and psychically homogeneous creatures."

Less than twenty years after the close of World War I the second, even more devastating, world war threatened. The conditions that contributed to the outbreak of World War II included the failure of the peace settlement that had ended World War I and the undiminished growth of nationalism and militarism. But the specific event that initiated a renewal of hostilities was Hitler's military advance into Poland in 1939.

Once again, two opposing alliances were formed: Germany, Italy, Bulgaria, and Hungary comprised the Axis powers (the term describing the imaginary line between Rome and Berlin), while France and Britain and, in 1941, the United States and the Soviet Union, constituted the major Allied forces. Germany joined forces with totalitarian regimes in Italy (under Benito Mussolini) and in Spain (under General Francisco Franco), and the hostilities quickly spread into North Africa, the Balkans, and elsewhere (Map **34.2**). The fighting that took place during the three-year civil war in Spain (1936–1939) and in the German attack on the Netherlands in 1940 anticipated the merciless aspects of total war. In Spain, Nazi dive-bombers destroyed whole cities, while in the Netherlands,

---

Mein Kampf, translated by Ralph Manheim. Boston: Houghton Mifflin, 1943, 324.

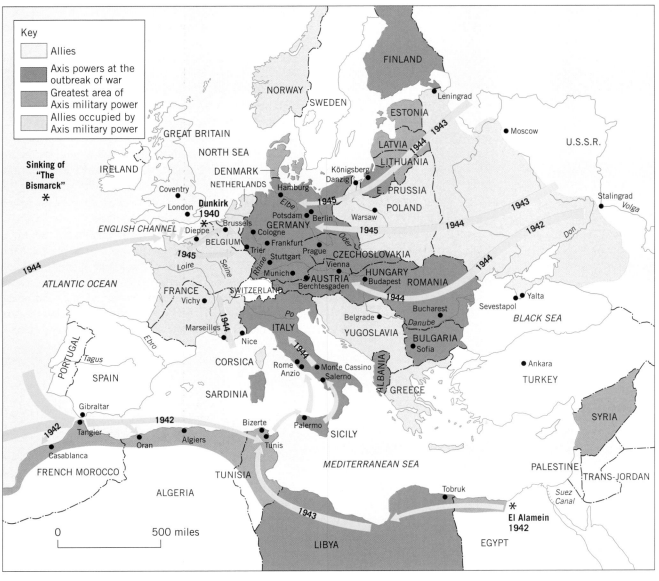

Map 34.2 World War II: The Defeat of the Axis, 1942–1945.

German tanks, parachute troops, and artillery overran the country in less than a week. The tempo of death was quickened as German air power attacked both military and civilian targets. France fell to Germany in 1940, and Britain became the target of systematic German bombing raids. At the same time, violating a Nazi–Soviet pact of 1939, Hitler invaded the Soviet Union, only to suffer massive defeat in the Battle of Stalingrad in 1942.

The United States, though supportive of the Allies, again tried to hold fast to its policy of "benevolent neutrality." It was brought into the war nevertheless by Japan, which had risen rapidly to power in the late nineteenth century. Japan had defeated the Russians in the Russo–Japanese War of 1904. The small nation had successfully invaded Manchuria in 1931 and established a foothold in China and Southeast Asia. In December 1941, in opposition to United States efforts at restricting Japanese trade, the Japanese naval air service dropped bombs on the American air base at Pearl Harbor in Hawaii. The United States, declaring war on Japan, joined the twenty-five other nations that opposed the Axis powers and sent combat

forces to fight in both Europe and the Pacific. The war against Japan was essentially a naval war, but it involved land and air attacks as well. Its terrible climax was America's attack on two Japanese cities, Hiroshima and Nagasaki, in August of 1945. The bombing, which annihilated over 120,000 people (mostly civilians) and forced the Japanese to surrender within a matter of days, ushered in the atomic age. Just months before, as German forces had given way to Allied assaults on all fronts, Hitler had committed suicide. World War II came to a close with the surrender of both Germany and Japan in 1945.

World War II Poetry

World War II poetry around the globe carried to new extremes the sentiments of despair and futility. The American poet and critic Randall Jarrell (1914–1965), who served in the army air force from 1942 to 1946, described military combat as dehumanizing and degrading. In the short poem "The Death of the Ball Turret Gunner," a World War II airman, speaking from beyond the grave, recounts his fatal experience as an air force gunner.

Encased in the Plexiglas bubble dome of an airplane ball turret—like an infant in his mother's womb—he "wakes" to "black flak" and dies; the startling image of birth in death fuses the states of dreaming and waking. Jarrell observed that modern combat, fueled by sophisticated technical instruments, neither fostered pride nor affirmed human nobility. Rather, such combat turned the soldier into a technician and an instrument of war. It robbed him of personal identity and reduced him to the level of an object—a thing to be washed out by a high-pressure steam hose. The note to the title of the poem was provided by the poet himself.

In Japan, lamentation preceded rage. The *haiku*, the light verse form that had traditionally enshrined such images as cherry blossoms and spring rain, now became the instrument by which Japanese poets evoked the presence of death. Kato Shuson (1905–1993) introduced the three *haikus* reproduced below with the following words: "In the middle of the night there was a heavy air raid. Carrying my sick brother on my back I wandered in the flames with my wife in search of our children."

READING 6.9   Poems Of World War II

Jarrell's "The Death of the Ball Turret Gunner"[1] (1945)

From my mother's sleep I fell into the State,
And I hunched in its belly till my wet fur froze.[2]
Six miles from earth, loosed from its dream of life,
I woke to black flak and the nightmare fighters.
When I died they washed me out of the turret with a hose.

Shuson's haikus (ca. 1945)

Hi no oku ni	In the depths of the flames
Botan kuzururu	I saw how a peony
Sama wo mitsu	Crumbles to pieces.

—◆—

Kogarashi ya	Cold winter storm—
Shōdo no kinko	A safe-door in a burnt-out site
Fukinarasu	Creaking in the wind.

—◆—

Fuyu kamome	The winter sea gulls—
Sei no ie nashi	In life without a house,
Shi no haka nashi	In death without a grave.

Q How is the motif of death developed in each of these poems?

Q How does verbal compression work in each poem?

---

[1] "A ball turret was a Plexiglas sphere set into the belly of a B-17 or B-24 and inhabited by two .50 caliber machine-guns and one man, a short, small man. When this gunner traced with his machine-guns a fighter attacking his bomber from below, he revolved with the turret; hunched upside-down in his little sphere, he looked like the fetus in the womb. The fighters which attacked him were armed with cannon firing explosive shells. The hose was a steam hose."
[2] The airman's fur-lined flight jacket.

World War II Fiction

As in the poetry of Jarrell, the novels of World War II were characterized by nihilism and resignation, their heroes robbed of reason and innocence. In such novels as *From Here to Eternity* (1951) by James Jones (1921–1977) and *The Naked and the Dead* (1948) by Norman Mailer (b. 1923), war makes men and machines interchangeable—the very brutality of total war dehumanizes its heroes. Mailer's raw, naturalistic novels, which are peppered with the four-letter words that characterize so much modern fiction, portray a culture dominated by violence and sexuality. Stylistically, Mailer often deviated from the traditional beginning-middle-and-end narrative format, using instead such cinematic techniques as flashback.

This episodic technique also prevails in the novels of Joseph Heller (1923–1999), Kurt Vonnegut (b. 1922), and other **gallows humor** writers. "Gallows" (or "black") humor is a form of literary satire that mocks modern life by calling attention to situations that seem too ghastly or too absurd to be true. Such fiction often describes the grotesque and the macabre in the passionless and nonchalant manner of a contemporary newspaper account. Like an elaborate hate joke, the gallows humor novel provokes helpless laughter at what is hideous and awful. Modern war, according to these humorists, is the greatest of all hate jokes: dominated by bureaucratic capriciousness and mechanized destruction, it is an enterprise that has no victors, only victims.

Heller's *Catch-22* (1955), one of the most popular gallows humor novels to emerge from World War II, marks the shift from the realistic description of modern warfare (characteristic of the novels of Remarque, Jones, and Mailer) to its savage satirization. Heller based the events of *Catch-22* on his own experiences as an air force bombardier in World War II. The novel takes place on an air base off the coast of Italy, but its plot is less concerned with the events of the war than with the dehumanizing operations of the vast military bureaucracy that runs the war. Heller describes this bureaucracy as symbolic of "the humbug, hypocrisy, cruelty and sheer stupidity of our mass society." Heller's rendering of the classic armed forces condolence form-letter satirizes the impersonal character of modern war and provides a brief example of his biting style:

> Dear Mrs.,/Mr.,/Miss,/or Mr. and Mrs.— — —:
> Words cannot express the deep personal grief I experienced when your husband,/son,/father,/or brother was killed,/wounded,/or reported missing in action.

Catch-22 is a caustic blend of nihilism and forced cheerfulness. The characters in the novel—including a navigator who has no sense of direction and an aviator who bombs his own air base for commercial advantage—operate at the mercy of a depersonalizing system. As they try their best to preserve their identity and their sanity, they become the enemies of the very authorities that sent them to war.

FILM IN THE WAR ERA

Film provided a permanent historical record of the turbulent military and political events of the early twentieth century. It also became an effective medium of political propaganda. In Russia, Lenin envisioned film as an invaluable means of spreading the ideals of communism. Following the Russian Revolution, he nationalized the fledgling motion-picture industry. In the hands of the Russian filmmaker Sergei Eisenstein (1898–1948), film operated both as a vehicle for political persuasion and as a fine art. He shaped the social and artistic potential of cinema by combining realistic narrative with symbolic imagery. In *The Battleship Potemkin* (1925), his silent film masterpiece, Eisenstein staged the 1905 mutiny of the Tzar's soldiers to resemble an on-the-spot documentary. He used to brilliant effect the technique of **montage**—the assembling of cinematic shots in rapid succession. In the final sequence of the film, the events of a riot in the city of Odessa are captured with graphic force. Eisenstein interposed images of the advancing Tzarist police with a series of alternating close-ups and long shots of civilian victims, including those of a mother who is killed trying to save her infant in a baby carriage that careens down a broad flight of stairs (Figure **34.8**). The so-called "Odessa Steps sequence," whose rapidly increasing tempo works to evoke apprehension and terror, is an ingenious piece of editing that has been imitated with great frequency by modern filmmakers. Two years later, in 1927, Eisenstein made the Russian Revolution itself the subject of the film *Ten Days That Shook the World*. Both in his silent movies and in those he made later with sound, Eisenstein developed techniques that drew the viewer into the space of the film. He deliberately cut off parts of faces to bring attention to the eyes, played one shot off the next to build a conflicting and often discontinuous sequence, and devised visual angles that, in true constructivist fashion, produced startling asymmetrical abstractions. The masterpiece of Eisenstein's post-silent film career was *Alexander Nevsky* (1938), a film that exalted the thirteenth-century Russian prince who defended the motherland against the onslaught of the Teutonic knights. Here Eisenstein linked the musical score (composed by Sergei Prokofiev) to the pacing of the cinematic action: specifically, to the compositional flow of individual shots in the visual sequence—a technique known as "vertical montage." In place of the operatic crowd scenes of his earlier films, he framed the protagonist within landscapes and battle scenes that were as gloriously

stylized as monumental paintings. *Alexander Nevsky* earned the approval of Joseph Stalin and the acclaim of the Russian people. It survives as a landmark in the history of inventive filmmaking.

While Eisenstein used film to glorify the collective and individual heroism of the Soviet people, German filmmakers working for Hitler turned motion pictures into outright vehicles of state propaganda. The filmmaker and former actress Leni Riefenstahl (1902–2003) received unlimited state subsidies to produce the most famous propaganda film of all time, *The Triumph of the Will* (1934). She engaged a crew of 135 people to film the huge rallies and ceremonies staged by Hitler and the Nazi party, including their

Figure 34.8 SERGEI M. EISENSTEIN, *The Battleship Potemkin*, 1925. Film stills from Act IV, "The Odessa Steps Massacre." Courtesy, The Museum of Modern Art/Film Stills Library.

Figure 34.9 LENI RIEFENSTAHL, *The Triumph of the Will*, 1934. Film still showing Himmler, Hitler, and Lutze framed by columns of people as they approach the memorial monument in Nuremberg, Germany. Kobal Collection, London.

first meeting in Nuremberg. *The Triumph of the Will* is a synthesis of documentary fact and sheer artifice. Its bold camera angles and stark compositions seem in themselves totalitarian—witness the absolute symmetry and exacting conformity of the masses of troops that frame the tiny figures of Hitler and his compatriots at the Nuremberg rally (Figure **34.9**).

In America, film served to inform, to boost morale, and to propagandize for the Allied cause; but it also served as entertainment and escape. At the height of the Depression as well as during the war era

millions of Americans flocked to movie-theaters each week. While such prize-winning movies as *All Quiet on the Western Front* (1930) and *From Here to Eternity* (1953) were painfully realistic, numerous other films romanticized and glamorized the war. An exception to the standard war-movie fare was *The Great Dictator* (1940), which was directed by the multitalented British-born actor and filmmaker Charlie Chaplin (1889–1977). In this hilarious satire of Fascist dictatorship, Adolf Hitler (known in the film as Adenoic Hynkel and played by Chaplin) rises to power as head of the "Double Cross Party," only to be arrested by his own troops, who mistake him for a Jewish barber.

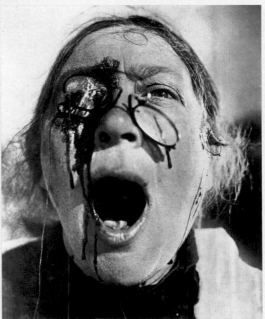

Responses to Totalitarianism

While total war became a compelling theme in twentieth-century fiction, so too did totalitarianism, especially as it was described by those who had experienced it firsthand. Until Stalin's death in 1953, a reign of terror prevailed in the Soviet Union. As many found out, the slightest deviation from orthodox Marxist-Stalinist decorum resulted in imprisonment, slave labor, or execution. Between 1929 and 1953 some 18 million people were sent to prison camps and another six million were exiled to remote parts of the Soviet Union. Aleksandr Solzhenitsyn (b. 1918) served in the Russian army during World War II, and although he had twice received recognition for bravery in combat, Solzhenitsyn was arrested in 1945 for veiled anti-Stalinist comments that he had made in a letter to a friend. He was sentenced to eight years of imprisonment, spending half the term in a *gulag* in Siberia and the other half teaching mathematics in a Moscow prison. His Siberian experience provided the eyewitness material for his first novel, *One Day in the Life of Ivan Denisovich* (1962), which was followed in 1973–1976 by *The Gulag Archipelago*, a documentary description of Soviet prison life. These dispassionate accounts of the grim conditions of totalitarianism are searing indictments of inhumanity, and testaments to the heroism of the victims of Soviet political oppression.

Like Stalin, Hitler wielded unlimited and often ruthless authority. He destroyed democratic institutions in Germany, condemned avant-garde art, modern architecture, atonal music, and jazz as "degenerate," attacked Einstein's theories as "Jewish physics," and proceeded to eliminate—by means of the *Gestapo* (the Nazi secret police)—all opposition to his program of mass conformity. In 1933, over 35,000 Germans died either by suicide or from "unexplained causes." Over the next ten years, concentration camps arose in Austria, Poland, and Germany to house Hitler's "impure" minorities. It is estimated that 6 million Jews and 5 million non-Jews were put to death in Nazi gas chambers—a hideous episode in European history known as the Holocaust.

In Germany, the voices of actual witnesses to the atrocities of the Holocaust were for the most part silenced by death, but drawings by camp inmates and documentary photographs taken just after the war (see Figure 34.10) provide shocking visual evidence of modern barbarism. One of the most eloquent survivors of the Holocaust is the writer Elie Wiesel (b. 1928), recipient of the Nobel Peace Prize in 1986. At the age of fifteen, Wiesel, a Romanian Jew, was shipped with his entire family to the concentration camp at Auschwitz, Poland. From there the family was split up, and Wiesel and his father were sent to a labor camp in Buchenwald, Germany, where the youth saw his father and hundreds of others killed by the Nazis. Liberated in 1945, Wiesel transmuted the traumatic experiences of his childhood into prose. "Auschwitz," wrote Wiesel, "represents the negation and failure of human progress: it negates the human design and casts doubts on its validity." *Night*, Wiesel's autobiographical record of the Nazi terrors, is a graphic account of Hitler's barbarism. The brief excerpt that follows reveals the anguish Wiesel and other Jews experienced in confronting what appeared to be "God's silence" in the face of brutal injustice.

READING 6.10 From Wiesel's *Night* (1958)

One day, the electric power station at Buna was blown up. The [1] Gestapo, summoned to the spot, suspected sabotage. They found a trail. It eventually led to the Dutch Oberkapo.[1] And there, after a search, they found an important stock of arms.

The Oberkapo was arrested immediately. He was tortured for a period of weeks, but in vain. He would not give a single name. He was transferred to Auschwitz. We never heard of him again.

But his little servant had been left behind in the camp in prison. Also put to torture, he too would not speak. Then the SS[2] sentenced him to death, with two other prisoners who had [10] been discovered with arms.

One day when we came back from work, we saw three gallows rearing up in the assembly place, three black crows. Roll call. SS all round us, machine guns trained: the traditional ceremony. Three victims in chains—and one of them, the little servant, the sad-eyed angel.

The SS seemed more preoccupied, more disturbed than usual. To hang a young boy in front of thousands of spectators was no light matter. The head of the camp read the verdict. All eyes were on the child. He was lividly pale, almost calm, [20] biting his lips. The gallows threw its shadow over him.

This time the Lagerkapo[3] refused to act as executioner. Three SS replaced him.

The three victims mounted together onto the chairs.

The three necks were placed at the same moment within the nooses.

"Long live liberty!" cried the two adults.

But the child was silent.

"Where is God? Where is He?" someone behind me asked.

At a sign from the head of the camp, the three chairs tipped [30] over.

Total silence throughout the camp. On the horizon, the sun was setting.

"Bare your heads!" yelled the head of the camp. His voice was raucous. We were weeping.

"Cover your heads!"

Then the march past began. The two adults were no longer alive. Their tongues hung swollen, blue-tinged. But the third rope was still moving; being so light, the child was still alive. . . .

For more than half an hour he stayed there, struggling [40] between life and death, dying in slow agony under our eyes. And we had to look him full in the face. He was still alive when I passed in front of him. His tongue was still red, his eyes were not yet glazed.

Behind me, I heard the same man asking:

"Where is God now?"

---

[1] The foreman of the prisoners, selected from among them by the Nazis.

[2] A special police force that operated the camps.

[3] The prisoner who acted as foreman of the warehouse.

And I heard a voice within me answer him:
"Where is He? Here He is—He is hanging here on this
gallows. . . ."
That night the soup tasted of corpses. . . .   **50**

Q What similarities and differences do you
detect between the circumstances described
here and those described by Remarque
(Reading 6.8)?

Q How do the styles of Wiesel and Remarque
compare?

The Visual Arts in the War Era

Photojournalism

The realities of World War II were recorded by an international array of photojournalists. One of the most gifted was Lee Miller (1907–1977), an American debutante who became the first female wartime photojournalist and an early witness to the horrors of the German concentration camps (Figure **34.10**). The American photographer Robert Capa (1897–1954) produced notable pictures of World War II paratroopers, and the French photographer Henri Cartier-Bresson (1908–2004) immortalized the plight of war-torn Europe in hundreds of aesthetically compelling social realist photographs.

In the Soviet Union, photography came under the totalitarian knife, as Stalin's propagandists carefully excised from official photographs unseemly images of political brutality. The "remaking" of history via photomanipulation—a technique that would become popular among American filmmakers at the end of the century—had its ignoble beginnings in the war era.

Picasso's *Guernica*

On the afternoon of April 26, 1937, during the Spanish Civil War (1936–1939) that pitted republican forces against the Fascist dictatorship of General Francisco Franco, the German air force (in league with the Spanish Fascists) dropped incendiary bombs on Guernica, a small Basque market town in northeast Spain. News of the event—the world's first aerial bombardment of a civilian target—reached Paris, where the horrified Picasso read illustrated newspaper accounts of the attack as the death toll mounted. Earlier in the year, the artist had been invited to contribute a painting for the Spanish Pavilion of the Paris World's Fair. The bombing of Guernica provided him with inspiration for the huge mural that would become the twentieth century's most memorable antiwar image (Figure **34.11**).

More powerful than any literary description, *Guernica* captures the grim brutality and suffering of the wartime era. Picasso used monochromatic tones—the ashen grays of incineration—which also call to mind the documentary media of mass communication: newspapers, photographs, and film. However, *Guernica* is far from documentary. Indeed, its abstract treatment of flattened, distorted forms contrasts sharply with the social realist truth-to-nature style that dominated much of the art produced in Europe and America between the wars. Picasso invests cubism's strong, angular motifs with expressive fervor. The bull and horse of the Spanish bullfight—Picasso's lifelong metaphor for savage discord—share the shallow stage with a broken statue of a warrior and four women, one of whom holds a dead infant. This figure, her upturned head issuing a voiceless scream, is the physical embodiment of human grief. At the center of the painting, the horse, whose body bears the gaping wound of a spear, rears its head as if to echo the woman's anguished cry. The shattered warrior at the bottom of the composition symbolizes war's corrupting effect on the artifacts of high culture, while mocking the militant idealism represented by traditional war monuments. Sharp contrasts of light and dark establish the geometric structure that gives drama to the composition in a manner that recalls Goya's *The Third of May, 1808* (see Figure 29.2). Like Goya's powerful painting, but phrased in the vocabulary of modern abstraction, *Guernica* is a universal symbol of protest. It illustrates Picasso's insistent argument for art as a "weapon against the enemy."

Figure 34.10 LEE MILLER, *Buchenwald, Germany*, 30 April 1945. Photograph. Photo: © Lee Miller Archive, Penrose Film Productions, Chiddingly, East Sussex.

Figure 34.11 PABLO PICASSO, *Guernica*, 1937. Oil on canvas, 11 ft. 5½ in. × 25 ft. 5¾ in. Museo Nacional de Arte Reina Sofia, Madrid.
© Succession Picasso/DACS, London, 2005.

Music in the War Era

Every totalitarian government in history has feared the power of music and condemned those musical styles that threatened mass conformity. In Nazi Germany, jazz was forbidden on the basis of its free and improvised style and its association with black musicians; in communist China, Beethoven's music was banned as the sound of the independent spirit. In Soviet Russia, Lenin's regime laid down the specific rule that composers write only music that "communicated" to the people; since atonality was associated with elitism and inscrutability, it was to be avoided, along with other expressions of Western "decadence." "Music," observed Lenin, "is a means of unifying great masses of people."

Music, which rarely has meaning beyond sound itself, allows for ambiguity of meaning, as the career of the eminent Russian composer, Dmitri Shostakovich (1906–1975), illustrates. Enrolled at thirteen in the Leningrad Conservatory, Shostakovich was the product of rigorous classical training. His compositions, including fifteen symphonies, fifteen string quartets, and numerous scores for ballet, opera, plays, and motion pictures, incorporate songlike melodies and insistent rhythmic repetition. They are essentially tonal, but they make dramatic use of dissonance and frequently evoke a reflective, melancholic mood. Although Shostakovich appeared to be a loyal adherent to Russian communism, his music received constant criticism for its "bourgeois formalism." In 1948, he was denounced by the government and dismissed from his posts at the Moscow and Leningrad Conservatories. Earlier, upon the performance of his Seventh ("Leningrad") Symphony in 1941, Soviet leaders had hailed his work as a celebration of the Soviet triumph against the Nazi invasion of Leningrad. Only in 1979, when Shostakovich's memoirs were smuggled out of the Soviet Union, did it become apparent that the composer intended the piece as an attack on Stalin's inhumanity toward his own people.

The career of the Russian composer Sergei Prokofiev (1891–1953) was equally turbulent. Permitted to leave Russia in 1918, he was persuaded to return in 1936. Defending Soviet principles, he proclaimed ". . . the composer . . . is in duty bound to serve man, the people. He must be a citizen first and foremost, so that his art may consciously extol human life and lead man to a radiant future." In 1948, the Soviets nevertheless denounced Prokofiev's music as "too modern." Prokofiev's compositions, most of which reveal his preference for classical form, are tonal and melodic, but they are boldly inventive in modulation and harmonic dissonance. In his scores for the ballets *Romeo and Juliet* (1935) and *Cinderella* (1944), in his cantata for the Eisenstein film *Alexander Nevsky* (1938), and in such shorter, modern-day classics as the witty *Lieutenant Kije Suite* (1934) and the orchestral fairy tale *Peter and the Wolf* (1936), Prokofiev demonstrated a talent for driving rhythms, sprightly marches, and unexpected, often whimsical shifts of tempo and melody.

Twentieth-century composers were frequently moved to commemorate the horrors of war in music. The most monumental example of such music is the *War Requiem* (1963) written by the British composer Benjamin Britten (1913–1976) to accompany the opening of England's new Coventry Cathedral, built alongside the ruins of the fourteenth-century cathedral, which had been virtually destroyed by German bombs in World War II. Britten was a master at setting text to music. In the *War Requiem* he juxtaposed the Roman Catholic Mass for the Dead (the Latin Requiem Mass) with the war poems of Wilfred Owen so that Owen's lines offer ironic commentary on traditional religious thought. Britten's imaginative union of sacred ritual and secular song calls for orchestra, chorus, boys' chorus, and three soloists. Poignant in spirit and dramatic in effect, Britten's oratorio may be seen as the musical analogue of Picasso's *Guernica*.

If it were possible to capture in music the agony of war, the Polish composer Krzystof Penderecki (b. 1933) has come closest to doing so. His *Threnody in Memory of the Victims of Hiroshima* (1960) consists of violent torrents of dissonant, percussive sound, some of which is produced by beating on the bodies of the fifty-two stringed instruments for which the piece is scored. The ten-minute song of lamentation for the dead begins with a long, screaming tone produced by playing the highest pitches possible on the violins; it is followed by passages punctuated by **tone clusters** (groups of adjacent dissonant notes). The rapid shifts in densities, timbres, rhythms, and dynamics are jarring and disquieting—effects consistent with the subject matter of the piece. *Threnody* was said to be the "anguished cry" that proclaimed the birth of the musical avant-garde behind the Iron Curtain. Penderecki's angry blurring of tones also characterizes his *Dies Irae* (1967), subtitled *Oratorio Dedicated to the Memory of those Murdered at Auschwitz*. Like Britten's *War Requiem*, Penderecki's composition draws on Christian liturgy—here the traditional hymn of Last Judgment (the "Day of Wrath")—to convey a mood of darkness and despair. The *Dies Irae*—first performed on the grounds of a former concentration camp— is punctuated by clanking chains and piercing sirens. Painfully harsh and abrasive, it remains a symbol of the Holocaust's haunting impact.

Copland and the American Sound

One of America's finest twentieth-century composers, Aaron Copland (1900–1990) turned away from the horrors of war; however, just as the music of Shostakovich and Prokofiev was rooted in Russian soil, so that of Copland drew nourishment from native American idioms. The New York composer spiced his largely tonal compositions with the simple harmonies of American folk songs, the clarity of Puritan hymns, and the lively and often syncopated rhythms of jazz and Mexican dance. In 1941, Copland advised American composers to find alternatives to the harsh and demanding serialism of their European colleagues: "The new musical audiences will have to have music they can comprehend," he insisted. "It must therefore be simple and direct . . . Above all, it must be fresh in feeling." Copland achieved these goals in all his compositions, especially in the ballet scores *Billy the Kid* (1938), *Rodeo* (1940), and *Appalachian Spring* (1944). *Appalachian Spring*, commissioned by the Martha Graham Dance Company, features five variations on the familiar Shaker song, "'Tis the Gift to Be Simple." In directing an orchestral rehearsal for the piece in 1974, Copland urged, "Make

♪ See Music Listening Selection at end of chapter.

it more American in spirit, in that the sentiment isn't shown on the face." Copland also composed for film, winning an Oscar in 1949 for his score for *The Heiress*. Like the murals of Thomas Hart Benton, Copland's music wedded American themes to a vigorous and readily accessible language of form.

The Communist Revolution in China

The history of totalitarianism is not confined to the West. In the course of the twentieth century, modern tyrants wiped out whole populations in parts of Cambodia, Vietnam, Iraq, Africa, and elsewhere. Of all the Asian countries, however, China experienced the most dramatic changes. In 1900, less than ten percent of the Chinese population owned almost eighty percent of the land. Clamoring for reform, as well as for independence from foreign domination, nationalist forces moved to redistribute land among the enormous peasant population. By 1911, the National People's Party had overthrown the Manchu leaders (see chapter 21) and established a republican government. But the Nationalists failed to provide an efficient land redistribution program and, after 1937, they lost much of their popular support. Following World War II, the communist forces under the leadership of Mao Zedong (1893–1976) rose to power. In 1949 they formed the People's Republic of China.

In China as in Russia, the Communist Party gained exclusive control of the government, with Mao serving as both chairman of the party and head of state. Mao called upon the great masses of citizens to work toward radical reform. "The theory of Marx, Engels, Lenin and Stalin is universally applicable," wrote Mao; however, he added, "We should regard it not as a dogma, but as a guide to action." A competent poet and scholar, Mao drew up the guidelines for the new society of China, a society that practiced cooperative endeavor and self-discipline. These guidelines were published in 1963 as the *Quotations from Chairman Mao*. Mao's "little red book" soon became the "bible" of the Chinese Revolution. On youth, Mao wrote, "The world is yours, as well as ours, but in the last analysis, it is yours. You young people, full of vigor and vitality, are in the bloom of life, like the sun at eight or nine in the morning. Our hope is placed in you." On women: "In order to build a great socialist society, it is of the utmost importance to arouse the broad masses of women to join in productive activity. Men and women must receive equal pay for equal work in production." On the masses: "The masses have boundless creative power . . . the revolutionary war is a war of the masses; it can be waged only by mobilizing the masses and relying on them."*

_____

Mao Tse-Tung's Quotations: The Red Guard's Handbook, introduction by Stewart Fraser. Nashville, Tenn.: Peabody International Center, 1967, 118, 256, 288, 297.

Figure 34.12 LI HUA, *Roar!* 1936. Woodcut, 8 × 6 in. Lu Xun Memorial, Shanghai.

Mao's ambitious reforms earned the support of the landless masses, but his methods for achieving his goals struck at the foundations of traditional Chinese culture. He moved to replace the old order, and especially the Confucian veneration of the family, with new socialist values that demanded devotion to the local economic unit—and ultimately to the state. To carry out his series of five-year plans for economic development in industry and agriculture, he instituted numerous totalitarian practices, such as indoctrination, exile, and repeated purges of the voices of opposition. Between 1949 and 1952, Mao authorized the execution of some 2 to 5 million people, including the wealthy landowners themselves.

Like the century's other totalitarian leaders, Mao directed artists to infuse literature with ideological content that celebrated the creative powers of the masses. To some extent, however, the movement for a "people's literature" furthered reforms that had been launched during the political revolution of 1911: at that time, traditional styles of writing, including the "book language" of the classics, gave way to the language of common, vernacular speech. The new naturalistic style was strongly influenced by Western literature and journalism. Chinese writers responded enthusiastically to modern European novels, short stories, and psychological dramas—poets even imitated such Western forms as the sonnet. In the visual arts, the influence of late nineteenth-century Western printmakers such as Käthe Kollwitz (see chapter 30), helped to shape the powerful social realist style of many Chinese artists, including Li Hua (1907–1994). Li's stark and searing woodcut of a bound man (Figure **34.12**)—a metaphor for modern China—reiterates the silent scream of Munch (see Figure 33.1) and Eisenstein (see Figure 34.8). During the Cultural Revolution (1966–1976) China's communist regime reinstated the official policy of socialist realism as it had been defined by the First All-Union Congress of Soviet Writers in 1934. The consequences of this policy would work to foment the liberation movements of the last decades of the century.

SUMMARY

The twentieth century was molded in the crucible of total war and totalitarianism. World Wars I and II were more devastating in nature and effect than any previous wars in world history. The Russian Revolution of 1917 marked the beginnings of Soviet communism and ushered in decades of totalitarian rule. Revolutions in China and Mexico were equally effective in destroying age-long traditions. In Europe, the Nazi policy of militant racism under Adolf Hitler brought about the brutal deaths of millions.

Artists responded to these events with rage, disbelief, and compassion. Bitter indictments of World War I are found in literature and the visual arts. World War II literature emphasized the dehumanizing effects of war. In the poems of Jarrell, as in the novels of gallows humor fiction writers, war became a metaphor for all modern-day varieties of cruelty and perversion; the firsthand experiences of Solzhenitsyn in the Russian *gulags* and Wiesel in Nazi concentration camps are no less poignant and shocking.

In America, during the period between the wars, the effects of the Great Depression encouraged the rise of social realism, a style that dominates the novels of Steinbeck and the paintings of Benton. Throughout the world, photographs and film documented twentieth-century warfare, even as they served ideological ends. Working in Paris, Picasso produced the quintessential antiwar painting, *Guernica*.

Composers of the wartime era also felt the effects of current political events. Living under the critical eye of the communist regime, Shostakovich and Prokofiev composed in distinctly different, but memorable, musical styles. In England, Benjamin Britten commemorated World War II in his *War Requiem*, while in Poland Penderecki immortalized the harsh realities of twentieth-century genocide. Total war and totalitarianism touched all of the arts of the twentieth century and left upon them the indelible imprint of despair.

MUSIC LISTENING SELECTION

CD Two Selection 19   Copland, *Appalachian Spring*, excerpt 1944.

GLOSSARY

gallows humor (or "black humor") the use of morbid and absurd situations for comic and satirical purposes in modern fiction and drama

montage in art, music, or literature, a composite made by freely juxtaposing usually heterogeneous images; in cinema, the production of a rapid succession of images to present a stream of interconnected ideas (see also Glossary, chapter 33 "photomontage")

tone cluster a group of adjacent dissonant notes, such as the notes of a scale, sounded together

totalitarian a political regime that imposes the will of the state upon the life and conduct of the individual

CHAPTER 35

The Quest for Meaning

"Man is nothing else but what he makes of himself."
Jean-Paul Sartre

The nightmare of World War II left the world's population in a state of shock and disillusion. The Western democracies had held back the forces of totalitarian aggression, but the future seemed as threatening as ever. Communism and capitalist democracy now confronted one another in hostile distrust. And both possessed atomic weapons with the potential to extinguish the human race. The pessimism that accompanied the two world wars was compounded by a loss of faith in the bedrock beliefs of former centuries. The realities of trench warfare, the Holocaust, and Hiroshima made it difficult to maintain that human beings were rational by nature, that technology would work to advance human happiness, and that the universe was governed by a benevolent God. There is little wonder that the events of the first half of the twentieth century caused a loss of confidence in moral absolutes. The sense of estrangement from God and reason produced a condition of anxious withdrawal that has been called "alienation." Like a visitor to a foreign country, the modern individual felt estranged from all that was secure and certain.

The condition of alienation was further aggravated by the depersonalizing influence of modern science and technology. In the mid-twentieth century, the breach between humanism and science seemed wider than ever; increasingly, intellectuals questioned the social value of scientific technology to human progress. Optimists still envisioned modern technology as a liberating force for humankind. The American behavioral psychologist B. F. Skinner (1904–1990), for instance, anticipated a society in which the behavior of human beings might be scientifically engineered for the benefit of both the individual and the community. In the futuristic novel *Walden Two* (1948), Skinner created a fictional society in which the "technology of behavior" replaced traditional "prescientific" views of freedom and dignity. *Walden Two* is typical of a large body of *utopian literature* that exalted science as a positive force in shaping the future.

Pessimists, on the other hand, feared—and still fear—that modern technology might produce catastrophes ranging from a nuclear holocaust to the absolute loss of personal freedom. *Dystopian literature*, that is, works that picture societies in which conditions are dreadful and bleak, reflect this negative outlook. *Brave New World* (1932) by the British writer Aldous Huxley (1894–1963), *1984* (1949) by England's George Orwell (the pen name of Eric Arthur Blair, 1903–1950), and *Fahrenheit 451* (1953) by the American Ray Bradbury (b. 1920) all present fictional totalitarian societies in which modern technology and the techniques of human engineering operate to destroy human freedom. *Brave New World* describes an imaginary society of the seventh century "A.F." ("after Henry Ford," the early twentieth-century American automobile manufacturer). In Huxley's futuristic society, babies are conceived in test tubes and, following the assembly line methods invented by Henry Ford for the manufacture of cars, individuals are behaviorally conditioned to perform socially beneficial tasks. From this "brave new world," the concept and practice of family life have been eradicated; human anxieties are quelled by means of *soma* (a mood-altering drug); and art, literature, and religion—all of which, according to the custodians of technology, threaten communal order and stability—have been ruthlessly purged.

Existentialism and Freedom

While *utopians* envisioned science and technology as potentially liberating and *dystopians* saw them as potentially threatening, both schools implicitly acknowledged that environment determined human behavior. "We are what we are conditioned to be," held the futurists. But partisans of the new humanist philosophy called *existentialism* argued otherwise. "We are what we choose to be," insisted the existentialists; "we create both ourselves and our freedom by our every choice." Existentialism, the most influential philosophic

bourgeois taste by creating artworks that were simply too large to hang in the average living room. As the movement developed, in fact, the size of the canvas grew as if to accommodate the heroic ambitions of the artists themselves. Ironically, however, these artworks, which scorned the depersonalizing effects of capitalist technology, came to be prized by the guardians of that very technology. Abstract expressionist paintings, which now hang in large numbers of corporate offices, hotels, and banks, have become hallmarks of modern sophistication.

The abstract expressionists represented a decisive break with the realist tradition in American painting and with social realism in particular. Nevertheless, throughout the century, representational art continued to flourish, especially among the regionalists, that is, those associated with specific geographic locations. The paintings of the New York artist Edward Hopper (1882–1967), for instance, present a figurative view of an urban America that is bleak and empty of meaningful relationships. Hopper's fondness for American cinema and theater is reflected in oddly cropped, artificially lit compositions that often resemble film stills. Like the film still, Hopper's frozen moments seems to belong to a larger narrative. In *Nighthawks* (Figure **35.8**), Hopper depicts a harshly lit all-night diner, whose occupants share the same small space but little intimacy. His characters, estranged and isolated in the mundane interiors of "one-night cheap hotels" and "sawdust restaurants," call to mind Eliot's Prufrock.

Across the Atlantic, the major figure in postwar European art was the Dublin-born painter Francis Bacon (1909–1992). Self-trained, Bacon infused European expressionism with an eccentric approach to form that

Figure 35.6 (above) **MARK ROTHKO**, *Untitled*, 1960. Oil on canvas, 5 ft. 9 in. × 4 ft. 2⅛ in. San Francisco Museum of Modern Art. Acquired through a gift of Peggy Guggenheim. © Kate Rothko Prizel and Christopher Rothko/DACS, London, 2005.

While Rothko's abstract shapes are usually self-contained, those of Helen Frankenthaler (b. 1928) tend to swell and expand like exotic blooms (Figure **35.7**). Frankenthaler cultivated the practice of pouring thin washes of paint directly from coffee tins onto raw or **unprimed** (without gesso undercoat) canvas. Her lyrical compositions, often heroic in scale, capture the transparent freshness of watercolors.

In a culture increasingly dominated by mass mechanization, abstract expressionists asserted their preference for an art of spontaneous action. They sought a balance between choice and chance that obeyed the existential credo of self-actualization. Here, the *process* of making art was elevated to a status that was almost as significant as the *product* itself. They seemed to turn their backs on

Figure 35.7 (right) **HELEN FRANKENTHALER**, *Before the Canes*, 1958. Oil on canvas, 8 ft. 6⅛ in. × 8 ft. 8⅜ in. University Art Museum, University of California, Berkeley, California.

Figure 35.8 EDWARD HOPPER, *Nighthawks*, 1942. Oil on canvas, 33⅛ in. × 5 ft. ⅛ in. Art Institute of Chicago. Chicago Friends of American Art Collection, 1942.51.

Figure 35.9 FRANCIS BACON, *Study after Velázquez's Portrait of Pope Innocent X*, 1953. Oil on canvas, 5 ft. ¼ in. × 3 ft. 10½ in. Des Moines Art Center. Nathan Emory Coffin Collection, purchased with funds from the Coffin Fine Arts Trust. Photo © Michael Tropea, Chicago. © Estate of Francis Bacon/ARS, New York and DACS, London, 2005.

turned human and animal figures into flayed carcasses and mangled skeletons. Like a sorcerer, he transformed his favorite images from film, magazine illustrations, and the history of art into grotesque and deformed (but sensuously painted) icons. In Bacon's resurrection of Diego Velázquez's famous *Portrait of Pope Innocent X* (1650), for example, the figure is imprisoned in a transparent cage and immobilized by ambiguous lines of force—an effect that may have been inspired by Bacon's fascination with X-ray imagery (Figure 35.9). Bacon's venerable pope has become a visceral statement of alienation and anguish. His raging, silent scream, a logo for despiritualized modernism, looks back to Munch, Eisenstein, and Picasso, all of whom Bacon admired.

Sculpture

The mood of existential anxiety also dominated international sculpture. What the art critic Herbert Read called a "geometry of fear" was evident in both the figurative and the nonfigurative sculpture of the Swiss artist Alberto Giacometti (1901–1966). In 1930 Giacometti came under the influence of surrealism, but in the postwar era he devised a new language with which to describe the human figure and the human condition. In both small and large clay works, thereafter cast in bronze, he transformed his subjects into haunting, spindly creatures that seem to symbolize the existential solitude of the individual amidst the modern metropolis (Figure 35.10). Giacometti's disengaged and ravaged figures were greatly admired by Sartre, who wrote the introduction to the catalogue for the artist's one-man exhibition in New York City in 1948. Giacometti's ties to existentialist writers secured his commission to design the set for the original production of Beckett's *Waiting for Godot*.

Figure 35.10 ALBERTO GIACOMETTI, *City Square (La Place)*, 1948. Bronze, 8½ × 25⅜ × 17¼ in. The Museum of Modern Art, New York. Purchase. Photograph © 2000 The Museum of Modern Art, New York. © ADAGP, Paris and DACS, London 2000.

In America, the haunting works of George Segal (1924–2000) captured the modern mood of alienation. Segal devised a unique method of constructing life-sized figures from plaster casts of live models—often friends and members of his own family. He installed these ghostly replicas in mundane settings staged with ordinary, uncast props: bar stools, streetlights, beds, bus seats (Figure **35.11**). These "assembled environments," as he called them, allowed Segal to comment on matters of alienation, social injustice, and the failure of communication in modern life. Stylistically, Segal's tableaux link the tradition of realist sculpture to the pop and performance art movements of the later twentieth century (see chapter 38).

The nonfigurative sculpture of the postwar era shared the improvisatory vitality of abstract expressionist painting. American sculptors, exploiting such industrial materials as welded iron and steel, constructed abstract objects that were monumental in size and dynamic in spirit. Among the pioneers of *constructed sculpture* was the Midwestern artist David Smith (1906–1965). Smith learned to weld while in college during a summer job at an automobile plant. He mastered a variety of other industrial processes while working in a wartime locomotive factory. His early pieces were large, welded iron forms sprayed with multiple layers of automobile enamel. During the 1950s, he began to construct boxlike stainless steel forms whose surfaces he burnished and scraped with motorized tools so that they reflected the colors of their surroundings (Figure **35.12**). Smith

forged a new structural style based on industrial techniques. His heroic forms share the calligraphic energy of Franz Kline's gestural abstractions: they capture a sense of aggressive movement that animates the space around them. While the art of Giacometti and Segal evokes a mood of existential despair, Smith's sculptures symbolize the optimistic spirit of postwar America.

The American sculptor Alexander Calder (1898–1976) was a contemporary of the surrealists, whom he met in Paris in 1926. Influenced by the work of Duchamp and

Figure 35.11 GEORGE SEGAL, *Bus Riders*, 1962. Plaster, cottongauze, steel, wood, and vinyl, 5 ft. 10 in. × 3 ft. 6⅝ in. × 7 ft. 6¾ in. Hirshhorn Museum and Sculpture Garden. Smithsonian Institution, Washington, D.C. Gift of Joseph H. Hirshhorn, 1966. Photo: Lee Stalsworth. © George Segal/DACS, London/VAGA, New York, 2005.

Figure 35.12 (above) **DAVID SMITH**, *Cubi XIX*, 1964. Stainless steel, 9 ft. 5⅛ in. × 21¾ × 20¾ in. Krauss #667. Collection, The Tate Gallery London. Photo: David Smith. © Estate of David Smith/DACS, London/VAGA, New York 2005.

Miró, Calder created whimsical wire constructions. These he motorized or hung from ceilings so that they floated freely in the air. Calder's wind-driven mobiles, which range from a few feet in size to enormous proportions, take advantage of the "chance" effects of air currents to create constantly changing relationships between volumes and voids, that is, between brightly colored, biomorphic aluminum shapes and the surrounding space (Figure **35.13**).

Architecture at Mid-Century

By the middle of the twentieth century, public architecture assumed a distinctly international character. The principles of international style architecture, based on the use of structural steel, ferroconcrete, and glass, had gained popularity through the influence of Bauhaus-trained architects and Le Corbusier (see chapter 32). Standardization and machinelike efficiency became the hallmarks of high-rise urban apartment buildings, constructed in their thousands to provide low-rent housing in the decades after 1930 (Figure **35.14**). In the building of schools, factories, and offices, the simplicity and austerity of the international style echoed the mood of depersonalization that prevailed in the arts. International style skyscrapers became symbols of corporate wealth and modern technocracy. They reflected the ideals of the twentieth century as powerfully as the Gothic cathedral summed up the spirit of the High Middle Ages. Among the most daring of the international style proponents was the Dutch architect (and the last director of the Bauhaus) Ludwig Mies van der Rohe (1886–1969). Mies' credo "less is more" inspired austere structures such as the Seagram Building in New York City, designed in partnership with Philip Johnson

Figure 35.13 (left) **ALEXANDER CALDER**, *Big Red*, 1959. Sheet metal and steel wire, 6 ft. 2 in. × 9 ft. 6 in. Collection of Whitney Museum of American Art, new York. Purchase with funds from the Friends of the Whitney Museum of American Art, and exchange. Photograph by Geoffrey Clements. © ADAGP, Paris and DACS, London, 2005.

Figure 35.15 (above) **LUDWIG MIES VAN DER ROHE**, Seagram Building, New York, 1954–1958. Metallic bronze and amber glass. Photo: Ezra Stoller/ © Esto. Courtesy Joseph E. Seagram & Sons, Inc.

Figure 35.14 (above) **IRWIN CHANIN** and **GILMORE CLARKE**, Stuyvesant Town and Peter Cooper Village, New York, 1947. Photo: © The Bettmann Archive, New York.

(1906–2005) in 1958 (Figure **35.15**). This sleek, unadorned slab of metallic bronze and amber glass was "the last word" in sophisticated machine engineering and a monument to the "form follows function" credo of the international style. The proportions of the building are as impeccable as those of any classical structure: the raised level at the bottom is balanced at the top by a four-story band of

Figure 35.16 (below) **EERO SAARINEN**, Trans World Airlines Terminal, Kennedy Airport, New York, 1962. Photo: Balthazar Korab, Troy, Michigan.

Figure 35.17 FRANK LLOYD WRIGHT, The Solomon R. Guggenheim Museum interior, 1957–1959. Photo: Robert E. Mates/Courtesy of the Solomon R. Guggenheim Museum. © ARS, New York and DACS, London 2005.

structures that were as gestural as the sculptures of Smith and as lyrical as the paintings of Frankenthaler. The Trans World Airlines Terminal at New York's Kennedy Airport (Figure **35.16**), for example, designed by the Finnish architect Eero Saarinen (1910–1961), is a metaphor for flight: its cross-vaulted roof—a steel structure surfaced with concrete—flares upward like a gigantic bird. The interior of the terminal unfolds gradually and mysteriously to embrace fluid, uninterrupted space. Equally inventive in both design and function is Frank Lloyd Wright's Guggenheim Museum in Manhattan. Its interior, which resembles the inside of a huge snail shell, consists of a continuous spiral ramp fixed around an open, central well (Figure **35.17**). A clear glass dome at the top allows natural light to bathe interior space, whose breathtaking enclosure competes seductively with most of the artwork exhibited therein. A ten-story limestone extension added in 1992 reduces the dramatic contrast between the rotunda and its urban setting, but it does not destroy the eloquence of the original design (Figure **35.18**). The Guggenheim remains the definitive example of the modern architectural imagination.

darker glass. For decades, the Seagram Building influenced glass-and-steel-box architecture; unfortunately, in many of its imitators, it was the cool, impersonal quality of the building and not its poetic simplicity that prevailed.

At mid-century, some of the world's leading architects reacted against the strict geometry and functional purism of international style architecture. Instead, they provided subjective, personal, and even romantic alternatives to the cool rationalism of the international style. Using the medium of cast concrete, they created organically shaped

Figure 35.18 FRANK LLOYD WRIGHT, The Solomon R. Guggenheim Museum, New York, 1957–1959. Photo: David Heald/Courtesy of the Solomon R. Guggenheim Museum.

Music and Dance at Mid-Century

The arts at mid-century shared the modernist quest for a balance between freedom and control, and between meaninglessness and purposeful action. In the domain of music, the American writer/composer John Cage (1912–1992) epitomized that quest. Cage styled himself a student of architecture and gardening, and a devotee of Zen Buddhism; he was also a concert pianist and one of the most influential avant-garde composers of the twentieth century. A leading spokesperson for inventive creativity in modern music, he embraced chance and experimentation as fundamental to artistic expression. "Everything we do is music," argued Cage; his dadaesque definition of music claimed it as a combination of sounds (specific pitches), noise (nonpitched sounds), and silence, with rhythm as the common denominator.

Cage's approach to music—like Pollock's to painting—made process and accident central to the work. In 1938 he invented the prepared piano, a traditional Steinway piano "prepared" by attaching to its strings pieces of rubber, bamboo slats, bolts, and other objects. When played, the prepared piano becomes something like a percussion instrument, the sounds of which resemble those of a Balinese orchestra; as Cage observed, "a percussive orchestra under the control of a single player." Influenced by Schoenberg as well as by Asian music, Cage's early compositions—including his *Sonata V* (1948)—are delicate in timbre and texture and elegant in percussive rhythms. However, his later works were radically experimental, especially in their effort to accommodate silence and nonpitched sound. In 1953, Cage composed *4' 33"*, a piece in which a performer sits motionless before the piano for four minutes and thirty-three seconds. The "music" of *4' 33"* consists of the fleeting, random sounds that occur during the designated time period—the breathing of the pianist, the shuffling of the audience's feet, or the distant hum of traffic outside of the concert hall.

Like *4' 33"*, much of Cage's music is **aleatory**, that is, based on chance or random procedures. To determine the placement of notes in a musical composition, Cage might apply the numbers dictated in a throw of the dice or incorporate the surface stains and imperfections on an otherwise blank piece of sheet music. He found inspiration for random techniques in the *I jing*, the ancient oracular Chinese *Book of Changes*, and in the psychic automatism of dada and surrealist art. These techniques are basic to his *Imaginary Landscape No. 4* (1951), a composition that calls for twelve radios playing simultaneously with twenty-four performers (two at each radio) randomly turning the volume and selector controls. Such antimusical music celebrates the absurd and random nature of the modern experience. At the same time, it blurs the traditional relationship between composers and performers, and between artistic conception and execution. Nevertheless, despite Cage's chance methods, each of his compositions is fully

scored: even the most unconventional passages follow Cage's explicit directions. Ultimately, Cage's "scored improvisations" embrace the existential notion that every creative act, and even the decision *not* to act, requires choice. The very decision in favor of chance engages the act of choosing and, further, of deciding whether to roll dice, toss coins, or employ some other random method.

Cage's ideas, as publicized in his numerous essays and lectures, had an enormous influence on younger artists. His "chance" aesthetic inspired the international neo-dada movement known as *Fluxus*. Fluxus artists, writers, filmmakers, and musicians experimented with minimal, performance-oriented works that left the viewer to complete the work of art (see chapter 38). In the mid-1940s, Cage met the American choreographer Merce Cunningham (b. 1922) and the young painter Robert Rauschenberg (b. 1925). At Black Mountain College in North Carolina, they collaborated in staging performances that employed improvisational techniques. As the director of Cunningham's dance company (founded in 1953), Cage combined dance, mime, poetry, music, slide projections, and moving pictures in some of the first and most innovative mixed media performances of the late twentieth century.

Cunningham's contribution to modern choreography was revolutionary because it separated dance from music. Rejecting the representational, storytelling dance style of his teacher, Martha Graham (see chapter 32), he concentrated exclusively on movement and form. In a Cunningham piece, music may coexist with dance, but its rhythms do not necessarily determine those of the dancers. All body movements, even such ordinary ones as running, jumping, and falling, are equally important, and such movements may be determined by improvisation or by chance. Cunningham's rigorous choreography calls for clean, expansive body gestures that unfold in large, lateral spatial fields. Thus his works share the raw energy and spontaneity that characterize the canvases of the abstract expressionists. Just as Cunningham disclaims traditional dance positions, so he ignores traditional staging (whereby dancers are assigned to specific spaces). He creates a spatial continuum, which—like a Pollock painting or a Cage composition—lacks a fixed center. In *Summerspace* (1958), for instance, for which Rauschenberg designed the sets and costumes, dancers travel confidently in different directions, often overlapping in space (Figure **35.19**). Cunningham explores the tensions between chance and choice and between freedom and control that lie at the heart of existential expression.

The modern approach to dance as an exercise in pure abstraction was shared by the noted Russian choreographer George Balanchine (1903–1983). Balanchine was deeply influenced by the musical innovations of his friend and compatriot, Igor Stravinsky, with whom he often collaborated—Stravinsky wrote the scores for at least four of his ballets. Like Stravinksy, he left Russia early in life. In Paris, he served as ballet master with the Ballets Russes (see chapter 32) until the company was dissolved in 1929. Soon after, he settled in New York, where he founded the New York City Ballet. Unlike Cunningham, Balanchine

In the visual arts, the movement known as abstract expressionism marked a heroic effort at self-actualization through the gestural and often brutal application of paint to canvas. The action paintings of Pollock, the color field paintings of Frankenthaler, and the constructions of David Smith and Alexander Calder explore the dynamic balance between chance and choice. While these artists worked in an abstract mode, others, such as Hopper, Giacometti, Segal, and Bacon, employed representational means to probe the modern condition. At mid-century, the international style in architecture culminated in classic glass-box skyscrapers and spawned thousands of soulless imitations that reinforced the cold, impersonal nature of the modern urban community. However, a new wave of seductive ferroconcrete buildings, as exemplified in Wright's Guggenheim Museum, challenged the austerity of that style.

In the domains of music and dance, as in the visual arts, the postwar generation took the absence of absolutes as the starting point for free experimentation. John Cage, the foremost member of the musical avant-garde, integrated silence, noise, and chance into his compositions. Merce Cunningham redefined modern dance as movement stripped of thematic and musical associations. While the mood of anxiety pervaded the postwar decades, artists struggled to sustain their faith in the human capacity for choice, and their hope that, as William Faulkner asserted in his Nobel Prize Address of 1950, "[Man] is immortal, not because he alone among creatures has an inexhaustible voice, but because he has a soul, a spirit of compassion and sacrifice and endurance."

favored musically-driven dance. He also remained loyal to the 350-year-old idiom of classical ballet, with its emphasis on structure and unmannered form, and its use of toe shoes. However, he rejected the dance-drama vocabulary of former centuries, investing classical ballet with a contemporary language that featured speed, energy, and compositional verve. His purist choreography, in the words of one critic, "pushed dance into the space age."

SUMMARY

Alienation and anxiety were the two principal conditions of the postwar mentality. Pessimists feared the destructive potential of modern technology and anticipated the demise of human freedom. Existentialism, a humanistic philosophy formulated by Jean-Paul Sartre, emphasized the role of individual choice in a world that lacked moral absolutes. Both secular and Christian existentialism charged human beings with full responsibility for their freely chosen actions.

Twentieth-century writers gave serious attention to the existential challenge and to the anguish produced by the freedom to choose. Modern antiheroes—Eliot's Prufrock and the burlesque tramps in Beckett's *Waiting for Godot*—contend with the despair of making choices in an essentially meaningless universe. Their survival seems to depend only upon an authentic commitment to action. Asian writers such as Tagore and Iqbal pursued the quest for meaning in parts of the world where modernism did as much to threaten as to reshape tradition.

MUSIC LISTENING SELECTION

CD Two Selection 20   Cage, *Sonata V*, 1948, excerpt.

GLOSSARY

aleatory (Latin, *alea*, "dice") any kind of music composed according to chance or random procedures

unprimed lacking the gesso undercoat normally applied to the surface of the canvas

PART 2

The Postmodern Turn

The "postmodern turn" describes a constellation of significant changes in all aspects of the global community. After the mid-twentieth century, many former colonial states claimed independence from imperial control, and ethnic and racial minorities, and other disenfranchised groups, have fought their way to positions of equality. In the postwar era, the world's nations came to be classified according to their level of economic achievement: the industrialized capitalistic nations, including the United States, most of Western Europe, Japan, and Canada, constituted the "First World." The less industrialized socialist states of the Soviet Union, Eastern Europe, and China made up the "Second World." The rest—over one hundred nations located primarily in Africa, Asia, and Latin America—were the poor or emerging nations of the "Third World." At mid-century, states were often polarized ideologically between the forces of democratic capitalism and soviet-style communism. Intense competition for world supremacy in political and military affairs marked the Cold War, a rivalry dominated by the two superpowers: the United States and the Soviet Union. The dismantling of the Berlin Wall (1989) and the collapse of Soviet communism (1991) marked the end of the Cold War and fed rising expectations for the future of democracy worldwide. While civil and religious wars within many regions prompted the intervention of First World powers during the late twentieth century, total war gave way to local and regional conflicts and new forms of aggression using the tactics of terror to intimidate and effect political change. Terrorism has become a tactical alternative to outright war. As the twenty-first century opened, Islamic radicals expanded their terrorist agenda to launch (on 9/11/01) a direct assault on the United States. This action opened a new chapter in history, most recently involving United States military intervention in Afghanistan and Iraq. These campaigns, along with ongoing rivalries between religious groups in the Middle East (and elsewhere) perpetuate instability and bloodshed. Nevertheless, the last fifty years have been an era of population growth, urbanization, expanding materialism, and progress toward political, economic, and social equality. As the twenty-first century unfolds, a higher quality of life and a more egalitarian social structure prevail in more parts of the global village than ever before in history.

With regard to the arts, the postmodern turn describes a shift away from what the critic Robert Hughes called "the Messianic era of modernism," and modernism's quest for a new world order. Modernist utopianism and the existential ideal of responsible action that infused the arts at mid-century have largely disappeared. They have given way to more skeptical claims for human progress—claims shaped by a knowing and often cynical view of the historical past. Some theorists date the end of modernism from the decade of the Holocaust—an episode they perceive as the crime that refuted modernism's utopian agenda. Others identify the new age with a shift in morality (linked to the discovery of effective birth control); while still others perceive postmodernism as a product of the information age, an age of high-speed developments in mass communication (television and computers), molecular physics, space exploration, and bio-technology, all of which have extended human knowledge and power beyond that of any previous era. At the onset of a new millennium, globalism—the condition of interdependence among all parts of the world—reflects the realities of increased human contact, communication, and competition. Information technology and globalism inspire and facilitate the arts of a media-shaped world culture.

(opposite) **LEON GOLUB**. *Interrogation II*, 1981. Acrylic on canvas, 10 × 14 ft. Gift of The Society for Contemporary Art, 1983.264 Reproduction, The Art Institute of Chicago.

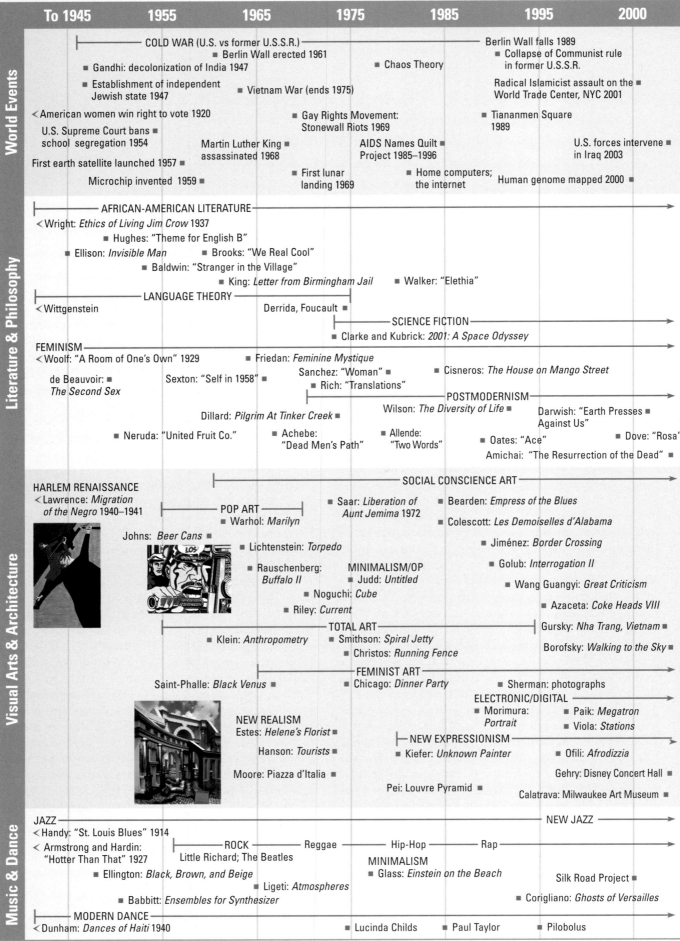

	To 1945	1955	1965	1975	1985	1995	2000

World Events

COLD WAR (U.S. vs former U.S.S.R.) —————————— Berlin Wall falls 1989

■ Berlin Wall erected 1961 — ■ Collapse of Communist rule in former U.S.S.R.

■ Gandhi: decolonization of India 1947 — ■ Chaos Theory

■ Establishment of independent Jewish state 1947 — ■ Vietnam War (ends 1975) — Radical Islamicist assault on the World Trade Center, NYC 2001 ■

< American women win right to vote 1920

■ Gay Rights Movement: Stonewall Riots 1969 — ■ Tiananmen Square 1989

U.S. Supreme Court bans ■ school segregation 1954

Martin Luther King ■ assassinated 1968 — AIDS Names Quilt ■ Project 1985–1996 — U.S. forces intervene ■ in Iraq 2003

First earth satellite launched 1957 ■

Microchip invented 1959 ■ — ■ First lunar landing 1969 — ■ Home computers; the internet — Human genome mapped 2000 ■

Literature & Philosophy

AFRICAN-AMERICAN LITERATURE ——————————→

< Wright: *Ethics of Living Jim Crow* 1937

■ Hughes: "Theme for English B"

■ Ellison: *Invisible Man* — ■ Brooks: "We Real Cool"

■ Baldwin: "Stranger in the Village"

■ King: *Letter from Birmingham Jail* — ■ Walker: "Elethia"

LANGUAGE THEORY ——————————

< Wittgenstein — Derrida, Foucault ■

SCIENCE FICTION ——————————→

■ Clarke and Kubrick: *2001: A Space Odyssey*

FEMINISM ——————————————————————→

< Woolf: "A Room of One's Own" 1929 — ■ Friedan: *Feminine Mystique*

Sanchez: "Woman" ■ — ■ Cisneros: *The House on Mango Street*

de Beauvoir: ■ *The Second Sex* — Sexton: "Self in 1958" ■ — ■ Rich: "Translations"

POSTMODERNISM ——————————→

Wilson: *The Diversity of Life* ■ — Darwish: "Earth Presses ■ Against Us"

Dillard: *Pilgrim At Tinker Creek* ■

■ Neruda: "United Fruit Co." — ■ Achebe: "Dead Men's Path" — ■ Allende: "Two Words" — ■ Oates: "Ace" — ■ Dove: "Rosa"

Amichai: "The Resurrection of the Dead" ■

Visual Arts & Architecture

HARLEM RENAISSANCE ————————————— SOCIAL CONSCIENCE ART ——————————→

< Lawrence: *Migration of the Negro* 1940–1941

POP ART ———————— ■ Saar: *Liberation of Aunt Jemima* 1972 — ■ Bearden: *Empress of the Blues*

■ Warhol: *Marilyn* — ■ Colescott: *Les Demoiselles d'Alabama*

Johns: *Beer Cans* ■

■ Lichtenstein: *Torpedo* — ■ Jiménez: *Border Crossing*

■ Rauschenberg: *Buffalo II* — MINIMALISM/OP — ■ Golub: *Interrogation II*

■ Judd: *Untitled*

■ Noguchi: *Cube* — ■ Wang Guangyi: *Great Criticism*

■ Riley: *Current* — ■ Azaceta: *Coke Heads VIII*

TOTAL ART ———————— Gursky: *Nha Trang, Vietnam* ■

■ Klein: *Anthropometry* — ■ Smithson: *Spiral Jetty* — Borofsky: *Walking to the Sky* ■

■ Christos: *Running Fence*

FEMINIST ART ——————————→

Saint-Phalle: *Black Venus* ■ — ■ Chicago: *Dinner Party* — ■ Sherman: photographs

ELECTRONIC/DIGITAL ——————————→

■ Morimura: *Portrait* — ■ Paik: *Megatron*

NEW REALISM — Estes: *Helene's Florist* ■ — ■ Viola: *Stations*

NEW EXPRESSIONISM ——————————

Hanson: *Tourists* ■ — ■ Kiefer: *Unknown Painter* — ■ Ofili: *Afrodizzia*

Moore: Piazza d'Italia ■ — Gehry: Disney Concert Hall ■

Pei: Louvre Pyramid ■ — ■ Calatrava: Milwaukee Art Museum

Music & Dance

JAZZ —————————————————————— NEW JAZZ ——————————→

< Handy: "St. Louis Blues" 1914

< Armstrong and Hardin: "Hotter Than That" 1927 — ROCK ———— Reggae —— Hip-Hop —— Rap

Little Richard; The Beatles — MINIMALISM

■ Ellington: *Black, Brown, and Beige* — ■ Glass: *Einstein on the Beach* — Silk Road Project ■

■ Ligeti: *Atmospheres*

■ Babbitt: *Ensembles for Synthesizer* — ■ Corigliano: *Ghosts of Versailles*

MODERN DANCE ——————————————————————→

< Dunham: *Dances of Haiti* 1940 — ■ Lucinda Childs — ■ Paul Taylor — ■ Pilobolus

Liberation and Equality

"This world is white no longer, and it will never be white again."
James Baldwin

While the mood of despair pervaded much of the postwar era, a second, more positive, spirit fueled movements for liberation in many parts of the world. Movements to reform conditions of oppression and injustice ranged from anticolonial drives for independence from foreign control to crusades for racial and gender equality. The drive toward liberation, one of the most potent themes of the twentieth century, inspired many of its most significant works of art. And while all art must, in the long run, be judged without reference to the politics, race, or gender of the artists, the value of such art may be better appreciated in the light of the historical circumstances out of which it emerged.

Two major types of liberation movement marked the second half of the twentieth century: the effort by colonial nations to achieve political, economic, religious, and ethnic independence; and the demand for racial and sexual equality. The first of these—the move toward political and economic independence—resulted from postwar efforts in Third World countries to reduce poverty and raise the standard of living to that of the more highly developed nations. After World War II, the weakened European nations were unable to maintain the military forces necessary to sustain their empires. At the same time, colonial subjects increased their efforts to free themselves of rule by Western nations, which, ironically, had fought for decades to liberate oppressed people from totalitarian dominion.

One of the earliest revolts against colonial rule took place in India. During World War I, the Indian National Congress came under the influence of the Hindu Mohandas Gandhi (1869–1948). Gandhi, whose followers called him "Mahatma," or "great soul," led India's struggle for independence from Great Britain. Guided by the precepts of Hinduism, as well as by the Sermon on the Mount and the writings of Thoreau and Tolstoy, Gandhi initiated a policy of peaceful protest against colonial oppression. His program of nonviolent resistance, including fasting and peaceful demonstrations, influenced subsequent liberation movements throughout the world. Gandhi's involvement was crucial to India's emancipation from British control,

which occurred in 1947, only one year before he was assassinated by a Hindu fanatic who opposed his conciliatory gestures toward India's Muslim minority. A related drive for liberation was well under way in India and other parts of Asia at that time: the pan-Islamic quest for a modern-day Muslim community on the Indian subcontinent resulted, in 1947, in an independent Pakistan. Similar efforts to advance Islam as a worldwide moral and religious force continue to flourish into the twenty-first century.

Between 1944 and 1960, many nations, including Jordan, Burma, Palestine, Sri Lanka, Ghana, Malaya, Cyprus, and Nigeria, freed themselves from British rule. Syria, Lebanon, Cambodia, Laos, North and South Vietnam, Morocco, Tunisia, Cameroon, Mali, and other African states won independence from France. And still other territories claimed their freedom from the empires of the United States, Japan, the Netherlands, Belgium, and Italy.

In Central America, Southeast Asia, and elsewhere, however, internal conflicts provoked military intervention by First World powers. For instance, between 1964 and 1975, the United States succeeded France in an unsuccessful effort to defend South Vietnam from communist control. The Vietnam War—the longest war in American history—cost the lives of some 50,000 Americans and more than 15 million Vietnamese. More recently, in Eastern Europe, the demise of Soviet authority has unleashed age-old ethnic conflicts, producing fragmentation and bloodshed. Sadly, liberation movements often broadcast seeds of tragedy.

Liberation and Literature in Latin America

From the time of Christopher Columbus, the peoples of Latin America have served the political and economic interests of First World countries more powerful than their own. And even after the European nations departed from the shores of Argentina, Brazil, Mexico, Peru, and other Latin American states in the early nineteenth century, the intolerable conditions that had prevailed in the long era of colonialism persisted: the vast majority of Latin Americans, including great masses of peasants of Native American descent, lived in relative poverty, while small, wealthy, landowning elites held power. These elites maintained their position by virtue of their alliance with the financial and industrial interests of First World nations, including (especially since the 1890s) the United States.

Spanish-speaking and predominantly Catholic, the rapidly growing populations of the more than two dozen nations of Latin America have suffered repeated social upheaval in their attempts to cope with persistent problems of inequality, exploitation, and underdevelopment. The long and bitter history of the Mexican Revolution, commemorated in the murals of Diego Rivera (see Figure 34.6), provides a vivid example. From country to country, political and social reformers have struggled to revolutionize the socioeconomic order, to liberate Latin America from economic colonialism, and to bring about a more equitable distribution of wealth. Support for these essentially socialist movements has come from representatives of the deprived elements of society, including organized labor and, often enough, from the Catholic Church, which has acted on behalf of the masses as an agent of social justice. The "liberation theology" preached by reformist elements in the clergy advanced a powerful new rendering of Christian dogma.

Latin America's artists rallied to support movements for liberation. During the 1960s, the outpouring of exceptionally fine Latin American prose and poetry constituted a literary boom, the influence of which is still being felt worldwide. Among the champions of Latin American reform was the Chilean Pablo Neruda (1904–1973), one of the most prolific and inventive poets in the history of the Spanish language. His poetry, often embellished by violent, surrealist images, endorses a radical, populist ideology. In the poem "The United Fruit Co." he describes the corruption of justice and freedom in the "Banana Republics" of Latin America. The poem, phrased as a mock Last Judgment, smolders with indignation at American policies of commercial exploitation in the nations south of its borders.

READING 6.17 Neruda's "United Fruit Co." (1950)

When the trumpets had sounded and all 1
was in readiness on the face of the earth,
Jehovah divided his universe:
Anaconda, Ford Motors,
Coca-Cola Inc., and similar entities: 5
the most succulent item of all,
The United Fruit Company Incorporated
reserved for itself: the heartland
and coasts of my country,
the delectable waist of America. 10
They rechristened their properties:

the "Banana Republics"—
and over the languishing dead,
the uneasy repose of the heroes
who harried that greatness, 15
their flags and their freedoms,
they established an *opéra bouffe*:
they ravished all enterprise,
awarded the laurels like Caesars,
unleashed all the covetous, and contrived 20
the tyrannical Reign of the Flies—
Trujillo the fly, and Tacho the fly,
the flies called Carias, Martinez,
Ubico[1]—all of them flies, flies
dank with the blood of their marmalade 25
vassalage, flies buzzing drunkenly
on the populous middens:
the fly-circus fly and the scholarly
kind, case-hardened in tyranny.
Then in the bloody domain of the flies 30
The United Fruit Company Incorporated
sailed off with a booty of coffee and fruits
brimming its cargo boats, gliding
like trays with the spoils
of our drowning dominions. 35
And all the while, somewhere in the sugary
hells of our seaports,
smothered by gases, an Indian
fell in the morning:
a body spun off, an anonymous 40
chattel, some numeral tumbling,
a branch with its death running out of it
in the vat of the carrion, fruit laden and foul.

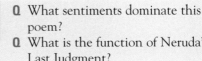

Q What sentiments dominate this poem?

Q What is the function of Neruda's mock Last Judgment?

The Quest for Racial Equality

The most turbulent liberation movement of the twentieth century addressed the issue of racial equality—an issue so dramatically reflected in the African-American* experience that some observers have dubbed the century "The Race Era." Since the days of slavery, millions of black Americans had existed as an underprivileged minority

[1]The twentieth-century dictators of Latin America: Rafael Molina Trujillo brutally dominated the Dominican Republic from 1930 to 1961; "Tacho" was the nickname for Anastasio Somoza, who controlled Nicaragua from 1937 until his assassination in 1956; Tiburcio Carias, self-styled dictator of Honduras, was supported during the 1930s and 1940s by the United Fruit Company; Maximilian Martinez was the ruthless dictator of El Salvador during the 1930s and 1940s; Jorge Ubico seized power in Guatemala in 1931 and served as a puppet of the United States until 1944.

*The current term for an American of African descent, which replaced "Negro," the popular designation of the early twentieth century and, after mid-century, "Black" or "Afro-American."

population living within an advanced industrial state. The Dutch took the first black Africans to America in 1619, and during the late seventeenth and eighteenth centuries, thousands of black slaves were imported to the American colonies, especially those in the South. For 250 years, until the end of the Civil War, slavery was a fact of American life. While the Emancipation Proclamation issued by Abraham Lincoln in 1863 facilitated the liberation of the slaves, it was not until 1865—with the Thirteenth Amendment to the United States Constitution—that all were finally freed. This and other constitutional amendments guaranteed the rights of black people; nevertheless, the lives of African-Americans continued to be harsh and poor by comparison with those of their former white masters. Separation of the races by segregated housing, inferior schools, and exclusion from voting and equal employment were only a few of the inequities suffered by this minority in the post-emancipation United States. It was to these issues and to the more general problem of racism that many African-Americans addressed themselves after World War I.

The Harlem Renaissance

World War I provided African-Americans with new opportunities in education and employment. During and after the war, over 5 million African-Americans migrated from the South to the Northern states. New York City became the center of economic opportunity, as well as the melting pot for black people from other parts of the world. But white frustration and fear of black competition for jobs led to race riots in over twenty-five cities during the "bloody summer" of 1919 (Figure **36.1**). Between 1920 and 1940, the quest for racial equality and a search for self-identity among African-Americans inspired an upsurge of creative expression in the arts. Centered in Harlem—a part of Manhattan occupied largely by African-Americans—poets, painters, musicians, and dancers forged the movement that came to be called the Harlem Renaissance.

One of the most eloquent voices of the Harlem Renaissance was Langston Hughes (1902–1967). He was born in Missouri and moved to New York in 1921, where he became the first African-American to support himself as a professional writer. A musician as well as a journalist and a novelist, Hughes became the rare poet whose powerful phrases ("a dream deferred," "a raisin in the sun," and "black like me") have become enshrined in the canon of American literature and in the English language. His poems, which capture the musical qualities of the African oral tradition, fuse everyday speech with the rhythms of blues and jazz. Hughes, who regarded poets as "lyric historians," drew deeply on his own experience: his "Theme for English B" records his response to the education of blacks in a dominantly white culture. In "Harlem," a meditation on the "bloody summer" of 1919, Hughes looks to the immediate past to presage the angry riots that have recurred regularly since the 1960s in America's black ghettos.

Like the writers of the Harlem Renaissance, the Chicago-born poet Gwendolyn Brooks (1917–2000) drew upon the idioms of jazz and street slang to produce a

Figure 36.1 JACOB LAWRENCE, "Race riots were numerous. White workers were hostile toward the migrants who had been hired to break strikes." Panel 50 from "The Migration" series, 1940–1941; text and title revised by the artist, 1993. Tempera on gesso on composition board, 18 × 12 in. The Museum of Modern Art, New York. Gift of Mrs. David M. Levy. © 2004 Digital Image MoMA, New York/Scala, Florence. © ARS, New York and DACS, London, 2005.

vivid picture of the black ghettos in her city. The first African-American to receive the Pulitzer Prize for poetry (1949), Brooks brought to attention the plight of blacks—especially young black men and women—in American society. The two poems reproduced below are representative of the early part of her long and productive career.

READING 6.18 The Poems of Hughes and Brooks

Hughes' "Theme for English B" (1949)

The instructor said,   1

   Go home and write
   a page tonight.
   And let that page come out of you—
   Then, it will be true.   5

I wonder if it's that simple?

I am twenty-two, colored, born in Winston-Salem.
I went to school there, then Durham, then here
to this college on the hill above Harlem.

I am the only colored student in my class.   10
The steps from the hill lead down into Harlem,
through a park, then I cross St. Nicholas,
Eighth Avenue, Seventh, and I come to the Y,
the Harlem Branch Y, where I take the elevator
up to my room, sit down, and write this page: 15

It's not easy to know what is true for you or me
at twenty-two, my age. But I guess I'm what
I feel and see and hear, Harlem, I hear you:
hear you, hear me—we two—you, me, talk on this page.
(I hear New York, too.) Me—who?   20
Well, I like to eat, sleep, drink, and be in love.
I like to work, read, learn, and understand life.
I like a pipe for a Christmas present,
or records—Bessie, bop, or Bach.
I guess being colored doesn't make me *not* like   25
the same things other folks like who are other races.
So will my page be colored that I write?
Being me, it will not be white.
But it will be
a part of you, instructor.   30
You are white—
yet a part of me, as I am a part of you.
That's American.
Sometimes perhaps you don't want to be a part of me.
Nor do I often want to be a part of you.   35
But we are, that's true!
I guess you learn from me—
although you're older—and white—
and somewhat more free.

This is my page for English B.   40

Hughes' "Harlem" (1951)

What happens to a dream deferred?   1

Does it dry up
like a raisin in the sun?
Or fester like a sore—
And then run?   5
Does it stink like rotten meat?
Or crust and sugar over—
like a syrupy sweet?
Maybe it just sags
like a heavy load.   10

Or does it explode?

Brooks' "The Mother" (1945)

Abortions will not let you forget.   1
You remember the children you got that you did not get,
The damp small pulps with a little or with no hair,
The singers and workers that never handled the air.
You will never neglect or beat   5
Them, or silence or buy with a sweet.
You will never wind up the sucking-thumb
Or scuttle off ghosts that come.
You will never leave them, controlling your luscious sigh,
Return for a snack of them, with gobbling mother-eye.   10

I have heard in the voices of the wind the voices of my
   dim killed children.
I have contracted. I have eased
My dim dears at the breasts they could never suck.
I have said, Sweets, if I sinned, if I seized
Your luck   15
And your lives from your unfinished reach,
If I stole your births and your names,
Your straight baby tears and your games,
Your stilted or lovely loves, your tumults, your marriages,
   aches, and your deaths,

If I poisoned the beginnings of your breaths,   20
Believe that even in my deliberateness I was not deliberate.
Though why should I whine,
Whine that the crime was other than mine?—
Since anyhow you are dead.
Or rather, or instead,   25
You were never made.

But that too, I am afraid,
Is faulty: oh, what shall I say, how is the truth to be said?
You were born, you had body, you died.
It is just that you never giggled or planned or cried.   30

Believe me, I loved you all.
Believe me, I knew you, though faintly, and I loved,
   I loved you
All.

Brooks' "We Real Cool" (1959)

The Pool Players.
Seven at the Golden Shovel.

    We real cool. We
    Left school. We

    Lurk late. We
    Strike straight. We

    Sing sin. We
    Thin gin. We

    Jazz June. We
    Die soon.

Q In what ways are these poems descriptive? Are they also didactic? How so?

Richard Wright and the Realities of Racism

Richard Wright (1908–1960) was born on a cotton plantation in Mississippi and came to New York City in 1937, just after the heyday of the Harlem Renaissance. Wright brought to his writings the anger of a man who had known physical punishment and repeated injustice at the hands of whites. In his novel *Native Son* (1940), the nightmarish story of a poor, young black who kills his white employer's daughter, Wright examined the ways in which the frustrated search for identity led some African-Americans to despair, defiance, and even violent crime. The novel won Wright immediate acclaim and was rewritten for the New York stage in 1941.

In the autobiographical sketch *The Ethics of Living Jim Crow* (1938), Wright records with grim frankness the experience of growing up in a racially segregated community in the American South. "Jim Crow," the stage name of a popular nineteenth-century minstrel performer, Thomas D. Rice, had come to describe anything pertaining to African-Americans, including matters of racial segregation.

READING 6.19 From Wright's *The Ethics of Living Jim Crow* (1938)

My first lesson in how to live as a Negro came when I was quite small. We were living in Arkansas. Our house stood behind the railroad tracks. Its skimpy yard was paved with black cinders. Nothing green ever grew in that yard. The only touch of green we could see was far away, beyond the tracks, over where the white folks lived. But cinders were good enough for me and I never missed the green growing things. And anyhow cinders were fine weapons. You could always have a nice hot war with huge black cinders. All you had to do was crouch behind the brick pillars of a house with your hands 10 full of gritty ammunition. And the first woolly black head you saw pop out from behind another row of pillars was your target. You tried your very best to knock it off. It was great fun. I never fully realized the appalling disadvantages of a cinder environment till one day the gang to which I belonged found itself engaged in a war with the white boys who lived beyond the tracks. As usual we laid down our cinder barrage, thinking that this would wipe the white boys out. But they replied with a steady bombardment of broken bottles. We doubled our cinder barrage, but they hid behind trees, hedges, 20 and the sloping embankment of their lawns. Having no such fortifications, we retreated to the brick pillars of our homes. During the retreat a broken milk bottle caught me behind the ear, opening a deep gash which bled profusely. The sight of blood pouring over my face completely demoralized our ranks. My fellow-combatants left me standing paralyzed in the center of the yard, and scurried for their homes. A kind neighbor saw me, and rushed me to a doctor, who took three stitches in my neck.

I sat brooding on my front steps, nursing my wound and 30 waiting for my mother to come from work. I felt that a grave injustice had been done me. It was all right to throw cinders. The greatest harm a cinder could do was leave a bruise. But broken bottles were dangerous; they left you cut, bleeding, and helpless.

When night fell, my mother came from the white folks' kitchen. I raced down the street to meet her. I could just feel in my bones that she would understand. I knew she would tell me exactly what to do next time. I grabbed her hand and babbled out the whole story. She examined my wound, then 40 slapped me.

"How come yuh didn't hide?" she asked me. "How come yuh awways fightin'?"

I was outraged, and bawled. Between sobs I told her that I didn't have any trees or hedges to hide behind. There wasn't a thing I could have used as a trench. And you couldn't throw very far when you were hiding behind the brick pillars of a house. She grabbed a barrel stave, dragged me home, stripped me naked, and beat me till I had a fever of one hundred and two. She would smack my rump with the stave, and, while the 50 skin was still smarting impart to me gems of Jim Crow wisdom. I was never to throw cinders any more. I was never to fight any more wars. I was never, never, under any conditions, to fight *white* folks again. And they were absolutely right in clouting me with the broken milk bottle. Didn't I know she was working hard every day in the hot kitchens of the white folks to make money to take care of me? When was I ever going to learn to be a good boy? She couldn't be bothered with my fights. She finished by telling me that I ought to be thankful to God as long as I lived that they didn't 60 kill me.

All that night I was delirious and could not sleep. Each time I closed my eyes I saw monstrous white faces suspended from the ceiling, leering at me.

From that time on, the charm of my cinder yard was gone. The green trees, the trimmed hedges, the cropped lawns grew very meaningful, became a symbol. Even today when I think of white folks, the hard, sharp outlines of white houses surrounded by trees, lawns, and hedges are present somewhere in the background of my mind. Through the years 70 they grew into an overreaching symbol of fear.

It was a long time before I came in close contact with white folks again. We moved from Arkansas to Mississippi. Here we had the good fortune not to live behind the railroad tracks, or close to white neighborhoods. We lived in the very heart of the local Black Belt. There were black churches and black preachers; there were black schools and black teachers; black groceries and black clerks. In fact, everything was so solidly black that for a long time I did not even think of white folks, save in remote and vague terms. But this could not last 80 forever. As one grows older one eats more. One's clothing costs more. When I finished grammar school I had to go to work. My mother could no longer feed and clothe me on her cooking job.

There is but one place where a black boy who knows no trade can get a job, and that's where the houses and faces are white, where the trees, lawns, and hedges are green. My first job was with an optical company in Jackson, Mississippi. The morning I applied I stood straight and neat before the boss, answering all his questions with sharp yessirs and nosirs. I 90 was very careful to pronounce my *sirs* distinctly, in order that he might know that I was polite, that I knew where I was, and that I knew he was a *white* man. I wanted that job badly.

He looked me over as though he were examining a prize poodle. He questioned me closely about my schooling, being particularly insistent about how much mathematics I had had. He seemed very pleased when I told him I had had two years of algebra.

"Boy, how would you like to try to learn something around here?" he asked me. 100

"I'd like it fine, sir," I said, happy. I had visions of "working my way up." Even Negroes have those visions.

"All right," he said. "Come on."

I followed him to the small factory.

"Pease," he said to a white man of about thirty-five, "this is Richard. He's going to work for us."

Pease looked at me and nodded.

I was then taken to a white boy of about seventeen.

"Morrie, this is Richard, who's going to work for us."

"Whut yuh sayin' there, boy!" Morrie boomed at me. 110

"Fine!" I answered.

The boss instructed these two to help me, teach me, give me jobs to do, and let me learn what I could in my spare time.

My wages were five dollars a week.

I worked hard, trying to please. For the first month I got along O.K. Both Pease and Morrie seemed to like me. But one thing was missing. And I kept thinking about it. I was not learning anything and nobody was volunteering to help me. Thinking they had forgotten that I was to learn something about the mechanics of grinding lenses, I asked Morrie one 120 day to tell me about the work. He grew red.

"Whut yuh tryin' t' do, nigger, get smart?" he asked.

"Naw; I ain' tryin' t' git smart," I said.

"Well, don't, if yuh know whut's good for yuh!"

I was puzzled. Maybe he just doesn't want to help me, I thought. I went to Pease.

"Say, are yuh crazy, you black bastard?" Pease asked me, his gray eyes growing hard.

I spoke out, reminding him that the boss had said I was to be given a chance to learn something. 130

"Nigger, you think you're *white*, don't you?"

"Naw, sir!"

"Well, you're acting mighty like it!"

"But, Mr. Pease, the boss said . . ."

Pease shook his fist in my face.

"This is a *white* man's work around here, and you better watch yourself!"

From then on they changed toward me. They said good-morning no more. When I was just a bit slow in performing some duty, I was called a lazy black son-of-a-bitch. 140

Once I thought of reporting all this to the boss. But the mere idea of what would happen to me if Pease and Morrie should learn that I had "snitched" stopped me. And after all the boss was a white man, too. What was the use?

The climax came at noon one summer day. Pease called me to his workbench. To get to him I had to go between two narrow benches and stand with my back against a wall.

"Yes, sir," I said.

"Richard, I want to ask you something," Pease began pleasantly, not looking up from his work. 150

"Yes, sir," I said again.

Morrie came over, blocking the narrow passage between the benches. He folded his arms, staring at me solemnly.

I looked from one to the other, sensing that something was coming.

"Yes, sir," I said for the third time.

Pease looked up and spoke very slowly.

"Richard, *Mr.* Morrie here tells me you called me *Pease.*"

I stiffened. A void seemed to open up in me. I knew this was the showdown. 160

He meant that I had failed to call him Mr. Pease. I looked at Morrie. He was gripping a steel bar in his hands. I opened my mouth to speak, to protest, to assure Pease that I had never called him simply *Pease*, and that I had never had any intentions of doing so, when Morrie grabbed me by the collar, ramming my head against the wall.

"Now be careful, nigger!" snarled Morrie, baring his teeth. "*I* heard yuh call 'im *Pease*! 'N' if yuh say yuh didn't, yuh're callin' me a *lie*, see?" He waved the steel bar threateningly.

If I had said: No, sir, Mr. Pease, I never called you *Pease* I 170 would have been automatically calling Morrie a liar. And if I said: Yes, sir, Mr. Pease, I called you *Pease*, I would have been pleading guilty to having uttered the worst insult that a Negro can utter to a southern white man. I stood hesitating, trying to frame a neutral reply.

"Richard, I asked you a question!" said Pease. Anger was creeping into his voice.

"I don't remember calling you *Pease*, Mr. Pease," I said cautiously. "And if I did, I sure didn't mean . . ."

"You black son-of-a-bitch! You called me *Pease*, then!" he 180 spat, slapping me till I bent sideways over a bench. Morrie was on top of me, demanding:

"Didn't you call 'im *Pease*? If yuh say yuh didn't, I'll rip yo' gut string loose with this bar, yuh black granny dodger! Yuh can't call a white man a lie 'n' git erway with it, you black son-of-a-bitch!"

I wilted. I begged them not to bother me. I knew what they wanted. They wanted me to leave.

"I'll leave," I promised. "I'll leave right *now*."

They gave me a minute to get out of the factory. I was 190 warned not to show up again, or tell the boss.

I went.

When I told the folks at home what had happened, they called me a fool. They told me that I must never again attempt to exceed my boundaries. When you are working for white folks, they said, you got to "stay in your place" if you want to keep working. . . .

Q Which of the details in this selection bring to life the plight of young blacks in the American South?

Q Describe the character, Pease: is he a believable figure?

The Civil Rights Movement

Well after World War II, racism remained an undeniable fact of American life. Ironically, while Americans had fought to oppose Nazi racism in Germany, black Americans endured a system of inferior education, restricted jobs, ghetto housing, and generally low living standards. High crime rates, illiteracy, and drug addiction were evidence of affluent America's awesome failure to assimilate a Third World population that suffered in its midst. The fact that African-Americans had served in great numbers in World War II inspired a redoubled effort to end persistent discrimination and segregation in the United States. During the 1950s and 1960s, that effort came to flower in the civil rights movement.

Civil rights leaders of the 1950s demanded enforcement of all the provisions for equality promised in the United States Constitution. Their demands led to a landmark Supreme Court decision in 1954 that banned school segregation; by implication, this undermined the entire system of legalized segregation in the United States. Desegregation was met with fierce resistance, especially in the American South. In response, the so-called "Negro Revolt" began in 1955 and continued for over a decade. It took the form of nonviolent, direct-action protests, including boycotts of segregated lunch counters, peaceful "sit-ins," and protest marches. Leading the revolt was Dr. Martin Luther King, Jr. (1929–1968), a Protestant pastor and civil rights activist who modeled his campaign of peaceful protest on the example of Gandhi. As president of the Southern Christian Leadership Conference, King served as an inspiration to all African-Americans.

The urgency of their cause is conveyed in a letter King wrote while confined to jail for marching without a permit in the city of Birmingham, Alabama. It addressed a group of local white clergy, who had publicly criticized King for breaking laws that prohibited blacks from using public facilities and for promoting "untimely" demonstrations. After King's letter was published in *The Christian Century* (June 12, 1963), it became (in a shorter version edited by King himself) the key text in a nationwide debate over civil rights: it provided philosophic justification for the practice of civil disobedience as a means of opposing injustice. King's measured eloquence and reasoned restraint stand in ironic contrast to the savagery of the opposition, who had used guns, hoses, and attack dogs against the demonstrators, 2,400 of whom were jailed along with King.

READING 6.20 From King's *Letter from Birmingham Jail* (1963)

My dear Fellow Clergymen,
While confined here in the Birmingham City Jail, I came   **1**
across your recent statement calling our present activities
"unwise and untimely." Seldom, if ever, do I pause to answer
criticism of my work and ideas. But since I feel that you are
men of genuine goodwill and your criticisms are sincerely set
forth, I would like to answer your statement in what I hope
will be patient and reasonable terms.

I think I should give the reason for my being in Birmingham,
since you have been influenced by the argument of "outsiders
coming in." Several months ago our local affiliate here in   **10**
Birmingham invited us to be on call to engage in a nonviolent
direct action program if such were deemed necessary. We
readily consented and when the hour came we lived up to our
promises. So I am here, along with several members of my
staff, because we were invited here. Beyond this, I am in
Birmingham because injustice is here.

Moreover, I am cognizant of the interrelatedness of all
communities and states. I cannot sit idly by in Atlanta and not
be concerned about what happens in Birmingham. Injustice
anywhere is a threat to justice everywhere. We are caught in   **20**

an inescapable network of mutuality tied in a single garment
of destiny. Never again can we afford to live with the narrow,
provincial "outsider agitator" idea. Anyone who lives inside
the United States can never be considered an outsider
anywhere in this country.

You deplore the demonstrations that are presently taking
place in Birmingham. But I am sorry that your statement did
not express a similar concern for the conditions that brought
the demonstrations into being. I would not hesitate to say that
it is unfortunate that so-called demonstrations are taking   **30**
place in Birmingham at this time, but I would say in more
emphatic terms that it is even more unfortunate that the white
power structure of this city left the Negro community with no
other alternative.

In any nonviolent campaign there are four basic steps:
1) collection of the facts to determine whether injustices are
alive; 2) negotiation; 3) self-purification; and 4) direct action.

You may well ask, "Why direct action? Why sit-ins,
marches, etc.? Isn't negotiation a better path?" You are exactly
right in your call for negotiation. Indeed, this is the purpose of   **40**
direct action. Nonviolent direct action seeks to create such a
crisis and establish such creative tension that a community
that has constantly refused to negotiate is forced to confront
the issue. So the purpose of the direct action is to create a
situation so crisis-packed that it will inevitably open the door
to negotiation.

My friends, I must say to you that we have not made a
single gain in civil rights without determined legal and
nonviolent pressure. History is the long and tragic story of the
fact that privileged groups seldom give up their privileges   **50**
voluntarily. Individuals may see the moral light and voluntarily
give up their unjust posture; but as Reinhold Niebuhr[1] has
reminded us, groups are more immoral than individuals.

We know through painful experience that freedom is never
voluntarily given by the oppressor; it must be demanded by the
oppressed. For years now I have heard the word "Wait!" It
rings in the ear of every Negro with a piercing familiarity. This
"wait" has almost always meant "never." We must come to
see with the distinguished jurist of yesterday that "justice too
long delayed is justice denied." We have waited for more than   **60**
three hundred and forty years for our constitutional and God-
given rights.

You express a great deal of anxiety over our willingness to
break laws. This is certainly a legitimate concern. Since we so
diligently urge people to obey the Supreme Court's decision of
1954 outlawing segregation in the public schools, it is rather
strange and paradoxical to find us consciously breaking laws.
One may well ask, "How can you advocate breaking some
laws and obeying others?" The answer is found in the fact
that there are two types of laws. There are *just* laws and   **70**
there are *unjust* laws. One has not only a legal but a moral
responsibility to obey just laws. Conversely, one has a moral
responsibility to disobey unjust laws.

Now what is the difference between the two? A just law is
a man-made code that squares with the moral law or the law
of God. An unjust law is a code that is out of harmony with

---

[1] An American Protestant theologian (1892–1971) who urged ethical realism in Christian approaches to political debate (see chapter 35).

the moral law. Any law that degrades human personality is unjust. All segregation statutes are unjust because segregation distorts the soul and damages the personality. It gives the segregator a false sense of superiority and the **80** segregated a false sense of inferiority.

Let us turn to a more concrete example of just and unjust laws. An unjust law is a code that a majority inflicts on a minority that is not binding on itself. This is *difference* made legal. On the other hand a just law is a code that a majority compels a minority to follow and that it is willing to follow itself. This is *sameness* made legal.

I hope you can see the distinction I am trying to point out. In no sense do I advocate evading or defying the law as the rabid segregationist would do. This would lead to anarchy. One who **90** breaks an unjust law *openly*, *lovingly*, and with a willingness to accept the penalty by staying in jail to arouse the conscience of the community over its injustice, is in reality expressing the very highest respect for law.

Of course there is nothing new about this kind of civil disobedience. It was seen sublimely in the refusal of Shadrach, Meshach, and Abednego to obey the laws of Nebuchadnezzar[2] because a higher moral law was involved. It was practiced superbly by the early Christians.

We can never forget that everything Hitler did in Germany **100** was "legal" and everything the Hungarian freedom fighters did in Hungary was "illegal." It was "illegal" to aid and comfort a Jew in Hitler's Germany.

In your statement you asserted that our actions, even though peaceful, must be condemned because they precipitate violence. But can this assertion be logically made? Isn't this like condemning the robbed man because his possession of money precipitated the evil act of robbery? We must come to see, as federal courts have consistently affirmed, that it is immoral to urge an individual to withdraw his efforts to gain **110** his basic constitutional rights because the quest precipitates violence. Society must protect the robbed and punish the robber.

Over the last few years I have consistently preached that nonviolence demands that the means we use must be as pure as the ends we seek. So I have tried to make it clear that it is wrong to use immoral means to gain moral ends. But now I must affirm that it is just as wrong, or even more so, to use moral means to preserve immoral ends. T. S. Eliot has said that there is no greater treason than to do the right deed for **120** the wrong reason.

I wish you had commended the Negro sit-inners and demonstrators of Birmingham for their sublime courage, their willingness to suffer, and their amazing discipline in the midst of the most inhuman provocation. One day the South will recognize its real heroes. They will include old, oppressed, battered Negro women, symbolized in a seventy-two-year-old woman of Montgomery, Alabama, who rose up with a sense of dignity and with her people decided not to ride the segregated buses, and responded to one who inquired about **130**

her tiredness with ungrammatical profundity: "My feets is tired, but my soul is rested." One day the South will know that when these disinherited children of God sat down at the lunch counters they were in reality standing up for the best in the American dream and the most sacred values in our Judeo-Christian heritage, and thus carrying our whole nation back to great wells of democracy which were dug deep by the founding fathers in the formulation of the Constitution and the Declaration of Independence.

I hope this letter finds you strong in the faith. I also hope **140** that circumstances will soon make it possible for me to meet each of you, not as an integrationist or a civil rights leader, but as a fellow clergyman and a Christian brother. Let us hope that the dark clouds of racial prejudice will soon pass away and the deep fog of misunderstanding will be lifted from our fear-drenched communities and in some not too distant tomorrow the radiant stars of love and brotherhood will shine over our great nation with all of their scintillating beauty.

Yours for the cause of
Peace and Brotherhood **150**
Martin Luther King, Jr.

Q What arguments does Dr. King make for nonviolence and negotiation?
Q Evaluate the claim (line 53) that "groups are more immoral than individuals."

As the Birmingham Letter confirms, Dr. King practiced the tactics of nonviolence to achieve the goals of racial integration and civil rights in America. Another black protest leader of the period took a very different tack: Malcolm Little (1925–1965), who called himself "Malcolm X," experienced firsthand the inequities and degradation of life in white America. For a time he turned to crime and drugs as a means of survival. Arrested and sentenced to prison in 1946, he took the opportunity to study history and religion, and most especially the teachings of Islam. By the time he was released in 1952, he had joined the Nation of Islam and was prepared to launch his career as a Muslim minister. Malcolm and other "Black Muslims" despaired over persistent racism in white America, and determined that blacks should pursue a very different course from that of Dr. King and the Southern Christian Leadership Conference. African-Americans, argued Malcolm, should abandon aspirations for integration. Instead, they should separate from American whites in every feasible way; they should create a black nation in which—through hard work and the pursuit of Muslim morality—they might live equally, in dignity, free of the daily affronts of white racism. These goals should be achieved by all available means, violent if necessary (armed self-defense was a first step). Only by fighting for black nationalism would African-Americans ever gain power and self-respect in racist America. Little wonder that Malcolm was feared and reviled by whites and deemed a dangerous radical by more moderate blacks as well.

---

[2]The Chaldean king of the sixth century B.C.E., who, according to the Book of Daniel, demanded that these Hebrew youths worship the Babylonian gods. Nebuchadnezzar cast them into a fiery furnace, but they were delivered unhurt by an angel of God (see Figure 9.7).

In 1963, Malcolm addressed a conference of black leaders in Detroit, Michigan. In this speech, which later came to be called "Message to the Grass Roots," Malcolm addressed a large audience representing a cross-section of the African-American community. The power and immediacy of his style is best captured on the tape of the speech published by the African-American Broadcasting and Record Company. Nevertheless, the following brief excerpt provides a glimpse into the ferocious eloquence that Malcolm exhibited throughout his brief career—until his death by assassination in 1965.

READING 6.21 From Malcolm X's *Message to the Grass Roots* (1963)

...America has a very serious problem. Not only does America have a very serious problem, but our people have a very serious problem. America's problem is us. We're her problem. The only reason she has a problem is she doesn't want us here. And every time you look at yourself, be you black, brown, red or yellow, a so-called Negro, you represent a person who poses such a serious problem for America because you're not wanted. Once you face this as a fact, then you can start plotting a course that will make you appear intelligent, instead of unintelligent.   10

What you and I need to do is learn to forget our differences. When we come together, we don't come together as Baptists or Methodists. You don't catch hell because you're a Baptist, and you don't catch hell because you're a Methodist. You don't catch hell because you're a Methodist or Baptist, you don't catch hell because you're a Democrat or a Republican, you don't catch hell because you're a Mason or an Elk, and you sure don't catch hell because you're an American; because if you were an American, you wouldn't catch hell. You catch hell because you're a black man. You catch hell, all of us catch   20 hell, for the same reason.

So we're all black people, so-called Negroes, second- class citizens, ex-slaves. You're nothing but an ex-slave. You don't like to be told that. But what else are you? You are ex-slaves. You didn't come here on the "Mayflower." You came here on a slave ship. In chains, like a horse, or a cow, or a chicken. And you were brought here by the people who came here on the "Mayflower," you were brought here by the so-called Pilgrims, or Founding Fathers. They were the ones who brought you here.   30

We have a common enemy. We have this in common: We have a common oppressor, a common exploiter, and a common discriminator. But once we all realize that we have a common enemy, then we unite—on the basis of what we have in common. And what we have foremost in common is that enemy—the white man....

As long as the white man sent you to Korea, you bled. He sent you to Germany, you bled. He sent you to the South Pacific to fight the Japanese, you bled. You bleed for white people, but when it comes to seeing your own churches being   40 bombed and little black girls murdered, you haven't got any blood. You bleed when the white man says bleed; you bite when the white man says bite; and you bark when the white man says bark. I hate to say this about us, but it's true. How are you going to be nonviolent in Mississippi, as violent as you were in Korea? How can you justify being nonviolent in Mississippi and Alabama, when your churches are being bombed, and your little girls are being murdered, and at the same time you are going to get violent with Hitler, and Tojo, and somebody else you don't even know?   50

If violence is wrong in America, violence is wrong abroad. If it is wrong to be violent defending black women and black children and black babies and black men, then it is wrong for America to draft us and make us violent abroad in defense of her. And if it is right for America to draft us, and teach us how to be violent in defense of her, then it is right for you and me to do whatever is necessary to defend our own people right here in this country....

Q How does Malcolm justify black violence?

Q How do his perceptions differ from King's?

The Literature of the Black Revolution

The passage of the Civil Rights Act in America in 1964 provided an end to official segregation in public places; but continuing discrimination and the growing militancy of some civil rights groups provoked a more violent phase of the protests during the late 1960s and thereafter. Even before the assassination of Martin Luther King, Jr., in 1968, the black revolution had begun to assume a transnational fervor. American voices joined those of their black neighbors in West India, South Africa, and elsewhere in the world. Fired by **apartheid**, the system of strict racial segregation that prevailed legally in the Union of South Africa until 1994, the poet Bloke Modisane (1923–1986) lamented:

> it gets awful lonely,
> lonely;
> like screaming,
> screaming lonely
> screaming down dream alley,
> screaming blues, like none can hear*

In *Black Skin, White Masks* (1958)—the handbook for African revolution—the West Indian essayist and revolutionary Franz Fanon (1925–1961) defended violence as necessary and desirable in overcoming the tyranny of whites over blacks in the colonial world. "At the level of individuals," he wrote, "violence is a cleansing force." In America, where advertising media made clear the disparity between the material comforts of blacks and whites, the black revolution swelled on a tide of rising expectations. LeRoi Jones (b. 1934), who in 1966 adopted the African name Imamu Amiri Baraka, echoed the message of Malcolm X in poems and plays that advocated militant

---

*From *Poems from Black Africa*, ed. Langston Hughes. Bloomington: Indiana University Press, 1963, 110.

action and pan-Africanism. Rejecting white Western literary tradition, Baraka called for "poems that kill"; "Let there be no love poems written," he entreats, "until love can exist freely and cleanly."

Two luminaries of American black protest literature were James Baldwin (1924–1987) and Ralph Ellison (1914–1994). Baldwin, the eldest of nine children raised in Harlem in conditions of poverty, began writing when he was fourteen years old. Encouraged early in his career by Richard Wright, he became a formidable preacher of the gospel of equality. For Baldwin, writing was a subversive act. "You write," he insisted, "in order to change the world, knowing perfectly well that you probably can't, but also knowing that literature is indispensable to the world. In some way, your aspirations and concern for a single man in fact do begin to change the world. The world changes according to the way people see it, and if you alter, even by a millimeter, the way a person looks or people look at reality, then you can change it."

In his novels, short stories, and essays, Baldwin stressed the affinity African-Americans felt with other poverty-stricken populations. Yet, as he tried to define the unique differences between blacks and whites, he observed that black people were strangers in the modern world—a world whose traditions were claimed by whites. As he explained in the essay "Stranger in the Village" (1953):

> [European Whites] cannot be, from the point of view of power, strangers anywhere in the world; they have made the modern world, in effect, even if they do not know it. The most illiterate among them is related, in a way that I am not, to Dante, Shakespeare, Michelangelo, Aeschylus, da Vinci, Rembrandt, and Racine; the cathedral at Chartres says something to them which it cannot say to me . . . . Out of their hymns and dances come Beethoven and Bach. Go back a few centuries and they are in their full glory—but I am in Africa, watching the conquerors arrive.

But Baldwin uncovered a much overlooked truth about the character of the modern world: that black culture has influenced white culture, and especially American culture, in a profound and irreversible manner:

> The time has come to realize that the interracial drama acted out on the American continent has not only created a new black man, it has created a new white man, too. . . . One of the things that distinguishes Americans from other people is that no other people has ever been so deeply involved in the lives of black men, and vice versa. . . . It is precisely this black–white experience which may prove of indispensable value to us in the world we face today. This world is white no longer, and it will never be white again.*

Baldwin's contemporary—Ralph Ellison, a native of Oklahoma and an amateur jazz musician, came to Harlem during the 1930s to study sculpture and musical composition. He was influenced by both Hughes and Wright and soon turned to writing short stories and newspaper reviews. In 1945, he began the novel *Invisible Man*, a fiction masterpiece that probes the black estrangement from white culture. The prologue to the novel, an excerpt of which follows, offers a glimpse into the spiritual odyssey of the "invisible" protagonist. It also broaches, with surrealistic intensity, some of Ellison's most important themes: the nightmarish quality of urban life and the alienation experienced by both blacks and whites in modern American society.

READING 6.22 From Ellison's *Invisible Man* (1952)

I am an invisible man. No, I am not a spook like those who   1
haunted Edgar Allan Poe;[1] nor am I one of your Hollywood-
movie ectoplasms. I am a man of substance, of flesh and
bone, fiber and liquids—and I might even be said to possess a
mind. I am invisible, understand, simply because people refuse
to see me. Like the bodiless heads you see sometimes in
circus sideshows, it is as though I have been surrounded by
mirrors of hard, distorting glass. When they approach me they
see only my surroundings, themselves, or figments of their
imagination—indeed, everything and anything except me.   10

Nor is my invisibility exactly a matter of a bio-chemical
accident to my epidermis. That invisibility to which I refer
occurs because of a peculiar disposition of the eyes of those
with whom I come in contact. A matter of the construction of
their *inner* eyes, those eyes with which they look through their
physical eyes upon reality. I am not complaining, nor am I
protesting either. It is sometimes advantageous to be unseen,
although it is most often rather wearing on the nerves. Then
too, you're constantly being bumped against by those of poor
vision. Or again, you often doubt if you really exist. You   20
wonder whether you aren't simply a phantom in other people's
minds. Say, a figure in a nightmare which the sleeper tries
with all his strength to destroy. It's when you feel like this
that, out of resentment, you begin to bump people back. And,
let me confess, you feel that way most of the time. You ache
with the need to convince yourself that you do exist in the real
world, that you're a part of all the sound and anguish, and you
strike out with your fists, you curse and you swear to make
them recognize you. And, alas, it's seldom successful.

One night I accidentally bumped into a man, and perhaps   30
because of the near darkness he saw me and called me an
insulting name. I sprang at him, seized his coat lapels and
demanded that he apologize. He was a tall blond man, and as
my face came close to his he looked insolently out of his blue
eyes and cursed me, his breath hot in my face as he struggled.
I pulled his chin down sharp upon the crown of my head,
butting him as I had seen the West Indians do, and I felt his

---

*"Stranger in the Village," in James Baldwin, *Notes of a Native Son.* New York: Bantam Press, 1964, 140, 148–149.

[1] A leading American poet, literary critic, and short-story writer (1809–1849), noted for his tales of terror and his clever detective stories.

flesh tear and the blood gush out, and I yelled, "Apologize!
Apologize!" But he continued to curse and struggle, and I
butted him again and again until he went down heavily, on his 40
knees, profusely bleeding. I kicked him repeatedly, in a frenzy
because he still uttered insults though his lips were frothy
with blood. Oh yes, I kicked him! And in my outrage I got out
my knife and prepared to slit his throat, right there beneath
the lamplight in the deserted street, holding him by the collar
with one hand, and opening the knife with my teeth—when it
occurred to me that the man had not *seen* me, actually; that
he, as far as he knew, was in the midst of a walking
nightmare! And I stopped the blade, slicing the air as I pushed
him away, letting him fall back to the street. I stared at him 50
hard as the lights of a car stabbed through the darkness. He
lay there, moaning on the asphalt; a man almost killed by a
phantom. It unnerved me. I was both disgusted and ashamed. I
was like a drunken man myself, wavering about on weakened
legs. Then I was amused. Something in this man's thick head
had sprung out and beaten him within an inch of his life. I
began to laugh at this crazy discovery. Would he have
awakened at the point of Death? Would Death himself have
freed him for wakeful living? But I didn't linger. I ran away into
the dark, laughing so hard I feared I might rupture myself. The 60
next day I saw his picture in the *Daily News*, beneath a
caption stating that he had been "mugged." Poor fool, poor
blind fool, I thought with sincere compassion, mugged by an
invisible man! . . .

Q What does Ellison's protagonist mean
when he says he is "an invisible man?"

In the literature of the black revolution, especially that of
that last three decades of the twentieth century, many of
the most powerful voices were female. Succeeding such
notable Harlem Renaissance writers as Zora Neale Hurston
(1891–1960) and Dorothy West (1912–1998), two contemporary figures—Toni Morrison (b. 1931) and Alice Walker
(b. 1944)—have risen to eminence for their courageous
and candid characterizations of black women facing the
perils of racism, domestic violence, and sexual abuse. Space
permits only a small example of the writings of Alice
Walker, whose novel *The Color Purple* won the Pulitzer
Prize for literature in 1982. As effective as many of Walker's
novels and poems, her short story "Elethia" probes the
dual issues of identity and liberation as they come to shape
the destiny of a young black female.

READING 6.23 Walker's "Elethia" (1981)

A certain perverse experience shaped Elethia's life, and made 1
it possible for it to be true that she carried with her at all
times a small apothecary jar of ashes.

There was in the town where she was born a man whose
ancestors had owned a large plantation on which everything
under the sun was made or grown. There had been many
slaves, and though slavery no longer existed, this grandson of
former slaveowners held a quaint proprietary point of view

where colored people were concerned. He adored them, of
course. Not in the present—it went without saying—but at 10
that time, stopped, just on the outskirts of his memory: his
grandfather's time.

This man, whom Elethia never saw, opened a locally famous
restaurant on a busy street near the center of town. He called
it "Old Uncle Albert's." In the window of the restaurant was a
stuffed likeness of Uncle Albert himself, a small brown dummy
of waxen skin and glittery black eyes. His lips were intensely
smiling and his false teeth shone. He carried a covered tray in
one hand, raised level with his shoulder, and over his other
arm was draped a white napkin. 20

Black people could not eat at Uncle Albert's, though they
worked, of course, in the kitchen. But on Saturday afternoons
a crowd of them would gather to look at "Uncle Albert" and
discuss how near to the real person the dummy looked. Only
the very old people remembered Albert Porter, and their
eyesight was no better than their memory. Still there was a
comfort somehow in knowing that Albert's likeness was here
before them daily and that if he smiled as a dummy in a
fashion he was not known to do as a man, well, perhaps both
memory and eyesight were wrong. 30

The old people appeared grateful to the rich man who
owned the restaurant for giving them a taste of vicarious
fame. They could pass by the gleaming window where Uncle
Albert stood, seemingly in the act of sprinting forward with his
tray, and know that though niggers were not allowed in the
front door, ole Albert was already inside, and looking mighty
pleased about it, too.

For Elethia the fascination was in Uncle Albert's fingernails.
She wondered how his creator had got them on. She
wondered also about the white hair that shone so brightly 40
under the lights. One summer she worked as a salad girl in the
restaurant's kitchen, and it was she who discovered the truth
about Uncle Albert. He was not a dummy; he was stuffed. Like
a bird, like a moose's head, like a giant bass. He was stuffed.

One night after the restaurant was closed someone broke in
and stole nothing but Uncle Albert. It was Elethia and her
friends, boys who were in her class and who called her "Thia."
Boys who bought Thunderbird and shared it with her. Boys
who laughed at her jokes so much they hardly remembered
she was also cute. Her tight buddies. They carefully burned 50
Uncle Albert to ashes in the incinerator of their high school,
and each of them kept a bottle of his ashes. And for each of
them what they knew and their reaction to what they knew
was profound.

The experience undercut whatever solid foundation Elethia
had assumed she had. She became secretive, wary, looking
over her shoulder at the slightest noise. She haunted the
museums of any city in which she found herself, looking,
usually, at the remains of Indians, for they were plentiful
everywhere she went. She discovered some of the Indian 60
warriors and maidens in the museums were also real, stuffed
people, painted and wigged and robed, like figures in the Rue
Morgue. There were so many, in fact, that she could not
possibly steal and burn them all. Besides, she did not know if
these figures—with their valiant glass eyes—would wish to
be burned.

About Uncle Albert she felt she knew.

What kind of man was Uncle Albert?

Well, the old folks said, he wasn't nobody's uncle and wouldn't sit still for nobody to call him that, either.

Why, said another old-timer, I recalls the time they hung a boy's privates on a post at the end of the street where all the black folks shopped, just to scare us all, you understand, and Albert Porter was the one took 'em down and buried 'em. Us never did find the rest of the boy though. It was just like always—they would throw you in the river with a big old green log tied to you, and down to the bottom you sunk.

He continued.

Albert was born in slavery and he remembered that his mama and daddy didn't know nothing about slavery'd done ended for near 'bout ten years, the boss man kept them so ignorant of the law, you understand. So he was a mad so-an'-so when he found out. They used to beat him *severe* trying to make him forget the past and grin and act like a nigger. (Whenever you saw somebody acting like a nigger, Albert said, you could be sure he seriously disremembered his past.) But he never would. Never would work in the big house as head servant, neither—always broke up stuff. The master at that time was always going around pinching him too. Looks like he hated Albert more than anything—but he never would let him get a job anywhere else. And Albert never would leave home. Too stubborn.

Stubborn, yes. My land, another one said. That's why it do seem strange to see that dummy that sposed to be old Albert

with his mouth open. All them teeth. Hell, all Albert's teeth was knocked out before he was grown.

Elethia went away to college and her friends went into the army because they were poor and that was the way things were. They discovered Uncle Alberts all over the world. Elethia was especially disheartened to find Uncle Alberts in her textbooks, in the newspapers and on t.v.

Everywhere she looked there was an Uncle Albert (and many Aunt Albertas, it goes without saying).

But she had her jar of ashes, the old-timers' memories written down, and her friends who wrote that in the army they were learning skills that would get them through more than a plate glass window.

And she was careful that, no matter how compelling the hype, Uncle Alberts, in her own mind, were not permitted to exist.

Q What are "Uncle Alberts"?
Q What social contradictions does Walker attack in this story?

African-Americans and the Visual Arts

During the Harlem Renaissance, African-American painters and sculptors made public the social concerns of black poets and writers. In picturing their experience, they drew

Figure 36.2 ROMARE BEARDEN, *Empress of the Blues*, 1974. Acrylic and pencil on paper and printed paper on paperboard, 3 ft. 10 in. × 4 ft. 2 in. Smithsonian American Art Museum, Washington, D.C., 1996.71. © Smithsonian American Art Museum/Art Resource, New York/Scala, Florence.

The first African-American to establish himself in Hollywood, Spike Lee (b. 1955) has won international acclaim for films that explore race conflicts in the inner city (*Do the Right Thing*, 1989), modern black history (*Malcolm X*, 1992), the black minstrel tradition (*Bamboozled*, 2000), and drug-dealing (*25th Hour*, 2002). Lee uses the camera inventively to underline social conflicts, as in his radical close-ups of faces caught in bitter, heated disputes. He favors short, disconnected scenes, the "accidental" effects of the handheld camera, and editing techniques that often leave the narrative themes of his films unresolved but filled with implications. Lee opened the door to a new wave of black filmmakers that include John Singleton (*Boyz in the Hood*, 1991) and Julie Dash (*Daughters of the Dust*, 1991).

on African folk idioms and colloquial forms of native expression; but they also absorbed the radically new styles of European modernism. Among these painters, there emerged a "blues aesthetic" that featured bold colors, angular forms, and rhythmic, stylized compositions. One of the most notable artists of the twentieth century, Jacob Lawrence (1917–2000) migrated to Harlem with his family in 1930. Lawrence's powerful style features flat, local colors and angular, abstract forms that owe as much to African art as to synthetic cubism and expressionism. At the same time, his lifelong commitment to social and racial issues made him heir to the nineteenth-century artist–critics Goya and Daumier, whom he admired. Paint-ing in tempera on masonite panels, Lawrence won early acclaim for serial paintings that deal with black history and with the lives of black American heroes and heroines. Among the most famous of these is a series of sixty panels known as *The Migration of the Negro* (1940–1941). For *The Migration*—an expressionistic narrative of the great northward movement of African-Americans after World War I—Lawrence drew on textual sources rather than firsthand visual experience. The drama of each episode (see Figure 36.1) is conveyed by means of bold rhythms and vigorous, geometric shapes that preserve what Lawrence called "the magic of the picture plane."

Lawrence's contemporary, Romare Bearden (1916–1988) was born in North Carolina, but grew up in Harlem. He knew the major figures of the Harlem Renaissance, including Lawrence himself, Langston Hughes, and the leading jazz musicians of New York. Bearden's favorite medium was collage. The earliest of these emerged against the backdrop of the civil rights movement and took as their theme the African-American experience. Much like Hannah Höch (see Figure 33.15), Bearden cut bits and pieces of images from popular magazines; but his semi-abstract compositions developed narrative themes drawn from everyday life. Their abrupt shifts in scale and strident colors call to mind the improvisational phrasing and syncopated rhythms of jazz. Music, in fact, provided the subject matter for some of his most notable works, such as *Train Whistle Blues* (1964), *Three Folk Musicians* (1967), *New Orleans Ragging Home* (1974), and *Empress of the Blues* (1974, Figure **36.2**).

Since the mid-twentieth century, African-American artists have taken ever more cynical approaches to themes of race discrimination and racial stereotyping. The sculptor Betye Saar (b. 1926) abandoned the African-inspired fetishlike sculptures of her early career and turned to

fabricating boxed constructions that attacked the icons of commercial white culture. In the mixed-media sculpture entitled *The Liberation of Aunt Jemima*, Saar transforms the familiar symbol of American pancakes and cozy kitchens into a gun-toting version of the "mammy" stereotype (Figure **36.3**). The satirist–artist Robert Colescott (b. 1925) creates parodies of famous paintings in which whites are recast as cartoon-style, stereotyped blacks. In doing so, Colescott calls attention to the exclusion of blacks from Western art history. His bitter parody of Delacroix's *Liberty Leading the People* (1976) features a crew of brashly painted African-American rebels commanded by a black-faced

Figure 36.3 BETYE SAAR, *The Liberation of Aunt Jemima*, 1972. Mixed media, 11¾ × 8 × 2¾ in. University Art Museum, University of California at Berkeley. Purchased with the aid of funds from the National Endowment for the Arts. Selected by the Committee for the Acquisition of African-American Art.

Figure 36.4 ROBERT COLESCOTT, *Les Demoiselles d'Alabama (Vestidas)*, 1985. Acrylic on canvas, 8 ft. × 7 ft. 8 in. Collection of Hanford Yang, New York. Photo courtesy Phyllis Kind Gallery, New York.

Liberty. Colescott's *Les Demoiselles d'Alabama* (Figure **36.4**), an obvious funk-art clone of Picasso's landmark painting (see Figure 32.2), slyly challenges contemporary definitions of primitivism and modernism. Colescott observes, "Picasso started with European art and abstracted through African art, producing 'Africanism' but keeping one foot in European art. I began with Picasso's Africanism and moved toward European art, keeping one foot in Africanism. . . ."*

African-Americans and Jazz

Possibly the most important contribution made by African-Americans to world culture occurred in the area of music, specifically in the birth and development of that unique form of modern music known as jazz. Jazz is a synthesis of diverse musical elements that came together in the first two decades of the twentieth century, but it was after World War I that jazz came to full fruition as an art form. Although some music historians insist that jazz is the product of place, not race, the primary role of African-Americans in the origins and evolution of jazz is indisputable.

Jazz is primarily a performer's rather than a composer's art. Dominated by Afro-Caribbean rhythmic styles, it incorporates a wide range of European and African-American concepts of harmony, melody, and tone color. In its evolution, jazz absorbed the musical idioms of the marching brass band, the minstrel stage, the blues, and the piano style known as *ragtime*. Ragtime is a form of piano composition and performance featuring highly syncopated rhythms and simple, appealing melodies. It apparently originated in the lower Mississippi Valley, but it migrated north after the Civil War and became popular during the 1890s. Its most inspired proponent (if not its inventor) was the black composer and popular pianist Scott Joplin (1868–1917). Early jazz performers, like "Jelly Roll" Morton (Ferdinand Joseph LaMonthe, 1885–1941), who claimed to have invented jazz, utilized ragtime rhythms in developing the essential features of the new form.

Blues, a formative element in the evolution of jazz, had begun as a vocal rather than an instrumental genre. Native to the United States, but possibly stemming from African song forms and harmonics, it is an emotive type of individual expression for lamenting one's troubles, loneli-

ness, and despair. A blues song may recall the wailing cries of plantation slaves; it may describe the anguish of separation and loss or the hope for deliverance from oppression. Such classics as W. C. Handy's "St. Louis Blues" (1914) begin with a line that states a simple plaint ("I hate to see the evening sun go down"); the plaint is repeated in a second line, and it is "answered" in a third ("It makes me think I'm on my last go-round")—a pattern derived perhaps from African call and response chants (see chapter 18). Technically, blues makes use of a special scale known as a "blues scale," which features (among other things) the flatted forms of E, G, and B within the standard scale.

Both ragtime and blues contributed substantially to the development of jazz as a unique musical idiom. But if jazz manifests any single defining quality, that quality would have to be improvisation—individual and collective. Most jazz performances are based in standard melodies—often familiar popular tunes; the individual performers (and sometimes a group of performers within an ensemble) "improvise" on the base melody. They invent passages while in the process of performing them—a form of "composing as you go"—or they incorporate bits of other (often familiar) melodies into their solos. Most scholars agree that improvisation, either individual or collective, constitutes the single element that most distinguishes jazz from

♪ See Music Listening Selections at end of chapter.

other musical idioms. Finally, jazz employs a unique variation on standard rhythms that performers and aficionados term "**swing**." While it is virtually impossible to define the concept of "swing," it may be described as the practice of playing just off the beat—slightly ahead or behind. "Swinging" normally involves achieving a certain rhythmic "groove"—a combination of rhythm and harmony that vitalizes the ensemble and propels the performance forward. (In the words of a 1940s popular song, "It don't mean a thing if it ain't got that swing!")

As a performance art, jazz depends on the interaction of the ensemble's members as they create an essentially new composition in the very act of performing it. Although syncopated rhythms, the blues motif, harmonic flexibility, and improvisation were not in themselves new, their combination—when vitalized by a "swinging" performance—produced an essentially new art form, one that would have a major impact on Western music for years to come.

The beginnings of American jazz are found in New Orleans, Louisiana, a melting pot for the rich heritage of Spanish, French, African, Caribbean, Indian, and Black Creole musical traditions. Here, black and white musicians drew on the intricate rhythms of African tribal dance and the European harmonies of traditional marching bands. The street musicians who regularly marched behind funeral or wedding processions, many of whom were neither formally trained nor could read music, might play trumpets, trombones, and clarinets; rhythm was provided by tubas as well as snare and bass drums. These musicians made up the "front line" of the parade; the crowd that danced behind them was called the "second line."* Parade bands performed perhaps the earliest version of what became jazz. Similar bands also played the popular music of the time in nightclubs and dance halls.

Louis Armstrong (1900–1971), a native of New Orleans who began playing the cornet at the age of twelve, emerged in the 1920s as the foremost jazz musician of the period. Armstrong's innovative solos provided the breakthrough by which solo improvisation became central to jazz performance. His ability to redirect harmonies and to invent reworkings of standard melodies in his solos—all performed with breathtaking virtuosity—elevated the jazz soloist to the foremost role in ensemble performance. "Satchmo" ("Satchelmouth") Armstrong was also a jazz singer with formidable musical gifts. He often embellished jazz with **scat singing**—an improvised set of nonsense syllables. His compelling personality and unfailing good

Figure 36.5 King Oliver's Creole Jazz Band, 1923. Honore Dutrey, Warren "Baby" Dodds, Joe Oliver, Louis Armstrong, Lil Hardin, Bill Johnson, and Johnny Dodds. Courtesy Hogan Jazz Archive, Tulane University.

spirits brought joy to millions and turned jazz into an internationally respected musical form. "Hotter Than That" (1927), a composition by Lillian Hardin (Armstrong's wife), exemplifies the style termed "hot jazz" (Figure **36.5**)—a style that the French in particular elevated to the status of a craze.

In the 1920s jazz spread north to the urban centers of Chicago, Kansas City, and New York. Armstrong moved to Chicago in 1922. In New York, extraordinary jazz and blues singers like Bessie Smith (1898–1937), known by her fans as the "Empress of the Blues" (see Figure 36.2) and Billie Holiday (1915–1959)—"Lady Day"—drew worldwide acclaim through the phenomena of radio and phonograph records. In the so-called "Jazz Age," jazz had a major impact on other musical genres. The American composer George Gershwin (1898–1937) incorporated the rhythms of jazz into the mesmerizing *Rhapsody in Blue* (1924), a concert piece for piano and orchestra. Gershwin's *Porgy and Bess* (1935), a fully composed opera dealing with the life of poverty-stricken Charleston African-Americans, combined jazz, blues, and spiritual and folk idioms to produce a new style of American musical theater featuring an all-black cast. Popular music of the 1930s and 1940s was closely tied to the vogue for big band jazz and the danceable rhythms of swing, a big-band jazz style that fed the dance craze of the 1940s. The white swing bands of Tommy Dorsey, Glenn Miller, and Benny Goodman (who later integrated his band—the first bandleader to do so) played a mix of instrumental swing and popular ballads, while black swing bands like that of William "Count"

---

*Not to be confused with a variant usage of the term which distinguishes the rhythm section of a band from the "front line" of reed and brass solo instrumentalists.

♪ See Music Listening Selections at end of chapter.

Figure 36.6 JEAN-MICHEL BASQUIAT, *Horn Players*, 1983. Acrylic and mixed media on canvas, 8 ft. × 6 ft. 3 in. The Broad Art Foundation, Santa Monica. Photograph © Douglas M. Parker Studio, Los Angeles. © ADAGP, Paris and DACs, London 2005.

Basie (1904–1984) leaned more toward blues and a dynamic big-band sound.

In the years following World War II, jazz took on some of the complex and sophisticated characteristics of "art music." The beguiling suite *Black, Brown, and Beige* (1948) composed by Edward Kennedy "Duke" Ellington (1899–1974) paved the way for concert hall jazz, a form that has enjoyed a revival since the 1990s. Ellington was a prolific musician, unquestionably the foremost composer in the jazz idiom (and arguably in *any* idiom) that the United States has produced.

On a smaller scale, among groups of five to seven instruments, the jazz of the late 1940s and 1950s engaged the unique improvisational talents of individual performers. New forms included "bebop" (or "bop")—a jazz style characterized by frenzied tempos, complex chord progressions, and dense polyrhythms—and "cool" jazz, a more restrained and gentler style associated with the West Coast. "Koko," performed by the saxophonist Charlie Parker (1920–1955) and the trumpeter John "Dizzy" Gillespie (1917–1993), epitomizes the bop style of the 1940s. Since the jazz renaissance of the 1980s, the New Orleans composer, trumpet prodigy, and teacher Wynton Marsalis (b. 1961) has reconfirmed the role of jazz as America's classical music. Awarded the Pulitzer Prize in 1995 for his jazz oratorio on slavery, *Blood on the Field*, Marsalis has become the world's most articulate spokesperson for the jazz genre. Likening jazz to the open exchange of ideas, Marsalis holds, "Jazz is more than the best expression there is of American culture; it is the most democratic of arts." To this day, jazz remains a unique kind of chamber music that combines the best of classical and popular musicianship.

Like the "blues aesthetic" in the poetry and painting of the Harlem Renaissance, a "jazz aesthetic" featuring spontaneity and improvisation infused the 1970s performance phenomenon known as *hip-hop*. A product of the inner-city American subculture, hip-hop brings together loud, percussive music (often electronically "mixed" by disc-jockeys), the spoken word, and street-dance, generating a raw vitality that border on the violent (see chapter 38). The paintings of the short-lived Jean-Michel Basquiat (1960–1988) embrace the free improvisations and borrowed "riffs" of modern jazz, even as they infuse the staccato rhythms and jarring lyrics of hip-hop. Basquiat's artworks conflate crude, childlike but familiar images, grim cartoon logos, and scrawled graffiti—an urban folk art style that vents the rage and joy of inner-city youths (like Basquiat himself). *Horn Players*, executed with portable oil sticks on a blackboard-like surface, pays

See Music Listening Selections at end of chapter.

homage to the jazz giants Dizzy Gillespie and Charlie Parker—the word "ornithology" a witty reference to the latter's nickname: "Bird" (Figure **36.6**).

African-Americans and Dance

The African-American impact on twentieth-century dance rivaled that of music. For centuries, dance served African-Americans as a primary language of religious expression and as a metaphor of physical freedom. By the late nineteenth century, as all-black theatrical companies and minstrel shows toured the United States, black entertainment styles began to reach white audiences. Popular black dances such as the high-kicking cakewalk became the international fad of the early 1900s, and dance techniques—especially tap dancing—influenced both social and theatrical dance.

With the pioneer African-American choreographer Katherine Dunham (b. 1909), black dance moved beyond the level of stage entertainment. An avid student of Caribbean dance, Dunham drew heavily on Afro-Caribbean and African culture in both choreography and the sets and costumes designed by her husband, John Pratt (Figure **36.7**). Dunham's troupe borrowed from Caribbean music the rhythms of the steel band, an instrumental ensemble consisting entirely of steel drums fashioned from oil containers. Originating in Trinidad, steel bands provided percussive accompaniment for calypso and other kinds of improvised dance forms. In her book *Dances of Haiti*,

Dunham examines the sociological function of dance—for instance, how communal dance captures the spirit of folk celebrations and how African religious dance interacts with European secular dance. Dunham's work inspired others: Pearl Primus (1919–1994) used her studies in choreography and anthropology (like Dunham, she earned a doctorate in this field) to become the world's foremost authority on African dance. Following a trip to Africa in the 1940s, she brought to modern dance the spirit and substance of native tribal rituals. She also choreographed theatrical versions of African-American spirituals and poems, including those of Langston Hughes. In her book *African Dance*, Primus declared: "The dance is strong magic. . . . It turns the body to liquid steel. It makes it vibrate like a guitar. The body can fly without wings. It can sing without voice."

The achievements of Dunham and Primus gave African-American dance theater international stature.

Since 1950, such outstanding choreographers as Alvin Ailey (1931–1989), Donald McKayle (b. 1930), and Arthur Mitchell (b. 1934) have graced the history of American dance. Ailey's *Revelations* (1960), a suite that draws on African-American spirituals, song-sermons, and gospel songs, is an enduring tribute to the cultural history of black Americans.

The Quest for Gender Equality

Throughout history, misogyny (the hatred of women) and the perception of the female sex as inferior in intelligence and strength have enforced conditions of gender inequality. While women make up the majority of the population in many cultures, they have exercised little significant political or economic power. Like many ethnic minorities, women have long been relegated to the position of second-class citizens. In 1900, women were permitted to vote in only one country in the world: New Zealand. By mid-century, women in most First World countries had gained voting rights; nevertheless, their social and economic status has remained far below that of men. As recently as 1985, the World Conference on Women reported that while women represent fifty percent of the world's population and contribute nearly two-thirds of all working hours, they receive only one-tenth of the world's income and own less than one percent of the world's property. Though female inequality has been a fact of history, it was not until the twentieth century that the quest for female liberation took the form of an international movement.

The Literature of Feminism: Woolf

The history of **feminism** (the principle advocating equal social, political, and economic rights for men and women) reaches back at least to the fourteenth century, when the French poet Christine de Pisan took up the pen in defense of women (see chapter 15). Christine had sporadic followers among Renaissance and Enlightenment humanists. The most notable of these was Mary Wollstonecraft (1759–1797), who published her provocative *Vindication of the Rights of Woman* in London in 1792 (see chapter 24). During the nineteenth century, Condorcet and Mill wrote reasoned pleas for female equality, as did the female novelist George Sand (see chapters 28 and 30). In America, the eloquence

Figure 36.7 Katherine Dunham in the 1945–1946 production of *Tropical Revue*. The Dance Collection, The New York Public Library for the Performing Arts. Astor, Lenox, and Tilden Foundations.

of Angelina Grimké (1805–1879) and other *suffragettes* (women advocating equality for women) was instrumental in winning women the right to vote in 1920.

Among the most impassioned advocates of the feminist movement that flourished in England during the early twentieth century was the novelist Virginia Woolf (1882–1941). Woolf argued that equal opportunity for education and economic advantage were even more important than the right to vote (British women gained the vote in 1918). In her novels and essays, Woolf proposed that women could become powerful only by achieving financial and psychological independence from men. Freedom, argued Woolf, is the prerequisite for creativity: for a woman to secure her own creative freedom, she must have money and the privacy provided by "a room of her own." In the feminist essay "A Room of One's Own," Woolf responds to a clergyman's remark that no female could have matched the genius of William Shakespeare. In the excerpt below, Woolf envisions Shakespeare's imaginary sister, Judith, in her sixteenth-century setting. She uses this fictional character to raise some challenging questions concerning the psychological aspects of female creativity.

READING 6.24 From Woolf's "A Room of One's Own" (1929)

. . . Let me imagine, since facts are so hard to come by, what 1
would have happened had Shakespeare had a wonderfully
gifted sister, called Judith, let us say. Shakespeare himself
went, very probably—his mother was an heiress—to the
grammar school, where he may have learnt Latin—Ovid, Virgil
and Horace—and the elements of grammar and logic. He was,
it is well known, a wild boy who poached rabbits, perhaps
shot a deer, and had, rather sooner than he should have done,
to marry a woman in the neighbourhood, who bore him a child
rather quicker than was right. That escapade sent him to seek 10
his fortune in London. He had, it seemed, a taste for the
theatre; he began by holding horses at the stage door. Very
soon he got work in the theatre, became a successful actor,
and lived at the hub of the universe, meeting everybody,
knowing everybody, practising his art on the boards, exercising
his wits in the streets, and even getting access to the palace
of the queen. Meanwhile his extraordinarily gifted sister, let
us suppose, remained at home. She was as adventurous, as
imaginative, as agog to see the world as he was. But she was
not sent to school. She had no chance of learning grammar 20
and logic, let alone of reading Horace and Virgil. She picked
up a book now and then, one of her brother's perhaps, and
read a few pages. But then her parents came in and told her
to mend the stockings or mind the stew and not moon about
with books and papers. They would have spoken sharply but
kindly, for they were substantial people who knew the
conditions of life for a woman and loved their daughter—
indeed, more likely than not she was the apple of her father's
eye. Perhaps she scribbled some pages up in an apple loft on
the sly, but was careful to hide them or set fire to them. Soon, 30
however, before she was out of her teens, she was to be
betrothed to the son of a neighbouring wool-stapler. She cried

out that marriage was hateful to her, and for that she was
severely beaten by her father. Then he ceased to scold her. He
begged her instead not to hurt him, not to shame him in this
matter of her marriage. He would give her a chain of beads or
a fine petticoat, he said; and there were tears in his eyes.
How could she disobey him? How could she break his heart?
The force of her own gift alone drove her to it. She made up a
small parcel of her belongings, let herself down by a rope one 40
summer's night and took the road to London. She was not
seventeen. The birds that sang in the hedge were not more
musical than she was. She had the quickest fancy, a gift like
her brother's, for the tune of words. Like him, she had a taste
for the theatre. She stood at the stage door; she wanted to
act, she said. Men laughed in her face. The manager—a fat,
loose-lipped man—guffawed. He bellowed something about
poodles dancing and women acting—no woman, he said,
could possibly be an actress. He hinted—you can imagine
what. She could get no training in her craft. Could she even 50
seek her dinner in a tavern or roam the streets at midnight?
Yet her genius was for fiction and lusted to feed abundantly
upon the lives of men and women and the study of their ways.
At last—for she was very young, oddly like Shakespeare the
poet in her face, with the same grey eyes and rounded
brows—at last Nick Greene the actor-manager took pity on
her; she found herself with child by that gentleman and so—
who shall measure the heat and violence of the poet's heart
when caught and tangled in a woman's body?—killed herself
one winter's night and lies buried at some cross-roads where 60
the omnibuses now stop outside the Elephant and Castle.

. . . any woman born with a great gift in the sixteenth
century would certainly have gone crazed, shot herself, or
ended her days in some lonely cottage outside the village, half
witch, half wizard, feared and mocked at. For it needs little
skill in psychology to be sure that a highly gifted girl who had
tried to use her gift for poetry would have been so thwarted
and hindered by other people, so tortured and pulled asunder
by her own contrary instincts, that she must have lost her
health and sanity to a certainty. No girl could have walked to 70
London and stood at a stage door and forced her way into the
presence of actor-managers without doing herself a violence
and suffering an anguish which may have been irrational—for
chastity may be a fetish invented by certain societies for
unknown reasons—but were none the less inevitable.
Chastity had then, it has even now, a religious importance in a
woman's life, and has so wrapped itself round with nerves and
instincts that to cut it free and bring it to the light of day
demands courage of the rarest. To have lived a free life in
London in the sixteenth century would have meant for a 80
woman who was poet and playwright a nervous stress and
dilemma which might well have killed her. Had she survived,
whatever she had written would have been twisted and
deformed, issuing from a strained and morbid imagination.
And undoubtedly, I thought, looking at the shelf where there
are no plays by women, her work would have gone unsigned.
That refuge she would have sought certainly. It was the relic
of the sense of chastity that dictated anonymity to women

---

[1]Currer Bell was the pseudonym for the British novelist Charlotte Brontë (1816–1855); for Eliot and Sand, see chapter 28.

even so late as the nineteenth century. Currer Bell,[1] George Eliot, George Sand, all the victims of inner strife as their writings prove, sought ineffectively to veil themselves by using the name of a man. Thus they did homage to the convention, which if not implanted by the other sex was liberally encouraged by them (the chief glory of a woman is not to be talked of, said Pericles, himself a much-talked-of man), that publicity in women is detestable. Anonymity runs in their blood. . . . 90

Q How does the figure of Shakespeare's fictional sister work to make Woolf's point?
Q How fragile, according to Woolf, is female creativity?

Postwar Feminism: de Beauvoir

In Western Europe and in America, the two world wars had a positive effect on the position of women. In the absence of men during wartime, women assumed many of the jobs in agriculture and in industry. As Woolf predicted, the newly found financial independence of women gave them a sense of freedom and stimulated their demands for legal and social equality. Women's roles in regions beyond the West were also changing. In the Soviet Union, the communist regime put women to work in industry and on the battlefields. In China, where women had been bought and sold for centuries, the People's Republic in 1949 closed all brothels, forbade arranged marriages, and enforced policies of equal pay for equal work. But the feminist movement in postwar Europe and the United States demanded psychological independence as well as job equality; its goals involved raising the consciousness of *both* sexes.

The new woman must shed her passivity and achieve independence through responsible action; this was the charge of the French novelist, social critic, and existentialist Simone de Beauvoir (1908–1986). In the classic feminist text *The Second Sex*, de Beauvoir dethroned the "myth of femininity"—the false and disempowering idea that women possess a unique and preordained "feminine" essence, which condemns them to a role of social and intellectual subordination to men. Reassessing the biological, psychological, and political reasons for women's dependency, she concluded that while Man defines Woman as "the Other" (or *second* sex), it is women themselves who complacently accept their subordinate position. De Beauvoir called on women everywhere "to renounce all advantages conferred upon them by their alliance" with men. She pursued this goal (unsuccessfully, according to some critics) in her own life: her fifty-year liaison with Jean-Paul Sartre constitutes one of the most intriguing partnerships of the century. Although both enjoyed love affairs with other people, they shared a lifelong marriage of minds.

In the following brief excerpt from *The Second Sex*, de Beauvoir explores the nature of female dependency upon men and the "metaphysical risk" of liberty.

If woman seems to be the inessential which never becomes the essential, it is because she herself fails to bring about this change. Proletarians say "We"; Negroes also. Regarding themselves as subjects, they transform the bourgeois, the whites, into "others." But women do not say "We," except at some congress of feminists or similar formal demonstration; men say "women," and women use the same word in referring to themselves. They do not authentically assume a subjective attitude. The proletarians have accomplished the revolution in Russia, the Negroes in Haiti, the Indo-Chinese are battling for it in Indo-China; but the women's effort has never been anything more than a symbolic agitation. They have gained only what men have been willing to grant; they have taken nothing, they have only received. 1 10

The reason for this is that women lack concrete means for organizing themselves into a unit which can stand face to face with the correlative unit. They have no past, no history, no religion of their own; and they have no such solidarity of work and interest as that of the proletariat. They are not even promiscuously herded together in the way that creates community feeling among the American Negroes, the ghetto Jews, the workers of Saint-Denis, or the factory hands of Renault. They live dispersed among the males, attached through residence, housework, economic condition, and social standing to certain men— fathers or husbands—more firmly than they are to other women. If they belong to the bourgeoisie, they feel solidarity with men of that class, not with proletarian women; if they are white, their allegiance is to white men, not to Negro women. The proletariat can propose to massacre the ruling class, and a sufficiently fanatical Jew or Negro might dream of getting sole possession of the atomic bomb and making humanity wholly Jewish or black; but woman cannot even dream of exterminating the males. The bond that unites her to her oppressors is not comparable to any other. The division of the sexes is a biological fact, not an event in human history. Male and female stand opposed within a primordial *Mitsein*,[1] and woman has not broken it. The couple is a fundamental unity with two halves riveted together, and the cleavage of society along the line of sex is impossible. Here is to be found the basic trait of woman: she is the *Other* in a totality of which the two components are necessary to one another. . . . 20 30 40

Now, woman has always been man's dependant, if not his slave; the two sexes have never shared the world in equality. And even today woman is heavily handicapped, though her situation is beginning to change. Almost nowhere is her legal status the same as man's, and frequently it is much to her disadvantage. Even when her rights are legally recognized in the abstract, long-standing custom prevents their full expression in the mores. In the economic sphere men and women can almost be said to make up two castes; other things being equal, the former hold the better jobs, get higher wages, and have more opportunity for success than their new 50

[1]German for "coexistence."

competitors. In industry and politics men have a great many more positions and they monopolize the most important posts. In addition to all this, they enjoy a traditional prestige that the education of children tends in every way to support, for the present enshrines the past—and in the past all history has been made by men. At the present time, when women are beginning to take part in the affairs of the world, it is still a **60** world that belongs to men— they have no doubt of it at all and women have scarcely any. To decline to be the Other, to refuse to be a party to the deal—this would be for women to renounce all the advantages conferred upon them by their alliance with the superior caste. Man-the-sovereign will provide woman-the-liege with material protection and will undertake the moral justification of her existence; thus she can evade at once both economic risk and the metaphysical risk of a liberty in which ends and aims must be contrived without assistance. Indeed, along with the ethical urge of **70** each individual to affirm his subjective existence, there is also the temptation to forego liberty and become a thing. This is an inauspicious road, for he who takes it—passive, lost, ruined—becomes henceforth the creature of another's will, frustrated in his transcendence and deprived of every value. But it is an easy road; on it one avoids the strain involved in undertaking an authentic existence. When man makes of woman the *Other*, he may, then, expect her to manifest deep-seated tendencies toward complicity. Thus, woman may fail to lay claim to the status of subject because she lacks definite **80** resources, because she feels the necessary bond that ties her to man regardless of reciprocity, and because she is often very well pleased with her role as the *Other*. . . .

Q What circumstances, according to de Beauvoir, work to make the female "the Other"?

Q Is it still "a world that belongs to men"? (line 60).

Feminist Poetry

During the 1960s, and especially in the United States, the struggle for equality between the sexes assumed a strident tone. Gender discrimination in both education and employment triggered demands for federal legislation on behalf of women. Even as new types of contraceptives gave women control over their reproductive functions and greater sexual freedoms, the campaign to secure legal and political rights continued, generating protest marches and a spate of consciousness-raising literature. In 1963, Betty Friedan (b. 1921) published *The Feminine Mystique*, which claimed that American society—and commercial advertising in particular—had brainwashed women to prefer the roles of wives and mothers to other positions in life. Friedan was one of the first feminists to attack the theories of Sigmund Freud (see chapter 33), especially Freud's patriarchal view of women as failed men. She challenged women to question

the existing order and to seek careers outside the home. With the founding of the National Organization for Women (NOW) in 1966, radical feminists called for a restructuring of all Western institutions.

Since the 1960s, there has been a virtual renaissance of poetry and fiction focused on the twin themes of gender equality and the search for female self-identity. As with the literature of black liberation, feminist writing often seethes with repressed rage and anger. Clearly, not all modern literature written by women addresses exclusively female issues—recent female writers have dealt with subjects as varied as boxing and the plight of the environment. Yet, in postwar literature produced by women, three motifs recur: the victimization of the female, her effort to define her role in a society traditionally dominated by men, and her displacement from her ancient role as goddess and matriarch.

The first generation of feminist poets includes Sylvia Plath (1932–1963) and Anne Sexton (1928–1975). Plath's searing verse reflects her sense of dislocation in male-dominated society. Much like Plath, Sexton probes problems related to the socialization of women and the search for female identity. Deeply confessional, her verse often reflects upon her own troubled life, which (like Plath's) ended in suicide—an ironic fulfillment of Woolf's prophecy concerning the fate of Shakespeare's imaginary sister. In the autobiographical poem "Self in 1958," Sexton explores the images that traditionally have defined women: dolls, apparel, kitchens, and, finally, herself as an extension of her mother. Sexton's poem, which contemplates the female struggle for self-identity in modern society, recalls both Nora's plight in Ibsen's *A Doll's House* (see chapter 30) and Woolf's observation that women "think through their mothers."

The African-American poet Sonia Sanchez (b. 1935) deals with the interrelated questions of racism and identity. Sanchez's poetry is more colloquial than Sexton's, and (like Baraka's) it is often fiercely confrontational. In the poem "Woman" Sanchez draws on the literary tradition in which eminent (and usually male) writers call upon the classical gods for inspiration: she invokes the spiritual powers of mother earth to infuse her with courage and creative energy.

The poems of Adrienne Rich (b. 1929) are among the most challenging in the feminist canon. They are, to a large extent, impassioned responses to her shifting and often conflicting roles as American, Southerner, Jew, wife, mother, teacher, civil rights activist, feminist, and lesbian. Many of Rich's poems explore the complexities of personal and political relationships, especially as they are affected by gender. In the poem "Translations," she draws attention to the ways in which traditional gender roles polarize the sexes and potentially disempower women. The youngest of the feminist poets in this group, Rita Dove (b. 1952), is the first African-American woman to have served as Poet Laureate in the United States (1993–1995). Dove's six collections of poetry, one of which was awarded the Pulitzer Prize (1987), reach into the domains of the black feminist experience. In the short poem "Rosa," from the sequence of poems entitled "On the Bus with Rosa Parks," Dove pays homage to the heroism of the black woman who, riding a Montgomery, Alabama bus, refused to give up her seat to a white man. (The incident triggered one of the earliest civil rights protests, a city-wide boycott led by Martin Luther King.)

READING 6.26 Feminist Poems

Sexton's "Self in 1958" (1966)

What is reality?   1
I am a plaster doll; I pose
with eyes that cut open without landfall or nightfall
upon some shellacked and grinning person,
eyes that open, blue, steel, and close.   5
Am I approximately an I. Magnin[1] transplant?
I have hair, black angel,
black-angel-stuffing to comb,
nylon legs, luminous arms
and some advertised clothes.   10

I live in a doll's house
with four chairs,
a counterfeit table, a flat roof
and a big front door.
Many have come to such a small crossroad.   15
There is an iron bed,
(Life enlarges, life takes aim)
a cardboard floor,
windows that flash open on someone's city,
and little more.   20

Someone plays with me,
plants me in the all-electric kitchen,
Is this what Mrs. Rombauer[2] said?
Someone pretends with me—
I am walled in solid by their noise—   25
or puts me upon their straight bed.
They think I am me!
Their warmth? Their warmth is not a friend!
They pry my mouth for their cups of gin
and their stale bread.   30

What is reality
to this synthetic doll
who should smile, who should shift gears,
should spring the doors open in a wholesome disorder,
and have no evidence of ruin or fears?   35
But I would cry,
rooted into the wall that
was once my mother,
if I could remember how
and if I had the tears.   40

---

[1] A fashionable department store.
[2] Irma S. Rombauer, author of the popular cookbook, *The Joy of Cooking.*

Sanchez's "Woman" (1978)

Come ride my birth, earth mother   1
tell me how i have become, became
this woman with razor blades between
her teeth.
        sing me my history O earth mother
about tongues multiplying memories   5
about breaths contained in straw.
pull me from the throat of mankind
where worms eat, O earth mother.
come to this Black woman. you.
rider of earth pilgrimages.   10
tell me how i have held five bodies
in one large cocktail of love
and still have the thirst of the beginning sip.
tell me. tellLLLLLL me. earth mother
for i want to rediscover me. the secret of me   15
the river of me. the morning ease of me.
i want my body to carry my words like aqueducts.
i want to make the world my diary
and speak rivers.

rise up earth mother   20
out of rope-strung-trees
dancing a windless dance
come phantom mother
dance me a breakfast of births
let your mouth spill me forth   25
so i creak with your mornings.
come old mother, light up my mind
with a story bright as the sun.

Rich's "Translations" (1972)

You show me the poems of some woman   1
my age, or younger
translated from your language

Certain words occur: *enemy, oven, sorrow*
enough to let me know   5
she's a woman of my time

obsessed

with Love, our subject
we've trained it like ivy to our walls
baked it like bread in our ovens   10
worn it like lead on our ankles
watched it through binoculars as if
it were a helicopter
bringing food to our famine
or the satellite   15
of a hostile power

I begin so see that woman
doing things: stirring rice
ironing a skirt
typing a manuscript till dawn   20
trying to make a call
from a phonebooth

The phone rings unanswered
in a man's bedroom
she hears him telling someone else   25
Never mind. She'll get tired.
hears him telling her story to her sister

who becomes her enemy
and will in her own time
light her own way to sorrow   30

ignorant of the fact this way of grief
is shared, unnecessary
and political

Dove's "Rosa"

How she sat there,   1
the time right inside a place
so wrong it was ready.

That trim name with
its dream of a bench   5
to rest on. Her sensible coat.

Doing nothing was the doing:
the clean flame of her gaze
carved by a camera flash.

How she stood up   10
when they bent down to retrieve
her purse. That courtesy.

Q What aspects of the female experience
do each of these poems address?

Q How might these poems "empower"
women?

Feminist Art

The history of world art includes only a small number of
female artists. Addressing this fact, the Australian-born
feminist Germaine Greer (b. 1939) explained,

> There is . . . no female Leonardo, no female Titian,
> no female Poussin, but the reason does not lie in the
> fact that women have wombs, that they can have
> babies, that their brains are smaller, that they lack
> vigor, that they are not sensual. The reason is simply
> that you cannot make great artists out of egos that
> have been damaged, with wills that are defective,
> with libidos that have been driven out of reach and
> energy diverted into neurotic channels.*

A sure indication of change, however, is the fact that,
since the middle of the twentieth century, the number of
women in the visual arts (and in music as well) has been
greater than ever before in history. And, as with feminist
poetry, much of the painting and sculpture produced by

The Obstacle Race: The Fortunes of Women Painters and their Work.
New York: Farrar, Straus, Giroux, 1979, 327.

Figure 36.8 **NIKI DE SAINT PHALLE**, *Black Venus*, 1965–1967. Painted polyester,
9 ft. 2 in. × 35 in. × 24 in. Whitney Museum of American Art, New York. Gift of the
Howard and Jean Lipman Foundation, Inc. Photograph © 2000 Whitney Museum of
American Art. Photography by Sandak, Inc/A Division of Macmillan Publishing. ©
ADAGP, Paris and DACS, London, 2005.

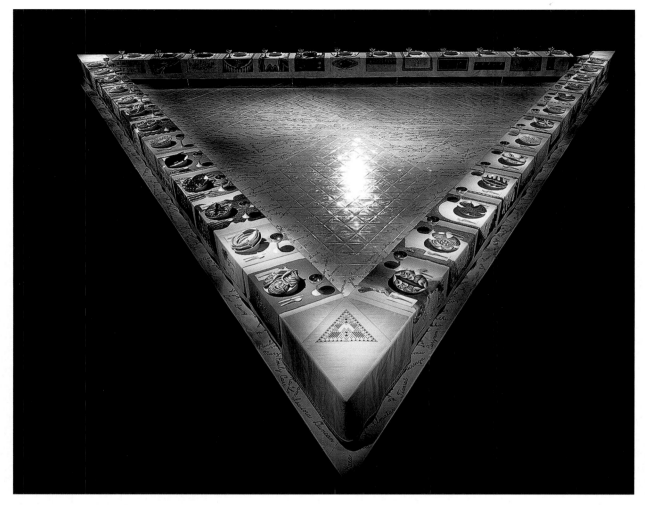

Figure 36.9 JUDY CHICAGO, *The Dinner Party*, 1974–1979. Multimedia, 48 × 48 × 48 ft. © Judy Chicago, 1979. Photo: Donald Woodman. © ARS, NY and DACS, London 2005.

women artists since the 1960s has been driven by feminist concerns. A few representative examples will suffice to make this point.

Bringing a feminist attention to the female body, the internationally acclaimed French sculptor Niki de Saint Phalle (1930–2003) fabricated gigantic sculptures that she called "Nanas." In 1963 Saint Phalle exhibited a monumental 80-foot-long, 20-foot-high, and 30-foot-wide Nana that viewers might enter through a doorway between the figure's legs. Inside was a cinema with Greta Garbo movies, a telephone, a refreshment bar, and taped voices of romantic conversations between a man and a woman. Saint Phalle's *Black Venus* (Figure **36.8**), a hugely proportioned polyester "earth mother," wears a heart on her belly and a flower on her breast. This exuberant creature is Saint Phalle's answer to Western stereotypes of female beauty. More closely resembling the ponderous fertility figures of prehistoric cultures (see Figure 0.3) than the refined marble goddesses of classical antiquity, Saint Phalle's *Venus* celebrates the joys of sensual freedom. She is the feminist reproof of the idealized and impassive images of womanhood that glut mainstream Western art history.

The militant American feminist Judy Gerowitz (b. 1939), who in 1969 assumed the surname of her native city (hence, Judy Chicago), has been a lifelong advocate of women's art. Chicago pioneered some of the first art communities in which women worked together to produce, exhibit, and sell art. Her efforts ignited the visual arts with the consciousness-raising politics of the feminist movement. Between 1974 and 1979, Chicago directed a project called *The Dinner Party*, a room-size sculpture consisting of a triangular table with thirty-nine place settings, each symbolizing a famous woman in myth or history (Figure **36.9**). The feminist counterpart of the Last Supper, *The Dinner Party* pays homage to such immortals as Nefertiti, Sappho, Queen Elizabeth I, and Virginia Woolf. To carry out this monumental project, Chicago studied the traditionally female arts of embroidery and china painting, inventing at the same time new techniques for combining such dissimilar materials as ceramics and lace. Over three hundred men and women contributed to this cooperative enterprise, which brought international attention to the cultural contributions of women in world history.

In searching for a feminist aesthetic, women artists have brought attention to the female body as representative of nature's procreative forces. The Cuban-born Ana Mendieta (1948–1985) used photography and film to document performances inspired by Afro-Caribbean fertility rituals. For the series known as *Silhouettes*, Mendieta immersed herself in pools of water, sand, and mud, and recorded 200 images of her body or its physical impressions on various earth surfaces. In the photograph *Tree of Life* from this series, the artist, encrusted with grass and mud, appears in the dual guises of dryad (a classical tree nymph) and ancient priestess (Figure **36.10**).

The career of the American photographer Cindy Sherman (b. 1954) addresses one of the more recent concerns of feminist artists: the fact that the traditional Western *image* of the female—sweet, sexy, and servile—has been shaped by male needs and values. Such images, say contemporary feminists, which dominate the world's "great artworks," reflect the controlling power of the (male) "gaze." Just as Colescott and Saar use art to attack racial stereotypes, so feminists like Sherman make visual assaults on gender stereotypes—those projected by the collective body of "great art" and by the modern-day phenomena of television, "girlie" magazines, and other mass media. Sherman's large, glossy studio photographs of the 1970s feature the artist herself in poses and attire that call attention to the body as a political or sexual object. In personalized narratives that resemble black-and-white movie stills, she recreates commercial stereotypes that mock the subservient roles that women play: the "little woman," the *femme fatale*, the baby doll, the "pinup," and the lovesick teenager. Since the 1980s, Sherman has used the newest

Figure 36.11 **CINDY SHERMAN**, *Untitled #276*, 1993. Color photograph, edition of six, 6 ft. 8½ in. × 5 ft. 1 in. framed. Courtesy of the artist and Metro Pictures, New York.

techniques in color photography to assault—often in visceral terms—sexual and historical stereotypes of women. She may replace the male image in a world-famous painting with a female image (often Sherman herself), use artificial body parts to "remake" the traditional nude, or flagrantly recast famous females from Western myth, history, and religion. In Figure **36.11**, a flaxen-haired Cinderella, holding the traditional symbol of purity (the lily), assumes the attitude and apparel of a prostitute. This vulgar figure Sherman "enshrines" in a manner usually reserved in Western art for images of the Virgin.

Well aware of the extent to which commercialism shapes identity, Barbara Kruger (b. 1945) creates photographs that deftly unite word and image to resemble commercial billboards. "Your Body is a Battleground," insists Kruger; by superimposing the message over the divided (positive and negative) image of a female face, the artist calls attention to the controversial issue of abortion in contemporary society (Figure **36.12**).

Sexual Identity

The dual quest for racial and gender equality has also worked to raise public consciousness concerning the ways

Figure 36.10 (below) **ANA MENDIETA**, *Tree of Life* from the *Silvetas* series, 1977. Color photographs, 20 × 13¼ in. Courtesy Galerie Lelong, New York. © The Estate of Ana Mendieta.

sex is used as a structuring principle in human culture and society. More so than race, gender* determines how people behave and how they are regarded by others. Assumptions concerning gender and, specifically, the sexual and social roles of males and females are rooted in traditions as old as Paleolithic culture and as venerated as the Bible. For many, sexual roles are fixed and unchanging. However, these assumptions, like so many others in the cultural history of the twentieth century, came to be challenged and reassessed. Gender issues accompanied a demand for equality on the part of those of untraditional sexual orientation—bisexuals, homosexuals (gays and lesbians), and other transgendered individuals. In America homosexuals date the birth of their "liberation" to June 1969, when they openly and violently protested a police raid on the Stonewall Inn, a gay bar in New York's Greenwich Village. Thereafter, the call for protection against harassment shifted to litigated demands for gender equality. While all societies have included a transgendered subculture, it was not until the last decades of the twentieth century that sexual and public issues intersected to produce some highly controversial questions. Should homosexuals serve in the armed forces? Should homosexual marriage be legalized? How does homosexuality affect the future of the traditional family? Should sexually explicit art receive public funding? The resolution of these and other gender-related questions continues to impact the development of the humanistic tradition.

There are a number of reasons why issues of human sexuality became so visible in the culture of the late twentieth century: increasing sexual permissiveness (the consequence of improved pharmaceutical methods of contraception); the activity of the media (especially TV and film) in broadcasting sexually explicit entertainment; and the appearance of the devastating pandemic called AIDS (Acquired Immune Deficiency Syndrome), a life-threatening disease resulting from a retrovirus named HIV that attacks the blood cells of the body, thus causing a failure of the autoimmune system. Collectively, these phenomena have represented an overwhelming challenge to traditional concepts of sexuality, sexual behavior, and (more generally) to conventional morality. They have also generated a provocative blurring of sex roles (which has been increasingly exploited in commercial advertising and the popular media). And they continue to complicate the task of distinguishing between forms of expression that have mere shock value and those that represent a substantial creative achievement. The photographs of Robert Mapplethorpe (1946–1989) are significant in this regard. Mapplethorpe's fine-grained silver gelatin prints display exquisitely composed images ranging from still life subjects to classically posed nudes. Although usually lacking explicit narrative, they reflect the artist's preoccupation with physical and sexual themes: male virility, sadomasochism, androgyny, and sexual identity. A sculptor in his early training, Mapplethorpe presents his subjects as pristine objects, occasionally transforming them into erotic symbols. His photographs depict contemporary sexuality in a manner that is at once detached and impassioned, but they often gain added power as gender-bending parodies of sexual stereotypes—witness the startling union of masculine and feminine cues in the portrait of Lisa Lyon—herself a weight-lifter (Figure **36.13**; see also Figure 38.26). Mapplethorpe fulfills the artist's mission to see things (in his words) "like they haven't been seen before."

Themes of human sexuality have also increasingly preoccupied twentieth and twenty-first century writers. In her science fiction fantasy *The Left Hand of Darkness* (1969), the African-American writer Ursula LeGuin (b. 1929) describes a distant planet, home to creatures with the sexual potential of both males and females. The ambisexuality of the characters in this fictional utopia calls into question human preconceptions about the defined roles of behavior for men and women. Through the device of science fiction, LeGuin suggests a shift in focus from the narrow view of male–female dualities (or opposites) to larger, more urgent matters of interdependence.

While LeGuin examines bisexuality in imaginary settings, others, and in particular gay artists, have dealt with the experience of homosexuality in their day-to-day lives.

Figure 36.12 BARBARA KRUGER, *Untitled ("Your body is a battleground")*, 1989. Photographic silkscreen on vinyl, 9 ft. 4 in. × 9 ft. 4 in. Courtesy Mary Boone Gallery, New York. Photo: Zindman/Freemont, New York.

---

*Unlike sex (which designates individuals as either male or female), gender (which distinguishes between masculinity and femininity) is culturally, not biologically, prescribed.

Figure 36.13 ROBERT MAPPLETHORPE, *Lisa Lyon*, 1982. Silver gelatin print. © 1998 Estate of Robert Mapplethorpe. Courtesy Robert Miller Gallery, New York.

The past three decades have been especially rich in the production of art that either examines sexual "otherness" or reflects (and celebrates) a "gay sensibility." Since the 1990s, these themes have received unprecedented attention in the popular entertainment media of television and film. They are also the subject of inquiry among scholars of a new discipline known as "queer representation."*

By drawing attention to the ways in which matters of sexuality affect society and its institutions, contemporary

art asserts that sexuality and power are as closely related as race and power or gender and power. For example, the Pulitzer prize-winning play *Angels in America: A Gay Fantasia on National Themes* (written in two parts: *Millennium Approaches*, 1990, and *Perestroika*, 1993) by Tony Kushner (b. 1957) offers a radical vision of American society set against the AIDS epidemic and the politics of conservatism. Kushner urges the old America—"straight," Protestant, and white—to look with greater objectivity at "the fringe" (the variety of ethnic, racial, and sexual minorities), which demands acceptance and its share of power. Kushner's landmark drama represents the movement for body-conscious politics and socially responsible art that animated the last decade of the twentieth century.

---

*See Martin Duberman, ed., *Queer Representations: Reading Lives, Reading Cultures.* New York: City University of New York Center for Lesbian and Gay Studies, 1997.

Beyond issues of sexual orientation and the struggle against discrimination on the part of the transgendered minority, the more immediate issue of the AIDS pandemic left its mark on the late twentieth century. The *Aids Memorial Quilt*, begun in 1985, engaged twenty thousand ordinary individuals, each of whom created a single 3- by 6-foot fabric panel in memory of someone who had died of an HIV-related disease. In 1992, AIDS activists assembled the panels in 16-foot squares and took them from San Francisco to Washington, D.C., to protest governmental inaction with regard to the AIDS crisis. Commemorating the deaths of some 150,000 Americans, the *Aids Memorial Quilt* covered 15 acres of ground between the Washington Monument and Lincoln Memorial. The Names Project continues: in 2004, the quilt panels numbered forty-four thousand, that is, more than double the figure of the original.

One of the most moving monuments to the AIDS crisis is the controversial *Still/Here* (1994), a performance work conceived by the African-American dancer Bill T. Jones (b. 1952). For the piece Jones, who is himself HIV-positive, combined choreography and vocal music with video imagery derived in part from workshops he conducted with AIDS victims. *Still/Here* has provoked heated debate concerning the artistic value of issue-driven art: does art that showcases sickness and death serve merely to manipulate viewers? This is only one of many questions that probe current efforts to wed art to social action.

SUMMARY

The quest for liberation from poverty, oppression, and inequality was a prevailing theme in twentieth-century history. In dozens of countries, movements for decolonization followed World War II. At the same time, and even into the twenty-first century, racial and ethnic minorities in various parts of the world fight valiantly to oppose discrimination as practiced by the majority culture. These crusades are yet ongoing among the populations of Eastern Europe, Latin America, and elsewhere.

The struggle of African-Americans to achieve freedom from the evils of racism has a long and dramatic history.

From the Harlem Renaissance in the early twentieth century through the civil rights movement of the 1960s, the arts have mirrored that history. In the poems of Langston Hughes and Gwendolyn Brooks, and in the novels of Richard Wright, James Baldwin, Ralph Ellison, and Alice Walker, the plight and the identity of the black in white America have been central themes. The impact of black culture on the visual arts, music, and dance has been equally formidable. Blues and jazz giants from Louis Armstrong to Wynton Marsalis have produced a living body of popular music, while choreographers from Katherine Dunham to Alvin Ailey have inspired generations of dancers to draw on their African heritage.

During the postwar era, women throughout the world worked to gain political, economic, and social equality. The writings of the feminists Virginia Woolf and Simone de Beauvoir influenced women to examine the psychological conditions of their oppression. In America, the feminist movement elicited a virtual golden age in literature. The self-conscious poetry of Anne Sexton, Sonia Sanchez, Rita Dove, and Adrienne Rich is representative of this phenomenon. In the visual arts, at least two generations of women have redefined traditional concepts of female identity: first, by celebrating womanhood itself, and, more recently, by attacking outworn stereotypes. One of the most controversial of the twentieth century's liberation movements centered on issues of sexual identity. Amidst the AIDS pandemic, Robert Mapplethorpe and Tony Kushner brought candor and perceptivity to matters of sexuality and sexual behavior. Clearly, the art inspired by the various liberation movements of the twentieth century was the tangible expression of a global search for personal freedom that continues to shape the humanistic tradition.

MUSIC LISTENING SELECTIONS

CD Two Selection 21 Handy, "St. Louis Blues," 1914.
CD Two Selection 22 Hardin Armstrong, "Hotter than That," 1927.
CD Two Selection 23 "Koko," Gillespie/Parker, 1945.

GLOSSARY

apartheid a policy of strict racial segregation and political and economic discrimination against the black population in the Union of South Africa

feminism the doctrine advocating equal social, political, and economic rights for women

scat singing a jazz performance style in which nonsense syllables replace the lyrics of a song

swing the jazz performer's practice of varying from the standard rhythms by playing just ahead or just behind the beat; also, a big-band jazz style developed in the 1920s and flourishing in the age of large dance bands (1932–1942)

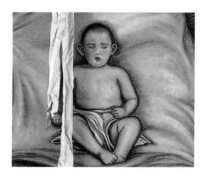

CHAPTER 37

The Information Age: Message and Meaning

"We talk because we are mortal: words are not signs, they are years."
Octavio Paz

We are still too close to the events of the past half century to distinguish the major cultural developments from the minor and ephemeral ones. However, it is clear that the history of the last five decades was altered dramatically by the shift from an industrial to an information age. In today's advanced industrial countries, more than two-thirds of the population is engaged in occupations related to high technology, rather than to farming, manufacturing, and service trades. The agents of high technology, the mass media, and electronic means of communicating, storing, and accessing information have facilitated an information explosion of vast proportions.

The tools of electronic technology have shrunk the distances between the inhabitants of the world community. At the same time, they have made more information more accessible to greater numbers of people, at greater speeds than ever before. In the sixteenth century, it was possible to have read every book ever printed, but such a feat would be patently impossible today. The number of books published between 1945 and 1970 alone equaled that issued during the entire 500-year period between the invention of the printing press and the end of World War I. Computer technology has radically accelerated the process of information production, storage, and retrieval: computer chips are capable of storing whole encyclopedias. Virtually unlimited amounts of information are available in databanks, and these in turn may be linked by way of the Internet—an international network of computers—and by satellite communication. The tools of electronic technology have thus brought all parts of the planet into the global village.

The Information Explosion

Television and computers—the primary vehicles of the information explosion—have altered almost every aspect of life in our time. The wonderchild of electronics and the quintessential example of modern mass media, television transmits sound and light by electromagnetic waves that carry information instantaneously into homes across the face of the earth. The very name "television" comes from the Greek word *tele*, meaning "far," and the Latin *videre*, meaning "to see"; hence "to see far." Television did not become common to middle-class life in the West until the 1950s, although it had been invented decades before then. By the 1960s the events of a war in the jungles of Vietnam were being relayed via electronic communications satellite into American living rooms. In 1969, in a live telecast, the world saw the first astronauts walk on the surface of the moon. And in the early 1990s, during the Middle Eastern conflict triggered by the Iraqi invasion of Kuwait, those with access to television witnessed the first "prime-time war"—a war that was "processed" by censorship and television newscasting.

The second major technological phenomenon of the information age is the computer. Digital computers—machines that process information in the form of numbers—were first used widely in the 1950s. By the 1960s, computers consisting of electronic circuits were able to perform millions of calculations per second. Smaller and more dependable than earlier models, electronic computers now facilitate various forms of instantaneous communication. Computers have also made possible the science of robotics and the creation of so-called artificial forms of intelligence, a phenomenon to which the artist Nam June Paik alludes in his witty "portrait" of George Boole (1815–1864), the brilliant mathematician whose work advanced the design of modern computers (Figure **37.1**).

The electronic media bring more information to more people, but they also alter the way in which information is presented. Communication in the information age is essentially image oriented. Film and television are fundamentally nonverbal modes of communication; they translate words into pictures. In contrast to print, a linear medium, electronic images are generated in diffuse, discontinuous bundles and rapidly dispatched fragments. The electronic media tend to homogenize images, that is, to make all images uniform and alike. As information is homogenized, it tends to become devalued; product and message may be sacrificed to process and medium. As the mass media recycle an ill-sorted variety of data, culture itself becomes what one critic has called "a vast garage sale." Electronic processing and the rapid diffusion of images via television and the Internet have worked to blur the differences between diverse kinds of information. In contemporary society, commonplace responses to everyday life—the stuff of "popular culture"—are often indistinguishable from forms of elite or "high" culture. Television has turned all information, from protest marches to breakfast cereals, into marketable commodities. Indeed, the electronic media have created a consumer society that often exercises little critical judgment with regard to the information it receives.

Electronically processed visual images bring together the world's population. Reared on television, contemporary society is, according to French sociologist Jacques Ellul (1912–1994), the society of "mass man." Modern technology, explains Ellul, has contributed to producing a "psychological collectivism" that has robbed human beings of freedom and self-esteem. Ellul singles out advertising as the most pernicious factor in the evolution of mass man. According to Ellul, advertising is a form of totalitarian control that—like the process of behavioral conditioning in Huxley's *Brave New World*—subordinates the individual to the technostructure, thus destroying the last vestiges of human freedom and dignity. In *The Technological Society* (1964), Ellul observed,

> Advertising [affects] all people; or at least an overwhelming majority. Its goal is to persuade the masses to buy. . . . The inevitable consequence is the creation of the mass man. As advertising of the most varied products is concentrated, a new type of human being, precise and generalized, emerges. We can get a general impression of this new human type by studying America, where human beings tend clearly to become identified with the ideal of advertising. In America, advertising enjoys universal popular adherence and the American way of life is fashioned by it.*

The Czechoslovakian writer Milan Kundera (b. 1929) takes a more positive view: he maintains that the global distribution of images has replaced all political ideologies with "imagology." In his novel, *Immortality* (1992), he describes the central place of the image in the global marketplace:

*Jacques Ellul, *The Technological Society*, translated by John Wilkinson. New York: Knopf, 1964, 407–408.

All ideologies have been defeated: in the end their dogmas were unmasked as illusions and people stopped taking them seriously. For example, communists used to believe that in the course of capitalist development the proletariat would gradually grow poorer and poorer, but when it finally became clear that all over Europe workers were driving to work in their own cars, they felt like shouting that reality was deceiving them. Reality was stronger than ideology. And it is in this sense that imagology surpassed it: imagology is stronger than reality.**

**Milan Kundera, *Immortality*, translated by Peter Kussi. New York: Grove Press, 1992, 114.

Figure 37.1 NAM JUNE PAIK, *George Boole*, 1995. 1 old Tektronic computer monitor, 1 old Goodyear Atomic metal cabinet, 15 KEC 9-inch television sets, 1 Samsung 13-inch television set, 2 Pioneer laser disk players, 2 original Paik laser disks, abacus, circuit board, aluminum, 7 ft. 6 in. × 4 ft. 8 in. × 30 in. Photo: Courtesy Carl Solway Gallery, Cincinnati, Ohio. Photographer: Chris Gomien.

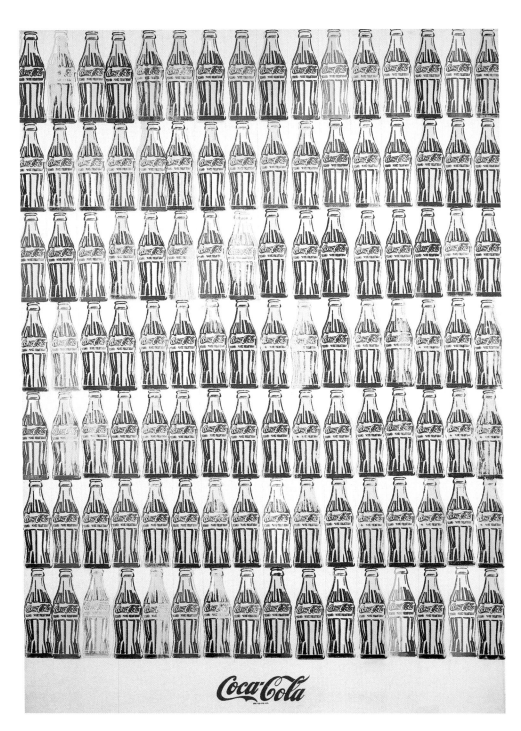

While the old way of life depended on direct human experience, distilled in linear and hierarchic formats, the new age, in which images are electronically transmitted and globally shared, is virtual: it takes the shape of a web, a network that links a wide range of disparate bits of information. Thanks to high-speed computers, the global community operates interactively, constantly weaving new networks for the exchange of information. Today's "imagologists" are participants in a continuously transforming web of message and meaning (Figure **37.2**).

New Directions in Science and Philosophy

The major developments of the last half century followed from scientific advances that have made possible investigations into outer space—the universe at large—and inner space, the province of our own bodies. Science and technology have propelled humankind beyond planet earth and into the cosmos. At the same time, they have provided an unprecedented understanding of the genetic patterns that govern life itself. These phenomena have worked to make the planet smaller, the universe larger, and methods of navigating the two ever more promising.

String Theory

Since the middle of the twentieth century, physicists have tried to reconcile the insights of the two great intellectual systems advanced early in the century: Einstein's theory of relativity, which applies to vast, cosmological space, and quantum physics, which describes the realms of the very small. They seek to establish "a theory of everything," one that might explain the "fundamental of fundamentals" that governs the organization and complexity of matter. A new (but yet unproven) theory proposes that all matter—from the page of this book to the skin of a peach—consists of tiny loops of vibrating strings. *String* (or *Superstring*) *Theory*, most eloquently explained by the American physicist Brian Greene (b. 1962), describes a multidimensional universe in which loops of strings and oscillating globules of matter unite all of creation into vibrational patterns.[*] Greene's "elegant universe" constitutes a cosmic model that Pythagoras would have found agreeable (see chapter 4). While the workings of such a universe can be simulated on a computer, human language seems too frail to serve as an explanatory medium. Yet it is in the arts, and possibly in aesthetic theory, that the design of this elegant universe may be best described. As the Norwegian physicist Niels Bohr observed, "When it comes to atoms, language can be used only as in poetry."

---

[*]Brian Greene, *The Elegant Universe: Superstrings, Hidden Dimensions and the Quest for the Ultimate Theory*. New York, Norton, 1999.

Science and Technology

1950 commercial color television becomes available

1953 the introduction of the first commercially successful computer

1957 the first artificial satellite (*Sputnik 1*) is put in orbit by the Soviet Union

1959 American engineers produce the first microchip (made from a silicon wafer)

1960 the first lasers are developed in America

1961 a Soviet astronaut becomes the first person to orbit the earth

1969 an American astronaut is the first person to walk on the moon

Chaos Theory

Equally fascinating are the speculations of those who explore the shape and structure of matter itself. The proponents of *Chaos Theory* find that universal patterns underlie all of nature, and repeat themselves in physical phenomena ranging from the formation of a snowflake to the rhythms of the human heart. Chaos theorists (not only physicists, but also astronomers, mathematicians, biologists, and computer scientists) observe that while these patterns appear random, unstable, and disorderly, they are actually self-similar in scale, like the zigs and zags of a lightning bolt, or oscillating, as in electric currents. To Einstein's famous assertion, "God does not play dice with the universe," these theorists might respond: "Not only does God play dice; but they are loaded."

The Human Genome

One of the major projects of the late twentieth century was the successful mapping of the *human genome*. By the year 2000, molecular biologists had been able (with the help of computers) to ascertain the order of nearly 3 billion units of DNA, thereby locating genes and determining their functions in the human cellular system. Ultimately, this enterprise is expected to revolutionize the practice of medicine, in both the preventive treatment of gene-related diseases and in the repair and regeneration of tissues. (Already, such gene-related research has diminished the number of AIDS deaths internationally.) The tools of genetic engineering have given scientists the ability to clone life forms. They also promise the mitigation of what Freud described as one of humankind's greatest threats: the suffering "from our own body, which is doomed to decay and dissolution." From sports medicine to psychoanalysis, society has come to perceive human beings as mechanisms that can be improved, if not perfected, by the right diet, drugs, exercise, and a healthy lifestyle. The 1990s brought exciting breakthroughs in the area of *cognitive neuroscience*, as new imaging technologies showed how brain waves can influence matter. In recent German experiments in neural consciousness, patients wearing electrodes on their scalp modulate electrical signals to choose letters from a video screen—thus communicating with nothing but one's own brain. These biofeedback experiments are reinforced by neurochemical research: the American biochemist Candace Pert (b. 1946) writes in her groundbreaking book *Molecules of Emotion* (1997), "We know that the immune system, like the central nervous system, has memory and the capacity to learn. Thus, it could be said that intelligence is located not only in the brain but in cells that are distributed throughout the body, and that the traditional separation of mental processes, including emotions, from the body, is no longer valid."* As the gap between mind and body grows narrower, Eastern notions of the symbiosis of matter and spirit have received increased attention in the West. By way of popular literature (such as *Quantum Healing: Exploring the Frontier of Mind/Body Medicine*, 1990), the Indian-born endocrinologist Deepak Chopra (b. 1946) introduced Western audiences to holistic models of meditation and body control that have flourished in India for 2,000 years.

Language Theory

While science moves forward optimistically to reveal the underlying natural order, philosophy has entered a phase of radical skepticism that denies the existence of any true or uniform system of thought. Contemporary philosophers have fastened on the idea, first popularized by the Austrian Ludwig Wittgenstein (1889–1951), that all forms of expression, and, indeed, all truths, are dominated by the limits of language as a descriptive tool. Wittgenstein, whose life's work was an inquiry into the ways in which language represents the world, argued that sentences (or propositions) were "pictures of reality." Following Wittgenstein, philosophers tried to unlock the meaning of the *text* (that is, any mode of cultural expression) by way of a close analysis of its linguistic structure. Language theorists suggested that one must "deconstruct" or "take apart" discourse in order to "unmask" its many meanings. The leaders of *deconstruction*, the French philosophers Jacques Derrida (1930–2004) and Michel Foucault (1926–1984), were influential in arguing that all human beings are prisoners of the very language they use to think and to describe the world. People erroneously believe, observed Foucault, that language is their servant; they fail to apprehend that they are forever submitting to its demands. Philosophers, he asserted, should abandon the search for absolute truths and concentrate on the discovery of meaning(s). The American philosopher Richard Rorty (b. 1931) is deeply troubled by the limits of both linguistic inquiry and traditional philosophy. Rorty has argued that the great thinkers of the post-philosophical age are not the metaphysicians or the linguists but, rather, those artists whose works provide others with insights into achieving postmodern self-transformation. What Rorty calls the "linguistic turn" describes the move (among writers and philosophers) to rethink language as verbal coding.

---

*Candace Pert, *Molecules of Emotion*, (New York: Scribners, 1997), 187.

Literature in the Information Age

Postmodernism

The term "postmodernism" came into use shortly before World War II to describe the reaction to or against modernism, but by the late 1960s it had come to designate the cultural condition of the late twentieth century. Whether defined as a reaction against modernism or as an entirely new form of modernism, postmodernism is a phenomenon that occurred principally in the West. As a style, it is marked by a bemused awareness of a historical past whose "reality" has been processed by mass communication and information technology. Postmodern artists appropriate (or borrow) pre-existing texts and images from history, advertising, and the media. They offer alternatives to the high seriousness and introversion of modernist expression, and move instead in the direction of parody (burlesque imitation), whimsy, paradox, and irony. Their playful amalgam of disparate styles mingles the superficial and the profound and tends to dissolve the boundaries between "high" and "low" art. At the same time, their seemingly incongruous "layering" of images calls to mind the fundamentals of Chaos Theory, which advances a geometry of the universe that is "broken up, twisted, tangled, intertwined."*

In contrast with elitist modernism, postmodernism is self-consciously populist, even to the point of inviting the active participation of the beholder. Whereas modern artists (consider Eliot or Kandinsky) exalt the artist as visionary and rebel, postmodern artists bring wry skepticism to the creative act. Less preoccupied than the modernists with formal abstraction and its redeeming power, postmodernists acknowledge art as an information system and a commodity shaped by the electronic media, its messages, and its modes of communication. The postmodern stance is more disengaged than authorial, its message more enigmatic than absolute. Postmodern writers share the contemporary philosopher's disdain for rational structure and the deconstructionist's fascination with the function of language. They tend to bypass traditional narrative styles in favor of techniques that parody the writer's craft. This genre has been called "metafiction"—fiction about fiction. It takes fragments of information out of their original literary/historical context and juxtaposes them with little or no commentary on their meaning. In a single story, a line from a poem by T. S. Eliot or a Shakespeare play may appear alongside a catchy saying or banal slogan from a television commercial, a phrase from a national anthem, or a shopping list, as if the writer were claiming all information as equally valuable. In postmodern fiction, characters undergo little or no development, plots often lack logical direction, and events—whether ordinary, perverse, or fantastic—may be described in the detached tone of a newspaper article. Like the television newscast, the language of postmodern fiction is often diffuse, discontinuous, and filled with innuendo and "commentary." For example, gallows humor novelist Kurt Vonnegut (b. 1922)

uses clipped sentences framed in the present tense. He creates a kind of "videofiction" that seems aimed at readers whose attention spans have been dwarfed by commercial television programming. The Italian novelist Italo Calvino (1923–1985) engages the reader in a hunt for meanings that lie in the spaces between the act of writing and the events the words describe. Calvino interrupts the story line of his novel *If On a Winter's Night a Traveler* (1979) to confront the reader, thus:

> For a couple of pages now you have been reading
> on, and this would be the time to tell you clearly
> whether this station where I have got off is a
> station of the past or a station of today; instead the
> sentences continue to move in vagueness, grayness,
> in a kind of no man's land of experience reduced
> to the lowest kind of denominator. Watch out:
> it is surely a method of involving you gradually,
> capturing you in the story before you realize it—a
> trap. Or perhaps the author still has not made up
> his mind, just as you, reader, for that matter,
> are not sure what you would most like to read.*

Postmodern writers seem to be seeking a universal voice shaped by the vernaculars of the world. Salman Rushdie (b. 1947), who was born in Bombay, India, but lives in New York, writes novels that mingle rock-and-roll lyrics with Hindu and Greek mythology. A chronicler of the global village, Rushdie joins other writers who reach back to cultural beginnings yet speak for their own time and place. Don Delillo (b. 1936) captures the cinematic rush of American life in novels that connect major worldwide phenomena—the atomic bomb, the Cold War—to such everyday events as baseball and waste management. Delillo's *Underworld* (1997) is *docufiction*, a genre that fictionalizes historical figures. His style, in which the narrative moves back and forth in time, reflects his (global) credo that "Everything is connected."

As with these prose stylists, so too among poets, there has been a preference for verse that has as much reference to language as to that which language describes. Postmodern poets convey the idea that language shapes and articulates the self. The Mexican poet and critic Octavio Paz (1914–1999) expresses this idea in the poem "To Talk," in which he defines language as sacred.

READING 6.27 Paz's "To Talk" (1987)

I read in a poem:	1
to talk is divine.	
But gods don't speak:	
they create and destroy worlds	
while men do the talking,	5
Gods, without words,	
play terrifying games.	

---

*James Gleick, *Chaos: Making a New Science*. New York: Viking, 1987, 94.

*Italo Calvino, *If On a Winter's Night a Traveler*, translated by William Weaver. New York: Harcourt Brace Jovanovich, 1981, 12.

The spirit descends,
untying tongues,
but it doesn't speak words: **10**
it speaks flames.
Language, lit by a god
is a prophecy
of flames and a crash
of burnt syllables: **15**
meaningless ash.

Man's word
is the daughter of death.
We talk because we are
mortal: words **20**
are not signs, they are years.
Saying what they say,
the names we speak
say time: they say us,
we are the names of time. **25**
To talk is human.

Q What insights concerning the powers and perils of language does Paz convey in this poem?

Magic Realism

The term "magic realism" originated in the context of the visual arts. It describes a surreal mode of representation that unites realistically depicted objects or settings, fantastical images (often from folklore or legend), unusual perspectives, and rich sensory detail (Figure **37.3**). However, the term has also come to characterize that mixture of fantasy and realism that dominates Latin American literature. Writers of the so-called Latin American "Boom," a literary explosion that began in the late 1960s, employ narrative techniques that evoke a dreamlike or mythic reality. Such is evident in the fiction writings of the Colombian novelist Gabriel García Marquéz (b. 1928) and the Chilean writer Isabel Allende (b. 1943). An experienced journalist, Allende is one of the most hypnotic storytellers of our time: her short stories begin with a single image that unfolds much like a folk or fairy tale. Allende credits the influence of film and television for the modern tendency to "think in images" and to write in short, tightly packed sentences. She claims, however, that the first sentences of her stories are "dictated" to her in a magical manner. In the story "Two Words," Allende combines terse, straightforward narrative and sensuous allegory to interweave universal themes of language, love, and the empowering role of women in Latin American society.

Figure 37.3 JULIO GALÁN, *What's Missing?*, 1990. Collage on canvas, 7 ft. 6 in. × 6 ft. 6 in. Courtesy of Annina Nosei Gallery, New York.

She went by the name of Belisa Crepusculario, not
because she had been baptized with that name or given it by
her mother, but because she herself had searched until she
found the poetry of "beauty" and "twilight" and cloaked
herself in it. She made her living selling words. She journeyed
through the country from the high cold mountains to the
burning coasts, stopping at fairs and in markets where she set
up four poles covered by a canvas awning under which she
took refuge from the sun and rain to minister to her customers.
She did not have to peddle her merchandise because from
having wandered far and near, everyone knew who she was.
Some people waited for her from one year to the next, and
when she appeared in the village with her bundle beneath her
arm, they would form a line in front of her stall. Her prices
were fair. For five centavos she delivered verses from memory;
for seven she improved the quality of dreams; for nine she
wrote love letters; for twelve she invented insults for
irreconcilable enemies. She also sold stories, not fantasies but
long, true stories she recited at one telling, never skipping a
word. This is how she carried news from one town to another.
People paid her to add a line or two: our son was born; so-
and-so died; our children got married; the crops burned in the
field. Wherever she went a small crowd gathered around to
listen as she began to speak, and that was how they learned
about each other's doings, about distant relatives, about what
was going on in the civil war. To anyone who paid her fifty
centavos in trade, she gave the gift of a secret word to drive
away melancholy. It was not the same word for everyone,
naturally, because that would have been collective deceit.
Each person received his or her own word, with the assurance
that no one else would use it that way in this universe or the
Beyond.

Belisa Crepusculario had been born into a family so poor
they did not even have names to give their children. She came
into the world and grew up in an inhospitable land where
some years the rains became avalanches of water that bore
everything away before them and others when not a drop fell
from the sky and the sun swelled to fill the horizon and the
world became a desert. Until she was twelve, Belisa had no
occupation or virtue other than having withstood hunger and
the exhaustion of centuries. During one interminable drought,
it fell to her to bury four younger brothers and sisters; when
she realized that her turn was next, she decided to set out
across the plains in the direction of the sea, in hopes that she
might trick death along the way. The land was eroded, split
with deep cracks, strewn with rocks, fossils of trees and
thorny bushes, and skeletons of animals bleached by the sun.
From time to time she ran into families who, like her, were
heading south, following the mirage of water. Some had
begun the march carrying their belongings on their backs or in
small carts, but they could barely move their own bones, and
after a while they had to abandon their possessions. They
dragged themselves along painfully, their skin turned to lizard
hide and their eyes burned by the reverberating glare. Belisa
greeted them with a wave as she passed, but she did not stop,
because she had no strength to waste in acts of compassion.

Many people fell by the wayside, but she was so stubborn
that she survived to cross through that hell and at long last
reach the first trickles of water, fine, almost invisible threads
that fed spindly vegetation and farther down widened into
small streams and marshes.

Belisa Crepusculario saved her life and in the process
accidentally discovered writing. In a village near the coast, the
wind blew a page of newspaper at her feet. She picked up the
brittle yellow paper and stood a long while looking at it,
unable to determine its purpose, until curiosity overcame her
shyness. She walked over to a man who was washing his
horse in the muddy pool where she had quenched her thirst.

"What is this?" she asked.

"The sports page of the newspaper," the man replied,
concealing his surprise at her ignorance.

The answer astounded the girl, but she did not want to
seem rude, so she merely inquired about the significance of
the fly tracks scattered across the page.

"Those are words, child. Here it says that Fulgencio Barba
knocked out El Negro Tiznao in the third round."

That was the day Belisa Crepusculario found out that words
make their way in the world without a master, and that
anyone with a little cleverness can appropriate them and do
business with them. She made a quick assessment of her
situation and concluded that aside from becoming a prostitute
or working as a servant in the kitchens of the rich there were
few occupations she was qualified for. It seemed to her that
selling words would be an honorable alternative. From that
moment on, she worked at that profession, and was never
tempted by any other. At the beginning, she offered her
merchandise unaware that words could be written outside of
newspapers. When she learned otherwise, she calculated the
infinite possibilities of her trade and with her savings paid a
priest twenty pesos to teach her to read and write; with her
three remaining coins she bought a dictionary. She pored over
it from A to Z and then threw it into the sea, because it was
not her intention to defraud her customers with packaged
words. One August morning several years later, Belisa
Crepusculario was sitting in her tent in the middle of a plaza,
surrounded by the uproar of market day, selling legal
arguments to an old man who had been trying for sixteen
years to get his pension. Suddenly she heard yelling and
thudding hoofbeats. She looked up from her writing and saw,
first, a cloud of dust, and then a band of horsemen come
galloping into the plaza. They were the Colonel's men, sent
under orders of El Mulato, a giant known throughout the land
for the speed of his knife and his loyalty to his chief. Both the
Colonel and El Mulato had spent their lives fighting in the civil
war, and their names were ineradicably linked to devastation
and calamity. The rebels swept into town like a stampeding
herd, wrapped in noise, bathed in sweat, and leaving a
hurricane of fear in their trail. Chickens took wing, dogs ran for
their lives, women and children scurried out of sight, until the
only living soul left in the market was Belisa Crepusculario.
She had never seen El Mulato and was surprised to see him
walking toward her.

"I'm looking for you," he shouted, pointing his coiled whip
at her; even before the words were out, two men rushed
her—knocking over her canopy and shattering her inkwell—

bound her hand and foot, and threw her like a sea bag across the rump of El Mulato's mount. Then they thundered off toward the hills.

Hours later, just as Belisa Crepusculario was near death, her heart ground to sand by the pounding of the horse, they stopped, and four strong hands set her down. She tried to stand on her feet and hold her head high, but her strength failed her and she slumped to the ground, sinking into a confused dream. She awakened several hours later to the murmur of night in the camp, but before she had time to sort out the sounds, she opened her eyes and found herself staring into the impatient glare of El Mulato, kneeling beside her.

"Well, woman, at last you've come to," he said. To speed her to her senses, he tipped his canteen and offered her a sip of liquor laced with gunpowder.

She demanded to know the reason for such rough treatment, and El Mulato explained that the Colonel needed her services. He allowed her to splash water on her face, and then led her to the far end of the camp where the most feared man in all the land was lazing in a hammock strung between two trees. She could not see his face, because he lay in the deceptive shadow of the leaves and the indelible shadow of all his years as a bandit, but she imagined from the way his gigantic aide addressed him with such humility that he must have a very menacing expression. She was surprised by the Colonel's voice, as soft and well-modulated as a professor's.

"Are you the woman who sells words?" he asked.

"At your service," she stammered, peering into the dark and trying to see him better.

The Colonel stood up, and turned straight toward her. She saw dark skin and the eyes of a ferocious puma, and she knew immediately that she was standing before the loneliest man in the world.

"I want to be President," he announced.

The Colonel was weary of riding across that godforsaken land, waging useless wars and suffering defeats that no subterfuge could transform into victories. For years he had been sleeping in the open air, bitten by mosquitoes, eating iguanas and snake soup, but those minor inconveniences were not why he wanted to change his destiny. What truly troubled him was the terror he saw in people's eyes. He longed to ride into a town beneath a triumphal arch with bright flags and flowers everywhere; he wanted to be cheered, and be given newly laid eggs and freshly baked bread. Men fled at the sight of him, children trembled, and women miscarried from fright; he had had enough, and so he had decided to become President. El Mulato had suggested that they ride to the capital, gallop up to the Palace, and take over the government, the way they had taken so many other things without anyone's permission. The Colonel, however, did not want to be just another tyrant; there had been enough of those before him and, besides, if he did that, he would never win people's hearts. It was his aspiration to win the popular vote in the December elections.

"To do that, I have to talk like a candidate. Can you sell me the words for a speech?" the Colonel asked Belisa Crepusculario. She had accepted many assignments, but none like this. She did not dare refuse, fearing that El Mulato would shoot her between the eyes, or worse still, that the Colonel would burst into tears. There was more to it than that, however; she felt the urge to help him because she felt a throbbing warmth beneath her skin, a powerful desire to touch that man, to fondle him, to clasp him in her arms.

All night and a good part of the following day, Belisa Crepusculario searched her repertory for words adequate for a presidential speech, closely watched by El Mulato, who could not take his eyes from her firm wanderer's legs and virginal breasts. She discarded harsh, cold words, words that were too flowery, words worn from abuse, words that offered improbable promises, untruthful and confusing words, until all she had left were words sure to touch the minds of men and women's intuition. Calling upon the knowledge she had purchased from the priest for twenty pesos, she wrote the speech on a sheet of paper and then signaled El Mulato to untie the rope that bound her ankles to a tree. He led her once more to the Colonel, and again she felt the throbbing anxiety that had seized her when she first saw him. She handed him the paper and waited while he looked at it, holding it gingerly between thumbs and fingertips.

"What the shit does this say?" he asked finally.

"Don't you know how to read?"

"War's what I know," he replied.

She read the speech aloud. She read it three times, so her client could engrave it on his memory. When she finished, she saw the emotion in the faces of the soldier who had gathered round to listen, and saw that the Colonel's eyes glittered with enthusiasm, convinced that with those words the presidential chair would be his.

"If after they've heard it three times, the boys are still standing there with their mouths hanging open, it must mean the thing's damn good, Colonel" was El Mulato's approval.

"All right, woman. How much do I owe you?" the leader asked.

"One peso, Colonel."

"That's not much," he said, opening the pouch he wore at his belt, heavy with proceeds from the last foray.

"The peso entitles you to a bonus. I'm going to give you two secret words," said Belisa Crepusculario.

"What for?"

She explained that for every fifty centavos a client paid, she gave him the gift of a word for his exclusive use. The Colonel shrugged. He had no interest at all in her offer, but he did not want to be impolite to someone who had served him so well. She walked slowly to the leather stool where he was sitting, and bent down to give him her gift. The man smelled the scent of a mountain cat issuing from the woman, a fiery heat radiating from her hips, he heard the terrible whisper of her hair, and a breath of sweetmint murmured into his ear the two secret words that were his alone.

"They are yours, Colonel," she said as she stepped back. "You may use them as much as you please."

El Mulato accompanied Belisa to the roadside, his eyes as entreating as a stray dog's, but when he reached out to touch her, he was stopped by an avalanche of words he had never heard before; believing them to be an irrevocable curse, the flame of his desire was extinguished.

During the months of September, October, and November the Colonel delivered his speech so many times that had it not been crafted from glowing and durable words it would have turned to ash as he spoke. He traveled up and down and across the country, riding into cities with a triumphal air, stopping in even the most forgotten villages where only the dump heap betrayed a human presence, to convince his fellow citizens to vote for him. While he spoke from a platform erected in the middle of the plaza, El Mulato and his men **240** handed out sweets and painted his name on all the walls in gold frost. No one paid the least attention to those advertising ploys; they were dazzled by the clarity of the Colonel's proposals and the poetic lucidity of his arguments, infected by his powerful wish to right the wrongs of history, happy for the first time in their lives. When the Candidate had finished his speech, his soldiers would fire their pistols into the air and set off firecrackers, and when finally they rode off, they left behind a wake of hope that lingered for days on the air, like the splendid memory of a comet's tail. Soon the Colonel was **250** the favorite. No one had ever witnessed such a phenomenon: a man who surfaced from the civil war, covered with scars and speaking like a professor, a man whose fame spread to every corner of the land and captured the nation's heart. The press focused their attention on him. Newspapermen came from far away to interview him and repeat his phrases, and the number of his followers and enemies continued to grow.

"We're doing great, Colonel," said El Mulato, after twelve successful weeks of campaigning.

But the Candidate did not hear. He was repeating his secret **260** words, as he did more and more obsessively. He said them when he was mellow with nostalgia; he murmured them in his sleep; he carried them with him on horseback; he thought them before delivering his famous speech; and he caught himself savoring them in his leisure time. And every time he thought of those two words, he thought of Belisa Crepusculario, and his senses were inflamed with the memory of her feral scent, her fiery heat, the whisper of her hair, and her sweetmint breath in his ear, until he began to go around like a sleepwalker, and his men realized that he might die **270** before he ever sat in the presidential chair.

"What's got hold of you, Colonel?" El Mulato asked so often that finally one day his chief broke down and told him the source of his befuddlement: those two words that were buried like two daggers in his gut.

"Tell me what they are and maybe they'll lose their magic," his faithful aide suggested.

"I can't tell them, they're for me alone," the Colonel replied.

Saddened by watching his chief decline like a man with a death sentence on his head, El Mulato slung his rifle over his **280** shoulder and set out to find Belisa Crepusculario. He followed her trail through all that vast country, until he found her in a village in the far south, sitting under her tent reciting her rosary of news. He planted himself, spraddle-legged, before her, weapon in hand.

"You! You're coming with me," he ordered.

She had been waiting. She picked up her inkwell, folded the canvas of her small stall, arranged her shawl around her shoulders, and without a word took her place behind El Mulato's saddle. They did not exchange so much as a word in **290**

all the trip; El Mulato's desire for her had turned into rage, and only his fear of her tongue prevented his cutting her to shreds with his whip. Nor was he inclined to tell her that the Colonel was in a fog, and that a spell whispered into his ear had done what years of battle had not been able to do. Three days later they arrived at the encampment, and immediately, in view of all the troops, El Mulato led his prisoner before the Candidate.

"I brought this witch here so you can give her back her words, Colonel," El Mulato said, pointing the barrel of his at rifle the woman's head. "And then she can give you back **300** your manhood."

The Colonel and Belisa Crepusculario stared at each other, measuring one another from a distance. The men knew then that their leader would never undo the witchcraft of those accursed words, because the whole world could see the voracious-puma eyes soften as the woman walked to him and took his hand in hers.

Q What does this story suggest about the power of words? About the power of women?

Q What two words might Belisa have given the Colonel?

Science Fiction

Science fiction has come to be one of our most entertaining genres. At its best, it evokes a sense of awe and a spirit of intellectual curiosity in the face of the unknown. It also is a vehicle by which writers express their concern for the future of the planet. During the twentieth century—a virtual golden age of science fiction—futurists contemplated the possibility of life in outer space, the interface between computers and human beings, the consequences of a nuclear disaster, and the potential for a bioengineered new species.

The beginnings of modern science fiction may be traced to the French novelist Jules Verne (1828–1905) and the British writer H. G. Wells (1866–1946). But the more recent flowering of the genre dates from the birth of space exploration—specifically the Soviet Union's historic launching of an artificial earth satellite (*Sputnik 1*)

Science and Technology

1962   Rachel Carson's *Silent Spring* argues that manmade chemicals are damaging the earth's ecosystem

1967   Christian Barnard (South African) performs the first human heart transplant

1973   American biochemists isolate genes to make genetic engineering possible

1974   American scientists demonstrate that chlorofluorocarbons (CFCs) are eroding the earth's ozone layer

1978   the world's first test-tube baby is born

SCIENCE FICTION FILM

Directed by one of America's most brilliant filmmakers, Stanley Kubrick (1928–1999), *2001: A Space Odyssey* (1968) builds on the intriguing hypothesis of most science fiction: that intelligent life exists in outer space. The plot, which loosely follows Arthur C. Clarke's short story "The Sentinel", involves the quest to locate a mysterious 4-million-year-old crystal monolith that appears to be emitting powerful radio waves in the direction of the planet Jupiter. Outfitted with a state-of-the-art spaceship called Discovery, which is engineered by a super computer named HAL-9000, the fictional heroes of the space odyssey set out for the planet Jupiter. Their adventures include a contest of wills between the astronauts and the ruthless and deviant HAL, breathtaking encounters with the perils of outer space, and a shattering revelation of regeneration and rebirth. Kubrick's *2001* is the modern counterpart of ancient myth and legend. Like Homer's *Odyssey*, the film celebrates the adventures of a hero who, as part of a quest, challenges the unknown by force of wit and imagination. The vast, mysterious realm of outer space is the twentieth-century equivalent of Gilgamesh's untamed wilderness, Odysseus' wine-dark sea, and Dante's Christian cosmos. Just as the ancients looked across the lands beyond the sea to the earth's outermost reaches, so for moderns extraterrestrial space constitutes the unprobed celestial fringe of the universe. "On the deepest psychological level," explained Kubrick, "the film's plot symbolizes the search for God, and it postulates what is little less than a scientific definition of God."

More recently, the American movie industry produced a compelling science fiction trilogy in which digital wizardry plays a major role. *The Matrix* (1999), followed by *The Matrix Reloaded* (2003) and *The Matrix Revolutions* (2003), picture a world dominated by an artificial intelligence that uses human beings as sources of energy. The known world—The Matrix—is actually a computer simulation, a virtual reality planted inside each human mind. Drawing elements from classical mythology, the Bible, Lewis Carroll's *Alice in Wonderland*, Zen Buddhism, and the choreography of gravity-defying martial arts, the film introduced a unique photographic technique ("flow motion") that employs more than 100 meticulously coordinated still cameras to create extraordinary special effects. *The Matrix*, which explores ideas of time and space by way of both content and form, is predicted to be the single greatest influence on science fiction film of the twenty-first century.

in 1957 and the American moon landing of 1969. These events triggered an outpouring of fiction related to space exploration. In 1950, Arthur C. Clarke (b. 1917), one of Britain's most successful writers, produced the intriguing science fiction story "The Sentinel," which in turn became the basis for an extraordinary cinematic conceptualization of the Space Age, *2001: A Space Odyssey*.

The Literature of Social Conscience

Urban violence, poverty, corporate greed, and the search for spiritual renewal in a commodity-driven world have inspired much of the literature of the late twentieth and early twenty-first centuries. Such writing is usually realistic and straightforward in its narrative style. One of the leading voices in this genre is the American writer Joyce Carol Oates (b. 1938). Oates deals with the violent under-layer of contemporary urban society. In the story "Ace," she makes use of a highly concentrated kind of prose fiction that she calls the "miniature narrative." Its tale of random violence—the familiar fare of the daily broadcast television news—unfolds with cinematic intensity, an effect embellished by powerful present-tense narrative and vivid characterization.

READING 6.29 Oates' "Ace" (1988)

A gang of overgrown boys, aged eighteen to twenty-five, has 1
taken over the northeast corner of our park again this summer.
Early evenings they start arriving, hang out until the park
closes at midnight. Nothing to do but get high on beer and

dope, the police leave them alone as long as they mind their
own business, don't hassle people too much. Now and then
there's fighting but nothing serious—nobody shot or stabbed.

Of course no girl or woman in her right mind would go
anywhere near them, if she didn't have a boyfriend there.

Ace is the leader, a big boy in his twenties with a mean 10
baby-face, pouty mouth, and cheeks so red they look fresh-
slapped, sly little steely eyes curling up at the corners like he's
laughing or getting ready to laugh. He's six foot two weighing
maybe two hundred twenty pounds—lifts weights at the
gym—but there's some loose flabby flesh around his middle,
straining against his belt. He goes bare-chested in the heat,
likes to sweat in the open air, muscles bunched and gleaming,
and he can show off his weird tattoos—ace of spades on his
right bicep, inky-black octopus on his left. Long shaggy hair
the color of dirty sand and he wears a red sweatband for looks. 20

Nobody notices anything special about a car circling the
park, lots of traffic on summer nights and nobody's watching
then there's this popping noise like a firecracker and right
away Ace screams and claps his hand to his eye and it's
streaming blood—what the hell? Did somebody shoot him?
His buddies just freeze not knowing what to do. There's a long
terrible minute when everybody stands there staring at Ace
not knowing what to do—then the boys run and duck for
cover, scattering like pigeons. And Ace is left alone standing
there, crouched, his hand to his left eye screaming, Help, Jesus, 30
hey, help, my eye—Standing there crouched at the knee like
he's waiting for a second shot to finish him off.

The bullet must have come at an angle, skimmed the side of
Ace's face, otherwise he'd be flat-out dead lying in the
scrubby grass. He's panicked though, breathing loud through

his mouth saying, O Jesus, O Jesus, and after a minute people start yelling, word's out there's been a shooting and somebody's hurt. Ace wheels around like he's been hit again but it's only to get away, suddenly he's walking fast stooped over dripping blood, could be he's embarrassed, doesn't want people to see him, red headband and tattoos, and now he's dripping blood down his big beefy forearm, in a hurry to get home. 40

Some young girls have started screaming. Nobody knows what has happened for sure and where Ace is headed people clear out of his way. There's blood running down his chest, soaking into his jeans, splashing onto the sidewalk. His friends are scared following along after him asking where he's going, is he going to the hospital, but Ace glares up out of his one good eye like a crazy man, saying, Get the fuck away! Don't 50 touch me! and nobody wants to come near.

On the street the cops stop him and there's a call put in for an ambulance. Ace stands there dazed and shamed and the cops ask him questions as if he's to blame for what happened, was he in a fight, where's he coming from, is that a bullet wound?—all the while a crowd's gathering, excitement in the air you can feel. It's an August night, late, eighty-nine degrees and no breeze. The crowd is all strangers, Ace's friends have disappeared. He'd beg the cops to let him go but his heart is beating so hard he can't get his breath. Starts swaying like a 60 drunk man, his knees so weak the cops have to steady him. They can smell the panic sweat on him, running in rivulets down his sides.

In the ambulance he's held in place and a black orderly tells him he's O.K., he's going to be O.K., goin' to be at the hospital in two minutes flat. He talks to Ace the way you'd talk to a small child, or an animal. They give him some quick first aid trying to stop the bleeding but Ace can't control himself can't hold still, he's crazy with fear, his heart gives a half-dozen kicks then it's off and going—like a drum tattoo right in his 70 chest. The ambulance is tearing along the street, siren going, Ace says O God O God O God his terrible heartbeat carrying him away.

He's never been in a hospital in his life—knows he's going to die there.

Then he's being hauled out of the ambulance. Stumbling through automatic-eye doors not knowing where he is. Jaws so tight he could grind his teeth away and he can't get his breath and he's ashamed how people are looking at him, right there in the lights in the hallway people staring at his 80 face like they'd never seen anything so terrible. He can't keep up with the attendants, knees buckling and his heart beating so hard but they don't notice, trying to make him walk faster, Come on man they're saying, you ain't hurt that bad, Ace just can't keep up and he'd fall if they weren't gripping him under the arms then he's in the emergency room and lying on a table, filmy white curtains yanked closed around him and there's a doctor, two nurses, What seems to be the trouble here the doctor asks squinting at Ace through his glasses, takes away the bloody gauze and doesn't flinch at what he 90 sees. He warns Ace to lie still, he sounds tired and annoyed as if Ace is to blame, how did this happen he asks but doesn't wait for any answer and Ace lies there stiff and shivering with

fear clutching at the underside of the table so hard his nails are digging through the tissue-paper covering into the vinyl, he can't see out of his left eye, nothing there but pain, pain throbbing and pounding everywhere in his head and the nurses—are there two? three?—look down at him with sympathy he thinks, with pity he thinks, they're attending to him, touching him, nobody has ever touched him so tenderly 100 in all his life Ace thinks and how shamed he is hauled in here like this flat on his back like this bleeding like a stuck pig and sweating bare-chested and his big gut exposed quivering there in the light for everybody to see—

The doctor puts eight stitches in Ace's forehead, tells him he's damned lucky he didn't lose his eye, the bullet missed it by about two inches and it's going to be swollen and blackened for a while, next time you might not be so lucky he says but Ace doesn't catch this, his heart's going so hard. They wrap gauze around his head tight then hook him up to a 110 machine to monitor his heartbeat, the doctor's whistling under his breath like he's surprised, lays the flat of his hand against Ace's chest to feel the weird loud rocking beat. Ace is broken out in sweat but it's cold clammy sick sweat, he knows he's going to die. The machine is going bleep-bleep-bleep high-pitched and fast and how fast can it go before his heart bursts?—he sees the nurses looking down at him, one of the nurses just staring at him, Don't let me die Ace wants to beg but he'd be too ashamed. The doctor is listening to Ace's heartbeat with his stethoscope, asks does he have any pain 120 in his chest, has he ever had an attack like this before, Ace whispers no but too soft to be heard, all the blood has drained from his face and his skin is dead-white, mouth gone slack like a fish's and toes like ice where Death is creeping up his feet: he can feel it.

The heart isn't Ace's heart but just something inside him gone angry and mean pounding like a hammer pounding pounding pounding against his ribs making his body rock so he's panicked suddenly and wants to get loose, tries to push his way off the table—he isn't thinking but if he could think 130 he'd say he wanted to leave behind what's happening to him here as if it was only happening in the emergency room, there on that table. But they don't let him go. There's an outcry in the place and two orderlies hold him down and he gives up, all the strength drained out of him and he gives up, there's no need to strap him down the way they do, he's finished. They hook him up to the heart monitor again and the terrible high-pitched bleeping starts again and he lies there shamed knowing he's going to die he's forgotten about the gunshot, his eye, who did it and was it on purpose meant for him and 140 how can he get revenge, he's forgotten all that covered in sick clammy sweat his nipples puckered and the kinky hairs on his chest wet, even his belly button showing exposed from the struggle and how silly and sad his tattoos must look under these lights where they were never meant to be seen.

One of the nurses sinks a long needle in his arm, and there's another needle in the soft thin flesh of the back of his hand, takes him by surprise, they've got a tube in there, and something coming in hot and stinging dripping into his vein the doctor's telling him something he can't follow, This is to 150 bring the heartbeat down the doctor says, just a tachycardia attack and it isn't fatal try to relax but Ace knows he's going to die, he can feel Death creeping up his feet up his legs like stepping out into cold water and suddenly he's so tired he can't lift his head, couldn't get up from the table if they unstrapped him. And he dies—it's that easy. Like slipping off into the water, pushing out, letting the water take you. It's that easy.

They're asking Ace if he saw who shot him and Ace says, Naw, didn't see nobody. They ask does he have any enemies 160 and he says, Naw, no more than anybody else. They ask can he think of anybody who might have wanted to shoot him and he says, embarrassed, looking down at the floor with his one good eye, Naw, can't think of nobody right now. So they let him go.

Next night Ace is back in the park out of pride but there's a feeling to him he isn't real or isn't the same person he'd been. One eye bandaged shut and everything looks flat, people staring at him like he's a freak, wanting to know What about the eye and Ace shrugs and tells them he's O.K., the bullet 170 just got his forehead. Everybody wants to speculate who fired the shot, whose car it was, but Ace stands sullen and quiet thinking his own thoughts. Say he'd been standing just a little to one side the bullet would have got him square in the forehead or plowed right into his eye, killed him dead, it's something to think about and he tries to keep it in mind so he'll feel good. But he doesn't feel good. He doesn't feel like he'd ever felt before. His secret is something that happened to him in the hospital he can't remember except to know it happened and it happened to him. And he's in a mean mood 180 his head half-bandaged like a mummy, weird-looking in the dark, picking up on how people look at him and say things behind his back calling him Ace which goes through him like a razor because it's a punk name and not really his.

   Mostly it's O.K. He hides how he feels. He's got a sense of humor. He doesn't mind them clowning around pretending they hear gunshots and got to duck for cover, nobody's going to remember it for long, except once Ace stops laughing and backhands this guy in the belly, low below the belt, says in his old jeering voice, What do you know?—you don't know shit. 190

Q How would you describe the character, Ace?

Q What aspects of contemporary American culture does Oates treat?

Globalism

The emerging new framework for the contemporary world—the global paradigm—centers on the reality of the interdependence of cultures and peoples everywhere on earth. This phenomenon has its roots in the nineteenth century: in the industrial and commercial technologies that brought all parts of the world closer together and by the policies of First World nations to introduce these technologies to the rest of the world—usually inspired by

some form of self-serving nationalism (see chapter 30). But the ready availability of jet travel, satellite communication, and the Internet has accelerated the globalization process enormously. In Second and Third World nations, some elements of the population have welcomed the new technologies and accepted their impact on traditional culture. Others have been reluctant to adjust to the paradigm shift and have assumed attitudes of careful moderation. Yet a third element has openly resisted both modernization and globalism.

A timely example of these circumstances is found in the recent history of Islam. Many of the West's cultural messages, such as political democracy, the separation of church and state, and equality for women, are unacceptable to devout Muslims. The most radical of the Muslim fundamentalists condemn Western-oriented modernism, insisting that Muslims must not stray from the path of the Prophet Muhammad. Like the poet Iqbal (see Reading 6.16), this element resists the intrusion of the "false ideals" of modernism that have replaced spirituality with secularism. However, unlike Iqbal, the radical minority rejects efforts to achieve a brotherhood of religious believers. Radical Islam's intolerance for other religions (evidenced in the February 2001 destruction of the colossal sculptures of the Buddha in Muslim Afghanistan) and the fundamentalist resistance to Western political, social, and economic norms have produced a dangerous rift within the Muslim world and a militant threat to "infidel encroachments" in Muslim regions. In the past twenty years, radical Islamic minorities have been responsible for repeated acts of terrorism, the most appalling of which was the brutal attack of 9/11/01 on the World Trade Center in Manhattan and the Pentagon building in Washington, D.C.

The Challenge of Globalism

While the Middle East remains the seedbed of Islamic turmoil, parts of continental Africa have also had a difficult time meeting the challenge of globalism. Following the end of colonialism and the withdrawal of Western powers from Africa, a void developed between African traditions and the modernist ways of life introduced by the European presence. Some African states have fallen into conflicts arising from this void. Power struggles in parts of Africa have resulted in the emergence of totalitarian dictatorships, and age-old ethnic conflicts have been reignited, all too often resulting in bloody civil war. Vast parts of Africa are thus caught in the sometimes devastating struggle between the old ways and the new. Africa's leading English-language writer, Chinua Achebe (b. 1930), has dealt sensitively with such problems. In the short story "Dead Men's Path," he examines the warp between premodern and modern traditions and the ongoing bicultural conflicts that plague many parts of black Africa. At the same time, he probes the elusive, more universal tensions between tradition and innovation, between spiritual and secular allegiance, and between faith and reason—tensions that continue to test human values in our time.

Michael Obi's hopes were fulfilled much earlier than he had **1** expected. He was appointed headmaster of Ndume Central School in January 1949. It had always been an unprogressive school, so the Mission authorities decided to send a young and energetic man to run it. Obi accepted this responsibility with enthusiasm. He had many wonderful ideas and this was an opportunity to put them into practice. He had had sound secondary school education which designated him a "pivotal teacher" in the official records and set him apart from the other headmasters in the mission field. He was outspoken in **10** his condemnation of the narrow views of these older and often less-educated ones.

"We shall make a good job of it, shan't we?" he asked his young wife when they first heard the joyful news of his promotion.

"We shall do our best," she replied. "We shall have such beautiful gardens and everything will be just *modern* and delightful. . . ." In their two years of married life she had become completely infected by his passion for "modern methods" and his denigration of "these old and superannuated **20** people in the teaching field who would be better employed as traders in the Onitsha market." She began to see herself already as the admired wife of the young headmaster, the queen of the school.

The wives of the other teachers would envy her position. She would set the fashion in everything. . . . Then, suddenly, it occurred to her that there might not be other wives. Wavering between hope and fear, she asked her husband, looking anxiously at him.

"All our colleagues are young and unmarried," he said with **30** enthusiasm which for once she did not share.
"Which is a good thing," he continued.

"Why?"

"Why? They will give all their time and energy to the school."

Nancy was downcast. For a few minutes she became sceptical about the new school; but it was only for a few minutes. Her little personal misfortune could not blind her to her husband's happy prospects. She looked at him as he sat folded up in a chair. He was stoop-shouldered and looked frail. **40** But he sometimes surprised people with sudden bursts of physical energy. In his present posture, however, all his bodily strength seemed to have retired behind his deep-set eyes, giving them an extraordinary power of penetration. He was only twenty-six, but looked thirty or more. On the whole, he was not unhandsome.

"A penny for your thoughts, Mike," said Nancy after a while, imitating the woman's magazine she read.

"I was thinking what a grand opportunity we've got at last to show these people how a school should be run." **50**

Ndume School was backward in every sense of the word. Mr. Obi put his whole life into the work, and his wife hers too. He had two aims. A high standard of teaching was insisted upon, and the school compound was to be turned into a place of beauty. Nancy's dream-gardens came to life with the coming

of the rains, and blossomed. Beautiful hibiscus and allamanda hedges in brilliant red and yellow marked out the carefully tended school compound from the rank neighbourhood bushes.

One evening as Obi was admiring his work he was scandalized to see an old woman from the village hobble right **60** across the compound, through a marigold flowerbed and the hedges. On going up there he found faint signs of an almost disused path from the village across the school compound to the bush on the other side.

"It amazes me," said Obi to one of his teachers who had been three years in the school, "that you people allowed the villagers to make use of this footpath. It is simply incredible." He shook his head.

"The path," said the teacher apologetically, "appears to be very important to them. Although it is hardly used, it connects **70** the village shrine with their place of burial."

"And what has that got to do with the school?" asked the headmaster.

"Well, I don't know," replied the other with a shrug of the shoulders. "But I remember there was a big row some time ago when we attempted to close it."

"That was some time ago. But it will not be used now," said Obi as he walked away. "What will the Government Education Officer think of this when he comes to inspect the school next week? The villagers might, for all I know, decide to use the **80** schoolroom for a pagan ritual during the inspection."

Heavy sticks were planted closely across the path at the two places where it entered and left the school premises. These were further strengthened with barbed wire.

Three days later the village priest of Ani called on the headmaster. He was an old man and walked with a slight stoop. He carried a stout walking-stick which he usually tapped on the floor, by way of emphasis, each time he made a new point in his argument.

"I have heard," he said after the usual exchange of **90** cordialities, "that our ancestral footpath has recently been closed. . . ."

"Yes," replied Mr. Obi. "We cannot allow people to make a highway of our school compound."

"Look here, my son," said the priest bringing down his walking-stick, "this path was here before you were born and before your father was born. The whole life of this village depends on it. Our dead relatives depart by it and our ancestors visit us by it. But most important, it is the path of children coming in to be born. . . ." **100**

Mr. Obi listened with a satisfied smile on his face.

"The whole purpose of our school," he said finally, "is to eradicate just such beliefs as that. Dead men do not require footpaths. The whole idea is just fantastic. Our duty is to teach your children to laugh at such ideas."

"What you say may be true," replied the priest, "but we follow the practices of our fathers. If you re-open the path we shall have nothing to quarrel about. What I always say is: let the hawk perch and let the eagle perch." He rose to go.

"I am sorry," said the young headmaster. "But the school **110** compound cannot be a thoroughfare. It is against our regulations. I would suggest your constructing another path, skirting our premises. We can even get our boys to help in building it. I don't suppose the ancestors will find the little detour too burdensome."

"I have no more words to say," said the old priest, already outside.

Two days later a young woman in the village died in childbed. A diviner was immediately consulted and he prescribed heavy sacrifices to propitiate ancestors insulted by the fence.   **120**

Obi woke up next morning among the ruins of his work. The beautiful hedges were torn up not just near the path but right round the school, the flowers trampled to death and one of the school buildings pulled down.

. . . That day, the white Supervisor came to inspect the school and wrote a nasty report on the state of the premises but more seriously about the "tribal-war situation developing between the school and the village, arising in part from the misguided zeal of the new headmaster."

 Q How does this story illustrate the conflict between tradition and innovation?
Q What might the path in this story symbolize?

The Global Ecosystem

The literature of our time draws increasing attention to the effects of bioscience and industrial technology upon the global environment and its inhabitants. While modern technology has brought vast benefits to humankind, it has also worked to threaten the global environment. The technology of any one region potentially affects the entire global village. For instance, sulphur dioxide and other industrial byproducts emitted in one area cause acid rain that damages forests, lakes, and soil in other parts of the world. Industrial pollution poisons rivers and oceans, global warming creates subtle changes in the earth's climate zones, and leaks in nuclear reactors endanger populations thousands of miles from their sites. Such realities have focused world attention on the destiny of the planet. Ecological concerns dominate the work of one of the world's most distinguished biologists, Edward Osborn Wilson (b. 1929). An evolutionary biologist whose early writing examined parallels between ants and other animal societies (including those of human beings), Wilson has become one of the leading defenders of conservation biology. In his elegantly written books, he defines our obligation to preserve the **ecosystem** that supports life in its vast diversity. Warning that the decline of biodiversity endangers not just the body but the spirit, he pleads for a practical ethic that will ensure the healthy future of the planet.

The poet Annie Dillard (b. 1945) shares Wilson's affection for the natural environment. To her essays and poems on nature and the environment of Virginia's Blue Ridge Mountains, she brings a dimension of awe that has been called "ecospirituality." A Roman Catholic convert whose outlook is essentially pantheistic, Dillard tests the objective facts of nature against her mystical appreciation of its wonders. An excerpt from her Pulitzer

prize-winning book *Pilgrim at Tinker Creek*, exemplifies the voice of the poet whose concerns are at once personal and global.

READING 6.31 From Wilson's *The Diversity of Life* (1992)

Every country has three forms of wealth: material, cultural, **1** and biological. The first two we understand well because they are the substance of our everyday lives. The essence of the biodiversity problem is that biological wealth is taken much less seriously. This is a major strategic error, one that will be increasingly regretted as time passes. Diversity is a potential source for immense untapped material wealth in the form of food, medicine, and amenities. The fauna and flora are also part of a country's heritage, the product of millions of years of evolution centered on that time and place and hence as **10** much a reason for national concern as the particularities of language and culture.

The biological wealth of the world is passing through a bottleneck destined to last another fifty years or more. The human population has moved past 5.4 billion, is projected to reach 8.5 billion by 2025, and may level off at 10 to 15 billion by midcentury. With such a phenomenal increase in human biomass, with material and energy demands of the developing countries accelerating at an even faster pace, far less room will be left for most of the species of plants and **20** animals in a short period of time.

The human juggernaut creates a problem of epic dimensions: how to pass through the bottleneck and reach midcentury with the least possible loss of biodiversity and the least possible cost to humanity. In theory at least, the minimalization of extinction rates and the minimization of economic costs are compatible: the more that other forms of life are used and saved, the more productive and secure will our own species be. Future generations will reap the benefit of wise decisions taken on behalf of biological diversity by our generation. **30**

What is urgently needed is knowledge and a practical ethic based on a time scale longer than we are accustomed to apply. An ideal ethic is a set of rules invented to address problems so complex or stretching so far into the future as to place their solution beyond ordinary discourse. Environmental problems are innately ethical. They require vision reaching simultaneously into the short and long reaches of time. What is good for individuals and societies at this moment might easily sour ten years hence, and what seems ideal over the next several decades could ruin future generations. To choose **40** what is best for both the near and distant futures is a hard task, often seemingly contradictory and requiring knowledge and ethical codes which for the most part are still unwritten.

If it is granted that biodiversity is at high risk, what is to be done? Even now, with the problem only beginning to come into focus, there is little doubt about what needs to be done. The solution will require cooperation among professions long separated by academic and practical tradition. Biology, anthropology, economics, agriculture, government, and law will have to find a common voice. Their conjunction has **50** already given rise to a new discipline, biodiversity studies, defined as the systematic study of the full array of organic diversity and the origin of that diversity, together with the methods by which it can be maintained and used for the benefit of humanity. The enterprise of biodiversity studies is thus both scientific, a branch of pure biology, and applied, a branch of biotechnology and the social sciences. It draws from biology at the level of whole organisms and populations in the same way that biomedical studies draw from biology at the level of the cell and molecule. Where biomedical studies **60** are concerned with the health of the living part of the planet and its suitability for the human species. . . .

The evidence of swift environmental change calls for an ethic uncoupled from other systems of belief. Those committed by religion to believe that life was put on earth in one divine stroke will recognize that we are destroying the Creation, and those who perceive biodiversity to be the product of blind evolution will agree. Across the other great philosophical divide, it does not matter whether species have independent rights or, conversely, that moral reasoning is uniquely a **70** human concern. Defenders of both premises seem destined to gravitate toward the same position on conservation.

The stewardship of environment is a domain on the near side of metaphysics where all reflective persons can surely find common ground. For what, in the final analysis, is morality but the command of conscience seasoned by a rational examination of consequences? And what is a fundamental precept but one that serves all generations? An enduring environmental ethic will aim to preserve not only the health and freedom of our species, but access to the world in **80** which the human spirit was born.

Q Why does Wilson contend that environmental problems are "innately ethical"?

Q Why does he regard "the stewardship of environment" as a global responsibility?

READING 6.32 From Dillard's *Pilgrim at Tinker Creek* (1974)

. . . . Our life is a faint tracing on the surface of mystery. The **1** surface of mystery is not smooth, any more than the planet is smooth; not even a single hydrogen atom is smooth, let alone a pine. Nor does it fit together; not even the chlorophyll and hemoglobin molecules are a perfect match, for even after the atom of iron replaces the magnesium, long streamers of disparate atoms trail disjointedly from the rims of the molecules' loops. Freedom cuts both ways. Mystery itself is as fringed and intricate as the shape of the air in time. Forays into mystery cut bays and fine fiords, but the forested **10** mainland itself is implacable both in its bulk and in its most filigreed fringe of detail. "Every religion that does not affirm that God is hidden," said Pascal flatly, "is not true."

What is man, that thou are mindful of him? This is where the great modern religions are so unthinkably radical: the love of God! For we can see that we are as many as the leaves of trees. But it could be that our faithlessness is a cowering cowardice born of our very smallness, a massive failure of imagination. Certainly nature seems to exult in abounding radicality, extremism, anarchy. If we were to judge nature by its common sense or likelihood, we wouldn't believe the **20** world existed. In nature, improbabilities are the one stock-in-trade. The whole creation is one lunatic fringe. If creation had been left up to me, I'm sure I wouldn't have had the imagination or courage to do more than shape a single, reasonably sized atom, smooth as a snowball, and let it go at that. No claims of any and all revelations could be so far-fetched as a single giraffe.

The question from agnosticism is, Who turned on the lights? The question from faith is, Whatever for? . . . .

Sir James Jeans, British astronomer and physicist, sug- **30** gested that the universe was beginning to look more like a great thought than a great machine. Humanists seized on the expression, but it was hardly news. We knew, looking around, that a thought branches and leafs, a tree comes to a conclusion. But the question of who is thinking the thought is more fruitful than the question of who made the machine, for a machinist can of course wipe his hands and leave, and his simple machine still hums; but if the thinker's attention strays for a minute, his simplest thought ceases altogether. And, as I have stressed, the place where we so incontrovertibly find **40** ourselves, whether thought or machine, is at least not in any way simple.

Q How does Dillard picture humankind's place in the natural world?

Q To what does she attribute modern "faithlessness"?

What Wilson calls "the stewardship of environment" has also captured the imagination of contemporary visual artists. Robert Smithson (1938–1973), for instance, pioneered one of the most important ecological landmarks of the late twentieth century, the piece known as *Spiral Jetty* (Figure **37.4**). Constructed on the edge of the Great Salt Lake in Utah, in waters polluted by abandoned oil mines, *Spiral Jetty* is a giant (1,500 foot-long) coil consisting of 6,650 tons of local black basalt, limestone, and earth. This snail-like symbol of eternity makes reference to ancient earthworks, such as those found in Neolithic cultures (see Figure 0.14), and to the origins of life in the salty waters of the primordial ocean; but it also calls attention to the way in which nature is constantly transforming the environment and its ecological balance. When Smithson created *Spiral Jetty* in 1970, the lake was unusually shallow because of drought. Submerged twice by rising waters, the piece can now be seen again from ground level, its galactic coil partially encrusted with white salt crystals that float in the algae-filled rose-colored shallows. Earthworks like *Spiral Jetty* are often best appreciated from the air. Tragically, it was in the crash of a small airplane surveying a potential site that Smithson was killed. Documentary drawings, photographs, and films of this and other earthworks, (along with the rehabilitation of *Spiral Jetty* itself), have heightened public awareness of the fragile balance between nature and culture.

The Literature of Globalism

The literature of globalism takes in many themes, from education to ecology and from travel to terrorism. It is a literature that, like its visual counterparts, reflects the conflicting demands of the multicultural present. The 1992 Nobel prize-winner Derek Walcott (b. 1930) writes poetry and plays that reflect his dual Caribbean and European heritage. A native of Saint Lucia in the West Indies, and a world traveler, Walcott considers himself a "mulatto of styles" (biblical, Classical, Shakespearean, and Creole) and a nomad between cultures (Caribbean, European, and African). He develops these themes in the long poem *Omeros* (1990), which places the drama of Homer's epics in a Caribbean setting. In his writings (but also evident in his watercolor studies), allusions to European high culture mingle with intensely visual imagery drawn from his native landscape. Walcott's union of everyday speech, folkloristic dialect, and richly metaphorical English reaches toward a hybridized voice, the multicultural voice of the information age. At the same time, however, his verse (as reflected, for instance, in the poem "Tomorrow, Tomorrow") describes his search for personal identity in the polyglot community of the global village.

Unlike Walcott, the Polish poet Wislawa Szymborska (b. 1923) has lived most of her life in communist-controlled Poland, a country that lost nearly one-fifth of its population during World War II. One of the global community's finest poets, Szymborska (pronounced "sheem-BOR-ska") uses straightforward, conversational speech to convey concerns that are both universal and personal. In the nervous, yet nonchalant "voice" of this poet, one detects a humane moral urgency. "The Terrorist, He Watches" represents Szymborska's prescient vision of our current global culture of unease and insecurity.

Walcott's "Tomorrow, Tomorrow" (1987)

I remember the cities I have never seen	1
exactly. Silver-veined Venice, Leningrad	
with its toffee-twisted minarets. Paris. Soon	
the Impressionists will be making sunshine out of shade.	
Oh! And the uncoiling cobra alleys of Hyderabad.[1]	5
To have loved one horizon is insularity;	
it blindfolds vision, it narrows experience.	
The spirit is willing, but the mind is dirty.	
The flesh wastes itself under crumb-sprinkled linens,	
widening the Weltanschauung[2] with magazines.	10
A world's outside the door, but how upsetting	
to stand by your bags on a cold step as dawn	
roses the brickwork and before you start regretting,	
your taxi's coming with one beep of its horn,	
sidling to the curb like a hearse—so you get in.	15

---

[1] A city in south-central India; also a city in Pakistan on the Indus River.
[2] A German word meaning "world view," one's personal philosophy of the universe.

Figure 37.4 ROBERT SMITHSON, *Spiral Jetty*, Great Salt Lake, Utah, 1970. Rock, salt crystals, earth algae; coil 1,500 ft.
© Estate of Robert Smithson/VAGA, New York/DACS, London 2005.

Szymborska's "The Terrorist, He Watches" (1976)

The bomb will explode in the bar at twenty past one.   1
Now it's only sixteen minutes past.
Some will still have time to enter,
some to leave.

The terrorist's already on the other side.   5
That distance protects him from all harm
and, well, it's like the pictures:

A woman in a yellow jacket, she enters.
A man in dark glasses, he leaves.
Boys in jeans, they're talking.   10
Sixteen minutes past and four seconds.
The smaller one, he's lucky, mounts his scooter,
but that taller chap, he walks in.

Seventeen minutes and forty seconds.
A girl, she walks by, a green ribbon in her hair.   15
But that bus suddenly hides her.
Eighteen minutes past.
The girl's disappeared.
Was she stupid enough to go in, or wasn't she.
We shall see when they bring out the bodies.   20

Nineteen minutes past.
No one else appears to be going in.
On the other hand, a fat bald man leaves.
But seems to search his pockets and
at ten seconds to twenty past one   25
he returns to look for his wretched gloves.

It's twenty past one.
Time, how it drags.
Surely, it's now.
No, not quite.   30
Yes, now.
The bomb, it explodes.

 Q What do these poems suggest about the life of the individual in the global village?

Globalism and Ethnic Identity

Ethnic identity—that is, the manner in which individuals define themselves as members of a group sharing the same culture and values—has become a leading issue in the contemporary global community. Such identity is a multi-dimensional phenomenon, a "cluster" of traits (gender, race, language, physical appearance, and religious values) that form one's self-image. The self-affirming significance of ethnic identity is well expressed in the ancient Yoruba proverb: "I am because we are; what I am is what we are." Perceiving oneself as part of an ethnic group is a major determinant of individual identity; it flowers in the freedom to exercise that identity, as it manifests itself in language, music, and other traditional and ritual forms. Ethnicity and the quest to maintain ethnic identity have inspired many of the creative projects of contemporary artists: Leslie Marmon Silko (b. 1948), for example (of Native American and

Mexican ancestry), draws on Pueblo tribal folktales in her poetry and prose; and in the stories of the Chinese-American writer Maxine Hong Kingston (b. 1940), family legends and native Chinese customs become conduits through which the author explores her identity. To these and many more contemporary writers, the oral tradition—stories handed down from generation to generation (often by and through women)—animates autobiographical themes that define a unique ethnic identity in modern society.

Similar examples occur in the visual arts. Photography and film are the favorite media of Iranian-born Shirin Neshat (b. 1957), who now lives in New York City. Neshat's art deals with conflicting ethnic values and lifestyles: Islamic and Western, ancient and modern, male and female. Her photographic series, *Women of Allah* (1993–1997) explores the role of militant women who fought in the 1979 revolution that overthrew Iran's ruling dynasty. Neshat makes dramatic use of the *chador* (the large veil of black cloth that has become an ethnic symbol of Muslim women) to frame her face, which, intersected by a rifle, becomes the site of a poem (by the feminist writer Forough Farrokhzad) transcribed in Farsi calligraphy (Figure **37.5**).

The process of globalization and the rise of ethnicity have accelerated yet another major phenomenon: Immigration—the age-old process of people moving from *mother* country to *other* country—has increased dramatically

Figure 37.5 SHIRIN NESHAT, *Rebellious Silence*, from "Women of Allah" series, 1994. Gelatin-silver print and ink. Courtesy of the Barbara Gladstone Gallery, New York.

in recent years. Every year, some 100 million people leave (or try to leave) their places of birth in search of political or economic advantage. This mass migration of peoples has resulted in the establishment of large ethnic communities throughout the world. The vast numbers of immigrants who have made the United States their home have had a dramatic impact: demographic changes, in the form of rising numbers of Asians and Latinos—persons from the various Latin American countries—have changed the face of the economy, the urban environment, and the culture. By the year 2009, Latinos are expected to supercede African-Americans as the largest ethnic minority in the United States. In all aspects of life, from literature and art to food and dance styles, there has been a flowering of Latino culture. With *The Mambo Kings Play Songs of Love* (1989), the first novel by a Hispanic to win the Pulitzer Prize, the Cuban-American Oscar Hijuelos (b. 1951) brought attention to the impact of Latin American music on American culture, and more generally, to the role of memory in reclaiming one's ethnic roots. Younger writers have given voice to personal problems of adjustment in America's ethnic mosaic and to the ways in which language and customs provide a vital sense of ethnic identity. These are the themes pursued by one of today's leading *Chicana* (Mexican-American female) authors, Sandra Cisneros (b. 1954). Cisneros, who describes the struggle of Chicana women in an alien society, writes in the familiar voice of everyday speech. Of her writing style, she says: "It's very much of an anti-academic voice—a child's voice, a girl's voice, a poor girl's voice, a spoken voice, the voice of an American Mexican. It's in this rebellious realm of antipoetics that I tried to create a poetic text with the most unofficial language I could find." Cisneros dates the birth of her own political consciousness from the moment (in a graduate seminar on Western literature) she recognized her "otherness," that is, her separateness from the dominant culture. An excerpt from *The House on Mango Street*, her now classic novel that describes, in a series of vignettes, the experience of a young girl growing up in the Latino section of Chicago, illustrates the shaping role of language and memory in matters of identity.

READING 6.34 Cisneros' "No Speak English" From *The House on Mango Street* (1984)

Mamacita[1] is the big mama of the man across the street,- third-floor front. Rachel says her name ought to be *Mamasota*,[2] but I think that's mean.   1

The man saved his money to bring her here. He saved and saved because she was alone with the baby boy in that country. He worked two jobs. He came home late and he left early. Every day.

Then one day *Mamacita* and the baby boy arrived in a yellow taxi. The taxi door opened like a waiter's arm. Out stepped a tiny pink shoe, a foot soft as a rabbit's ear, then   10 the thick ankle, a flutter of hips, fuchsia roses and green perfume. The man had to pull her, the taxicab driver had to push. Push, pull. Push, pull. Poof!

All at once she bloomed. Huge, enormous, beautiful to look at, from the salmon-pink feather on the tip of her hat down to the little rosebuds of her toes. I couldn't take my eyes off her tiny shoes.

Up, up, up the stairs she went with the baby boy in a blue blanket, the man carrying her suitcases, her lavender hatboxes, a dozen boxes of satin high heels. Then we didn't   20 see her.

Somebody said because she's too fat, somebody because of the three flights of stairs, but I believe she doesn't come out because she is afraid to speak English, and maybe this is so since she only knows eight words. She knows to say: *He not here* for when the landlord comes, *No speak English* if anybody else comes, and *Holy smokes*. I don't know where she learned this, but I heard her say it one time and it surprised me.

My father says when he came to this country he ate   30 hamandeggs for three months. Breakfast, lunch and dinner. Hamandeggs. That was the only word he knew. He doesn't eat hamandeggs anymore.

Whatever her reasons, whether she is fat, or can't climb the stairs, or is afraid of English, she won't come down. She sits all day by the window and plays the Spanish radio show and sings all the homesick songs about her country in a voice that sounds like a seagull.

Home. Home. Home is a house in a photograph, a pink house, pink as hollyhocks with lots of startled light. The man   40 paints the walls of the apartment pink, but it's not the same, you know. She still sighs for her pink house, and then I think she cries. I would.

Sometimes the man gets disgusted. He starts screaming and you can hear it all the way down the street.

Ay, she says, she is sad.

Oh, he says. Not again.

¿Cuándo, cuándo, cuándo?[3] she asks.

¡Ay, caray![4] We are home. This *is* home. Here I am and here I stay. Speak English. Speak English. Christ!   50

¡Ay, Mamacita, who does not belong, every once in a while lets out a cry, hysterical, high, as if he had torn the only skinny thread that kept her alive, the only road out to that country. And then to break her heart forever, the baby boy, who has begun to talk, starts to sing the Pepsi commercial he heard on T.V.

No speak English, she says to the child who is singing in the language that sounds like tin. No speak English, no speak English, and bubbles into tears. No, no, no, as if she can't believe here ears.   60

Q How does Cisneros bring Mamacita to life? What makes her a sympathetic figure?

---

[1] "Little Mama," also a term of endearment.
[2] "Big Mama."

[3] "When?"
[4] An exclamation, loosely: "Good grief."

Figure 37.6 YOLANDA M. LOPEZ, *Portrait of the Artist as the Virgin of Guadalupe*, part 3 from the "Guadalupe Triptych," 1978. Oil pastel on paper, 30 × 24 in. Collection of the artist.

No less than in literature, the visual arts display the Latino effort to preserve or exalt ethnic identity: Yolanda López (b. 1942) appropriates a popular Latin American icon of political resistance—our Lady of Guadalupe (see Figure 20.1). She transforms the Mother of God into the autobiographical image of an exuberant marathon athlete outfitted in track shoes and star-studded cape (redolent of both Our Lady and Wonder Woman, Figure **37.6**). The popular history of Latino culture also serves as inspiration for Luis Jiménez (b. 1940). Born to Mexican parents in El Paso, Texas, Jiménez constructs life-sized, brightly-colored fiberglass sculptures. These call attention to Mexican contributions to American culture and to the ongoing problems related to the migration of thousands of Mexicans across the United States/Mexican border. Dedicated to his father, who entered the United States legally in 1924, the ten-foot-high, totemlike sculpture called *Border Crossing* (*Cruzando El Rio Bravo*) evokes the heroic Mexican view of the crossing as a rite of passage heralding a transformation in status and lifestyle (Figure **37.7**).

The exercise of ethnic identity has become a powerful social and political force in the global paradigm. Having cast off the rule of foreign powers and totalitarian ideologies, ethnic peoples have sought to reaffirm their primary affiliations—to return to their spiritual roots. "Identity politics," the exercise of power by means of group solidarity, has—in its more malignant guise—pitted ethnic groups against each other in militant opposition. In Africa, the

Figure 37.7 LUIS JIMÉNEZ, *Border Crossing* (*Cruzando El Rio Bravo*), 1989. Fiberglass with urethane finish, 10 ft. 7 in. × 4 ft. 6 in. × 4 ft. 6 in. Courtesy the artist. Photo: Kirk Gittings, NM. © ARS, NY and DACS, London 2005.

Middle East, the Balkans, the Indian subcontinent, and the former Soviet Union, efforts to revive or maintain ethnic identity have coincided with the bitter and often militant quest for solidarity and political autonomy. Nowhere is this more evident than in the ongoing conflict between Palestinians and Israelis who lay claims to the same ancient territories of the Middle East. Hostilities between the Arab (and essentially Muslim) population of Palestine and the Jewish inhabitants of Israel preceded the establishment of an independent Jewish state in 1947. However, these have become more virulent in the past few decades, and the move toward peaceful compromise has only just begun.

The life of the Palestinian poet Mahmoud Darwish (b. 1942) has been one of displacement and exile. Born to Sunni Muslim parents in a Palestinian village that was destroyed by Israel in 1948, Darwish has lived in dozens of cities across the globe. Holding the bizarre status of a "present-absent alien," however, he has remained a refugee from his homeland. Regarded by Palestinians as their poet laureate, this "poet in exile" has published some twenty volumes of verse. His passion to redeem his lost homeland is expressed in a simple, yet eloquent, style illustrated in the poem "Earth Presses Against Us." Darwish's Israeli counterpart, Yehuda Amichai (1924–2000) was born in Germany but moved to Palestine in 1936. Raised as an Orthodox Jew amidst Israel's turbulent struggle to become a state, Amichai began writing poetry in 1948. Israel's favorite poet takes as his themes the roles of memory, homeland, and religious faith. His poem, "The Resurrection of the Dead," looks beyond the immediacy of ethnic turmoil to consider both the weight of past history and the promise of the future.

READING 6.35 The Poems of Darwish and Amichai

Darwish's "Earth Presses Against Us" (2003)

Earth is pressing against us, trapping us in the final passage. 1
To pass through, we pull off our limbs.
Earth is squeezing us. If only we were its wheat, we might die and yet live.
If only it were our mother so that she might temper us with mercy.
If only we were pictures of rocks held in our dreams like mirrors.
We glimpse faces in their final battle for the soul, of those who will be killed
by the last living among us. We mourn their children's feast. 10
We saw the faces of those who would throw our children out of the windows
of this last space. A star to burnish our mirrors.
Where should we go after the last border? Where should birds fly after the last sky?
Where should plants sleep after the last breath of air?
We write our names with crimson mist!
We end the hymn with our flesh.
Here we will die. Here, in the final passage.
Here or there, our blood will plant olive trees. 20

Amichai's "The Resurrection of the Dead" (2004)

We are buried below with everything we did, 1
with our tears and our laughs.
We have made storerooms of history out of it all,
galleries of the past, and treasure houses,
buildings and walls and endless stairs of iron and marble
in the cellars of time.
We will not take anything with us.
Even plundering kings, they all left something here.
Lovers and conquerors, happy and sad,
they all left something here, a sign, a house, 10
like a man who seeks to return to a beloved place
and purposely forgets a book, a basket, a pair of glasses,
so that he will have an excuse to come back to the beloved place.
In the same way we leave things here.
In the same way the dead leave us.

(Translated, from the Hebrew, by Leon Wieseltier.)

Q How does each of these poets deal with history, memory, and hope?
Q Why do you think there is no mention of religion in either poem?

SUMMARY

The last decades of the twentieth century witnessed a transformation from an industrially based world-culture to one shaped by mass media, electronic technology, space-travel, and advances in the biophysical sciences. Television and other electronic phenomena altered basic modes of communication and facilitated global homogeneity, while computer technology affected the structure and transmission of information itself. Propelled by high technology and by a condition of global homogeneity, the information age opened a new era in the arts—one that has persisted into the new millennium. The "postmodern turn" accompanied the shift away from the anxious subjectivity and high seriousness of modernism, toward a skeptical and bemused attention to the history of culture and its myriad texts. Postmodern writers have examined language as verbal coding and as a vehicle for both parody and social reform. In the short stories of Isabel Allende, the empowering roles of language and of women are intertwined. While some contemporary writers bring critical attention to the realities of urban violence and social inequity, others fabricate utopian scenarios of the science fiction genre. Still others address key issues associated with globalism: the ongoing effort to reconcile the culture of modernism with premodern traditions, the quest for ethnic identity among creolized and immigration populations, the threat of terrorism, and the ecological future of the planet. Stylistic diversity is the main feature of information-age literature; however, the search for a universal voice (the hybridized product of various vernaculars) is readily apparent.

GLOSSARY

ecosystem the ecological community and its physical environment

CHAPTER 38

Image and Sound in the Information Age

"Representing . . . information is going to be the main issue in the years ahead—how the world meets the mind, not the eye."
Bill Viola

The Visual Arts in the Information Age

In the last half century the visual arts have been overwhelmingly diverse in styles and techniques. Collectively, they are characterized by an indebtedness to mass media and electronic technology, by an emphasis on process and medium, and by such typically postmodern features as parody and irony. High-tech materials—fiberglass, Plexiglas, stainless steel, neon, and polyester resin—have become as commonplace in the artworld of the last fifty years as marble, clay, and oil paints were in the past five hundred. Performance and environmental art reach out of the studio and into daily life. The mixed-media experiments of the early modernists have expanded to include film, video, television, and the computer.

The electronic media have revolutionized the visual arts of our time: computer-manipulated photographs, virtual environments, and mixed-media installations are among the unique projects of the information age. The electronic synthesis of music, video, dance, and performance opens up

WARHOL AND EXPERIMENTAL FILM

Andy Warhol pioneered some of the most novel experiments in postmodern film. He focused a fixed camera on a single object and let it "roll" until the film ran out—thus bringing to film the (uniquely cinematic) "dead time" between "events," as John Cage had brought to music the "silence" between moments of sound. In *Outer and Inner Space* (1965), he experimented with double-screen formats to present multiple versions of his female "star" watching images of herself on televised videotape. Warhol also exploited the "long take": in the homoerotic film, *My Hustler* (1967), a single thirty-minute shot documents the interaction between two gay men who groom themselves before the bathroom sink.

new kinds of theatrical experience, some of which invite the participation of the audience. In the information age, the image, and especially the moving image, has assumed a position of power over the printed word. Indeed, the visual image has come to compete—in value and in authority—with all other forms of cultural expression.

Artists of the information age have joined popular musicians and world-class athletes in becoming the superstars of contemporary society. The art of prominent living painters, sculptors, and performance artists may command fortunes comparable to those of former industrial barons. Critics and gallery owners compete with websites to influence the marketing and commercialization of art, so that (for better or for worse) artists have become celebrities and art has become "big business."

Pop Art

The term *pop art* was coined in England in the 1950s, but the movement came to fruition in New York in the following decade—a time in which sixty percent of America's population owned television sets. Pop art became the quintessential style of the information age in that it embraced the imagery of consumer products, celebrities, and everyday events, as mediated by TV, film, and magazines. It presented commonplace goods and popular personalities in an overtly realistic style. By departing from postwar gestural abstraction, pop artists gave new life to the Western representational tradition. As Andy Warhol (1931–1987), the pioneer American pop artist, dryly pronounced: "Pop art is about liking things." Trained as a commercial artist, he took as his subject matter familiar and banal supermarket products such as Brillo, Campbell's soup, and Coca-Cola (see Figure 37.2); American superstars like Elvis Presley and Marilyn Monroe (Figure **38.1**); and media-documented episodes of social violence, such as the civil rights riots of the 1960s. He rendered celebrities and race-riots with the same deadpan objectivity. Warhol depersonalized images by enlarging them or by reproducing them in monotonous, postage-stamp rows that resem-

ble supermarket displays. He employed the slick advertising techniques of **silkscreen** and airbrush, thus blurring distinctions between fine and applied art. Warhol's Coke bottles and soup cans exalt the commercialism of contemporary life even as they assault the consumer mentality of Ellul's "mass society."

Jasper Johns (b. 1930), an artist whose career has spanned more than half a century, shared Warhol's interest in manipulating commonplace objects in ways that pose questions about the imitative power of art and the growing commercialism of the art object. When Willem de Kooning quipped that Johns' art dealer could sell anything—even two beer cans—Johns created *Painted Bronze* (1960), a set of bronze-cast, hand-painted cans of ale (Figure **38.2**). Johns' beer cans, like his flags and targets, are at once neodada tributes to Marcel Duchamp (see Figure 33.5), whom Johns knew personally, and postmodern parodies of the cherished icons of contemporary life. But they are also mock-heroic commentaries on the fact that art, like beer, is a marketable commodity.

Among the most intriguing vehicles of pop parody are the monumental soft vinyl sculptures of Claes Oldenburg (b. 1929)—gigantic versions of such everyday items as clothespins, hot dogs, table fans, typewriter erasers, and toilets. Often enlarged ten to twenty times their natural size, these objects assume a comic vulgarity that shatters our complacent acceptance of their presence in our daily

Figure 38.2 (right) **JASPER JOHNS**, *Painted Bronze (Beer Cans)*, 1960. Painted bronze, 5½ × 8 × 4¼ in. Private collection. © Jasper Johns/VAGA, New York/DACS, New York 2005.

lives (Figure **38.3**). With similar bravado, the oversized paintings of Roy Lichtenstein (1923–1997), modeled on comic-book cartoons, bring attention to familiar clichés and stereotypes of popular entertainment. Violence and romance are trivialized in the fictional lives of Lichtenstein's comic-book stereotypes—superheroes and helpless women (Figure **38.4**). Like other pop artists, Lichtenstein employs commercial techniques, including stencil and airbrush; he even imitates the Benday dots used in advertising design to achieve tonal gradation. The resulting canvases, with their slickly finished surfaces and flat, bold shapes, are burlesque versions of mass media advertisements. With tongue-in-cheek humor, however, the commercial world of the 1990s "reclaimed" pop art: just as Warhol and Lichtenstein appropriated the images of popular culture, so commercial advertising and the world of fashion design continue to "quote" from the works of these two artists.

Assemblage

Art that freely combines two- and three-dimensional elements has a history that reaches back to the early twentieth century—recall Picasso's collages and Duchamp's modified ready-mades. Since the middle of that century, however, the American artist Robert Rauschenberg (b. 1925) has monumentalized the art of *assemblage* in works that incorporate what he wryly referred to as "the excess of the world." Assembling bold, large-scale art objects out of old car tires, street signs, broken furniture, and other debris, he fathered pop artworks he called "combines." These creations attack the boundary between painting and sculpture. They work, as does the artist himself, "in the gap between art and life." Rauschenberg is a talented printmaker. For more than fifty years, he has experimented with a wide variety of transfer

techniques, lithograph, and silkscreen, to produce large-scale, provocative, two-dimensional kaleidoscopic masterworks drawn from contemporary magazines and newspapers (Figure **38.5**). His disparate bits and pieces of cultural

ART FILM

Traditional film usually obeys a narrative sequence or presents a story; experimental film, however, like Léger's *Ballet méchanique* (see chapter 34) and Warhol's *Outer and Inner*, explore the artistic potential of the medium itself. Narrative-free films, often called "art films," depend exclusively on the associational nuances evoked by sequences of imaginatively juxtaposed images. Like Rauschenberg's silkscreen collages, the experimental films of Bruce Conner (b. 1930) consist of footage assembled from old newsreels, pornographic movies, and Hollywood films. They may achieve additional effect by being "choreographed" to a specific musical score, such as with Conner's first film, *The Movie* (1958). As with music itself, Conner's films defy explicit meaning; the power to arouse emotions lies with an ingenious cinematic union of image and sound. Ushering in the new millennium is *Cremaster 3* (2002), the final piece in a five-part, ten-hour-long film cycle conceived by Matthew Barney (b. 1967). A ritualistic, non-narrative behemoth that interweaves many disparate subjects, from the construction of the Chrysler building to the differentiation of male and female sexuality, this complex work makes its impact by way of lush, disquieting, and (often) erotic images. The film is best compared to a fevered dream: powerful, perverse, haunting—and ultimately, inscrutable.

Figure 38.5 ROBERT RAUSCHENBERG, *Buffalo II*, 1964. Oil on canvas with silkscreen, 8 ft. × 6 ft. The Robert B. Mayer Fam ly Collection, Chicago, Illinois.
© Robert Rauschenberg/VAGA, New York/DACS, London, 2005.

boxes, filled them with discarded fragments of found and machine-made objects, and painted them a uniform black, white, or gold. Like decaying altarpieces, these structures enshrine the vaguely familiar and haunting objects of modern materialist culture (Figure **38.7**).

Geometric Abstraction, Op, Minimal, Neon, and Kinetic Art

Not all contemporary artists have embraced the ironic stance of pop and assemblage art. Some remained loyal to the nonobjective mode of *geometric abstraction*, first initiated in painting by Malevich and Mondrian (see chapter 32). Obedient to the credo of the Bauhaus architect Mies van der Rohe that "less is more," these artists have strived for the machinelike purity of elemental forms and colors, occasionally enlarging such forms to colossal sizes. Early in his career, the American artist Frank Stella (b. 1936) painted huge canvases consisting of brightly colored, hard-edged geometric patterns that look as though they are made with a giant protractor (Figure **38.8**). The canvases in the "Protractor" series, which are named after the ancient circular cities of Asia Minor, depart from the traditional square and rectangular format. Shaped like chevrons, circles, or triangles, they are fastened together to create unique geometric configurations. Stella's more recent artworks are flamboyant steel and aluminum pieces that capture in three dimensions the intensity of a Jackson Pollock painting. Nevertheless, the artist continues to reject value-oriented art in favor of a style that is neutral and impersonal. "All I want anyone to get out of my paintings, and all I ever get out of them, is the fact that you can see the whole thing without confusion," explains Stella: "What you see is what you see."

The idea that what one sees is determined by *how* one sees has been central to the work of Hungarian-born Victor

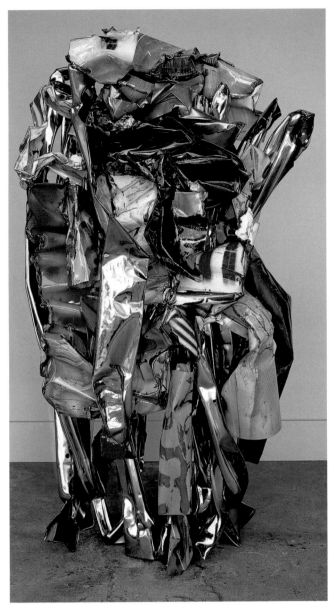

Figure 38.6 (above) **JOHN CHAMBERLAIN**, *Debonaire Apache*, 1991. Painted and chromium plated steel, 7 ft. 10 in. × 4 ft. 6¾ in. × 4 ft. 2½ in. Photo: Peter Foe/Fotoworks. Photograph courtesy of the Pace Gallery, New York. © ARS, New York and DACS, London 2005.

debris appear thrown together, as if all were equally valuable (or equally useless). But this bewildering array of visual information is assembled with an impeccable sensitivity to color, shape, and form. Rauschenberg's sly juxtaposition of familiar "found" images—like the visual scramble of post-modern channel-grazing—invite viewers to create their own narratives.

Numerous artists have used assemblage to bring attention to the random and violent aspects of contemporary society. John Chamberlain (b. 1927) has created seductive sculptures out of junked automobiles, whose corroded sheet-metal bodies and twisted steel bumpers suggest the transience of high-tech products and the dangers inherent in their misuse (Figure **38.6**). Louise Nevelson (1900–1988) collected wooden

Figure 38.7 (below) **LOUISE NEVELSON**, *Black Wall*, 1959. Wood, 9 ft. 4 in. × 7 ft. 3¼ in. Scottish National Gallery of Modern Art, Edinburgh.

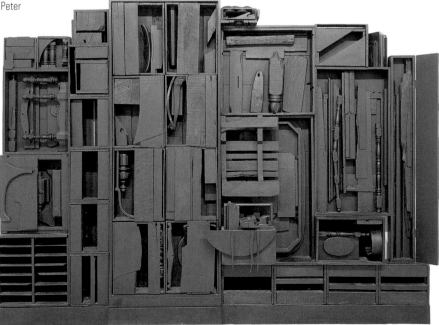

Figure 38.8 (above) **FRANK STELLA**, *Tahkt-i-Sulayman I*, from the "Protractor" series, 1967. Polymer and fluorescent paint on canvas, 10 ft ¼ in. × 20 ft. 2¼ in. Menil Collection Houston, Texas.

Figure 38.9 (below) **BRIDGET RILEY**, *Current*, 1964. Synthetic polymer paint on composition board, 4 ft. 10⅜ in. × 4 ft. 10⅞ in. The Museum of Modern Art, New York. Philip Johnson Fund. © 2004 Digital Image MoMA, New York/Scala, Florence.

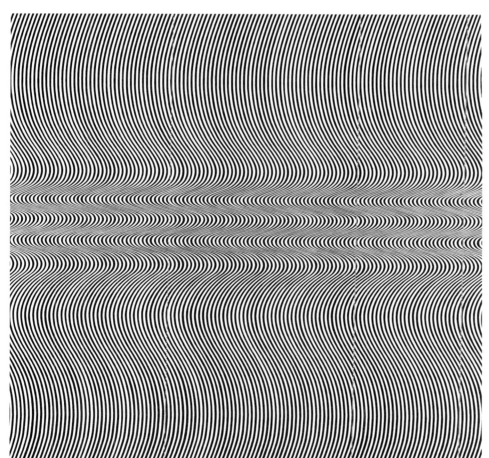

Vasarely (1908–1997) and Britain's Bridget Riley (b. 1931). Both Vasarely and Riley explore the operation of conflicting visual cues and the elemental effects of colors and shapes on the faculties of the human retina—a style known as *optical art*, or *op art*. In Riley's *Current* (Figure **38.9**), a series of curved black lines painted on a white surface creates the illusion of vibrating movement and elusive color—look for yellow by staring at the painting for a few minutes.

While Europeans pioneered optical abstractionism, Americans led the way in the development of *minimalism*. Minimalist sculptors developed a highly refined industrial aesthetic that featured elemental forms made of high-tech materials. The geometric components of minimalist artworks are usually factory-produced and assembled according to the artist's instructions. The untitled stainless steel and Plexiglas boxes of Donald Judd (1928–1994) protrude from the wall with mathematical clarity and perfect regularity (Figure **38.10**). They resemble a stack of shelves, yet they neither contain nor support anything. The visual rhythms of Judd's serial forms create a dialogue between space and volume, between flat, bright enamel colors and dull or reflective metal grays, and between subtly textured and smooth surfaces. More monumental in scale are the primal forms of the Japanese-American sculptor Isamu Noguchi (1904–1988). Poised on one corner

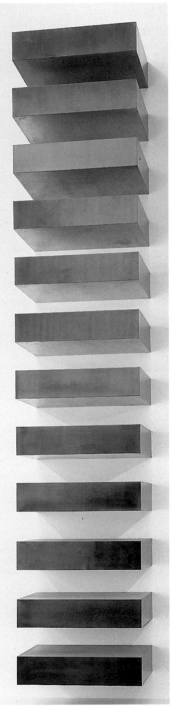

Figure 38.11 (above) **ISAMU NOGUCHI**, *Cube*, 1968. Steel subframe with aluminum panels, height 28 ft. Marine Midland Building, New York. Photo: Gloria Fiero.

Science and Technology

1962 the U.S.A. launches the first commercial communications satellite

1970 fiber optics technology is perfected to carry information thousands of times faster than copper cables

1974 Scientists demonstrate that chlorofluorocarbons (CFCs) are eroding the earth's ozone layer.

1977 the first international conference on Chaos Theory is organized

of its steel and aluminum frame, Noguchi's gigantic *Cube* (Figure **38.11**) shares the purity of form and the mysterious resonance of the Egyptian pyramids and the crystal monolith in the film *2001*.

Minimalists have enthusiastically embraced the tools of modern electronic technology. The Greek artist Chryssa (b. 1933) pioneered the use of fluorescent lights, trans-

forming them into powerful shapes inspired by commercial advertising. More abstract and iconic, however, are the fluorescent pieces of the American minimalist, Dan Flavin (1933–1996). In the course of his four-decade career, Flavin created light installations that, in their stark simplicity and utter refinement, have a gently transfixing effect (Figure **38.12**). The coloured fluorescents often

"bleed" into one another, reshaping the surrounding space. Other minimalists design anodized aluminum sculptures that move in response to currents of electricity or to the natural rhythms of wind and water. Constructed on the principle of movement, *kinetic* art looks back to the innovative mobiles of Alexander Calder (see Figure 35.13).

New Realism

During the 1970s, there emerged a new approach to figural realism that emphasized the stop-action stillness and sharp-focus immediacy of the photograph. *New realism* (also called *neorealism*, *hyperrealism*, and *photorealism*) differs from previous realist styles (including social realism and pop art) in its disavowal of narrative content and its indifference to moral, social, and political issues. Although decidedly representational, it is as impersonal as minimal art. New realist artists do not imitate natural phenomena; rather, they recreate the artificially processed view of reality captured by the photographic image. Richard Estes (b. 1936), for instance, paints urban still lifes based on fragments of the photographs that he himself makes (Figure **38.13**). A virtuoso painter, Estes tantalizes the eye with details refracted by polished aluminum surfaces and plate-glass windows. In his early works, Chuck Close (b. 1940) used an opaque projector to transfer the photographic image to canvas after both photograph and

Figure 38.12 (above) **DAN FLAVIN**, *Untitled (in honor of Harold Joachim) 3*, 1977. Pink, yellow, blue, and green fluorescent light, 8 ft. 1¹⁄₁₆ in. square across a corner. Gift of Kathan Brown, National Gallery of Art, Washington. Photo Billy Jim. Courtesy Dia Art Foundation. © ARS, New York and DACS, London, 2005.

Figure 38.13 (below) **RICHARD ESTES**, *Helene's Florist*, 1971. Oil on canvas, 4 ft. × 6 ft. The Toledo Museum of Art, Toledo, Ohio. Purchased with funds from the Libbey Endowment. Gift of Edward Drummond Libbey. © Richard Estes/VAGA, New York/DACS London 2005.

Figure 38.14 (above) **CHUCK CLOSE**, *Big Self-Portrait*, 1968. Acrylic on canvas, 8 ft. 11½ in. × 6 ft. 11½ in. Walker Art Center, Minneapolis.

canvas had been ruled to resemble graph paper; he then filled each square of the canvas with tiny gradations of color that resemble the pixels of a television screen (Figure **38.14**). The brutally impersonal tabloid quality of Close's oversized "mug-shots" is reinforced by his monochromatic palette.

High-tech materials and techniques have made possible the fabrication of new realist sculptures that are shockingly lifelike. Duane Hanson (1925–1996) used fiberglass-reinforced polyester resin to recreate the appearance of ordinary and often lower-class individuals in their everyday occupations (Figure **38.15**). He cast his polyester figures from live models, then added wigs, clothing, and accessories. Hanson's "living dead" are symbolic of modern life at its most prosaic.

New Expressionism

Dramatically different from the impassive objectivity of new realism, the paintings of Anselm Kiefer (b. 1945) manifest subjective distortions of form and color that—in their brutal, emotional fervor—revive the tradition of early twentieth-century German expressionism (see chapter 33). Painted in dark, thick colors, mixed with latex, straw, and shellac, these huge canvases conjure up memories of

Figure 38.15 (right) **DUANE HANSON**, *Tourists*, 1970. Fiberglass and polyester polychromed, 5 ft. 4 in. × 5 ft. 5 in. × 3 ft. 11 in. Scottish National Gallery of Modern Art, Edinburgh. © Estate of Duane Hanson/VAGA, New York/DACS, London, 2005

scorched earth and bombed villages—effects achieved with the use of a blowtorch. Kiefer draws his dark visions from the storehouse of German mythology and Nazi history. "I work with symbols," he explains, "that link our consciousness with the past." The ominous rectangular structure at the upper center of his paean *To the Unknown Painter* (Figure **38.16**)—at once a shrine, a gravesite, and a military bunker—suggests the painful ambiguity between humankind's creative and destructive ambitions.

Social Conscience Art

All art may be said to offer some perspective on the social scene; however, during the late twentieth century, many artists self-consciously assumed an activist, even missionary stance. Not overtly political nor even necessarily critical of the status quo, *social conscience art* seeks to transform society by awakening its visionary potential. Such art works holistically to reclaim the spiritual authority that art once held in ancient societies. Issue-driven art, like social conscience literature, draws attention to ecological ruin and widespread drug-use, to the threat of nuclear terrorism and the plight of marginalized populations, to decay in the quality of urban life and the erosion of moral values.

One of America's most outspoken social critics, Leon Golub (1922–2004), used figurative imagery based on classical models to bring attention to state-sponsored aggression and political repression. Opposing both the postmodern technology of war and the American presence in Vietnam, he painted large-sized canvases showing mercenary soldiers conducting acts of physical torture and gang violence (Figure **38.17**). Some of the assailants in

Figure 38.16 (left) ANSELM KIEFER, *To the Unknown Painter*, 1983. Oil, emulsion, woodcut, shellac, latex, and straw on canvas, 9 ft. 2 in. × 9 ft. 2 in. Carnegie Museum of Art, Pittsburgh. Richard M. Scaife Fund and A. W. Mellon Acquisition Endowment Fund. 85,53.

Figure 38.17 (below) LEON GOLUB, *Interrogation II* 1981. Acrylic on canvas, 10 ft. × 14 ft. Gift of The Society for Contemporary Art, 1983.264 Reproduction, The Art Institute of Chicago.

these paintings stare blatantly at the viewer as they intimidate or mutilate their victims. Golub's oversized figures, whose national affiliations are left unidentified, appear against the indeterminate (usually red) background of his canvases, which he scraped and abraded to resemble ancient frescoes. Regarded during his lifetime as an "existential activist," Golub left visual statements that seem timeless—as relevant to former decades as to our own.

The Cuban-born Luis Cruz Azaceta (b. 1942) combines figurative and expressionistic techniques to address the realities of arson, street crime, AIDS, and drug addiction (Figure **38.18**)—the evidence of a universal social disorder. His huge canvases are often splotched with harshly colored paint, their surfaces blistered, burned, cut, or collaged with wire and debris. In the tradition of the gallows-humor comedians Richard Pryor and Woody Allen, Azaceta delivers grotesque and macabre images that convey the need for reform.

In contrast with the aggressive activism of Azaceta, social conscience artworks from postwar Eastern Europe are subtle and understated. The Polish sculptor Magdalena Abakanowicz (b. 1930) draws on traditional methods of weaving and modeling to cast hulking, monumental figures that stage the drama of the human condition (Figure **38.19**). Sisal, jute, and resin-stiffened burlap make up the substance of these figures, whose scarred and patched surfaces call to mind earth, mud, and the dusty origins of primordial creatures. Abakanowicz installs her headless, sexless figures in groups that evoke a sense of collective anonymity and vulnerability, but at the same time underscore the kinship between human and natural forms. Abakanowicz regards art as potentially transformative and redeeming. She brings to these highly concentrated works her experience as a survivor of World War II (and Poland's repressive communist regime).

Figure 38.18 LUIS CRUZ AZACETA, *Coke Heads VIII*, 1991. Synthetic polymer paint on canvas, 8 ft. 11 in. × 10 ft. 2 in. Courtesy Frederick Snitzer Gallery, Coral Gables, Florida.

Figure 38.19 MAGDALENA ABAKANOWICZ, *Crowd 1* (detail), 1986–1987. Burlap and resin, 50 standing life-sized figures, each 5 ft. 6⅝ in. × 23⅜ in. × 11¾ in. Courtesy Marlborough Gallery, New York. 1997 © Magdalena Abakanowicz. Photography © Artur Starewicz.

In the People's Republic of China, activist art emerged within (and in spite of) repressive conditions. Despite popular efforts to modernize culture following the death of Mao Zedong in 1976, Chinese officials tightened control over intellectual and artistic expression: resolving in 1983 to eradicate "spiritual pollution," the state forbade all artworks that propagated religion, embraced "bourgeois" humanist values, or included pornographic material. Despite the repressive measures, young Chinese artists, imbued with a keen sense of mission and historical consciousness, continued to write and paint, either in exile or at their own peril. In June 1989, at Tiananmen Square in Beijing, thousands of student activists demonstrated in support of democratic reform. With Beethoven's Ninth Symphony blaring from loudspeakers, demonstrators raised a plaster figure of the Goddess of Democracy modeled on the *Statue of Liberty*. The official response to this overt display of freedom resulted in the massacre of some protesters and the imprisonment of others. Since Tiananmen Square, literary publication has remained

SOCIAL CONSCIENCE FILM

The late twentieth century was a golden age of cinematic creativity, an era in which the film medium (in alliance with television) reached a new level of social influence, its impact so great as to shape and even alter public opinion. The innovative films of the director/artists who emerged in the 1970s and 1980s reestablished the Hollywood film industry, which had faltered financially prior to the mid-1960s. The new directors, products of film schools rather than the Hollywood studio system, contributed to a reassessment of America's "master narratives" and dominant fictions: Arthur Penn's *Little Big Man* (1970), for example, exposed the myth of the Native American as "savage." Robert Altman, one of America's finest director/artists, launched a biting satire on the Korean War (and war in general) with the film *M*A*S*H* (1970). The image of the passive, male-dependent female was transformed in the film *Thelma and Louise* (1991), directed by Ridley Scott, and the plight of transgendered individuals was explored in Kimberly Peirce's *Boys Don't Cry* (1999). Filmmakers of the late twentieth century worked to develop signature styles, using cinematic and editing techniques (as sculptors use their media) to create affect and audience response. So, for instance, Altman favored the telephoto zoom lens to probe the faces of his (usually) socially troubled characters; fractured sounds and bits of dialogue overlap or intrude from off-camera. To achieve lifelike spontaneity, Altman often invited his actors to improvise as he filmed. In *Nashville* (1974), he traded the single cinematic protagonist for some two dozen characters involved in a presidential election. Postmodern in style, Altman's films are vast kaleidoscopic scenarios, the products of judiciously assembled fragments. Issue-driven subjects were common fare in the history of late modern American film. But they have rarely been treated as powerfully as in Steven Spielberg's *Schindler's List* (1993), a story of the Holocaust adapted from Thomas Keneally's prize-winning 1982 novel. A virtuoso filmmaker, Spielberg made brilliant use of the techniques of documentary newscasting to create visually shattering effects.

Social conscience film is by no means confined to the United States. In *Salaam Bombay!* (1988), filmed in the brothel district of Bombay, one of India's leading filmmakers, Mira Nair, exposed the sordid lives of that country's illiterate street urchins. China's internationally celebrated filmmaker and cinematographer Zhang Yimou (b. 1951) lived among the peasants of Shaanxi Province prior to making films about China's disenfranchised rural population (*The Story of Qiu Ju*, 1992) and in particular its courageous women, many of whom remain hostage to feudal and patriarchal traditions (*Raise the Red Lantern*, 1991). An admirer of Ingmar Bergman and Akira Kurosawa (see chapter 35), Zhang rejected the socialist realism of the communist era in favor of purity of vision and fierce honesty. His films, at least three of which have been banned in China, are noted for their sensuous use of color and their troubling insights into moral and cultural issues.

Figure 38.20 WANG GUANGYI, *Coca-Cola*, from the "Great Criticism" series, 1993. Enamel paint on canvas, 4 ft. 11 in. × 3 ft. 11 in. Collection of the artist.

of the early twentieth century (see Figure 34.4). In one sly and subversive painting from this series, three Maoist workers, armed with China's red flat and an oversized pen, boldly advance into the arena of commercial combat, their mission approved by official government stamps plastered on the surface of the painting. Here, the collective idealism of communism is replaced by the collective consumerism generated by popular commodities such as McDonalds hamburgers, Marlboro cigarettes, Coca-Cola, and Kodak film.

Total Art

The information age has generated creative strategies that reach beyond the studio and the art gallery and into the public domain. With *total art*, process (and conception) is often more important than product—the visual object itself. Somewhat like the Roman Catholic Mass or the African funeral, total art is a form of communal ritual that involves planned (though usually not rehearsed) performance. The beginnings of total art are found in the minimal and aleatory enterprises of John Cage (see chapter 35) and in the wildly experimental art of the postwar Japanese Gutai Group (see chapter 35), whose artist/performers engaged their materials violently—pounding the canvas with paint-filled boxing gloves or hurling themselves against wet canvases. In one of the earliest examples of *performance art*, a work entitled *Anthropometry* (Figure **38.21**), France's Yves Klein (1928–1962) employed nude women as "human brushes." Klein's contemporary Jean Tinguely (1925–1991) made a

under the watchful eye of the state, but efforts to control music and the visual arts have been relaxed. Some Chinese artists continue to pursue the traditional crafts of jade and porcelain, along with that favorite of Chinese genres, landscape painting. Others, however, have absorbed the confrontational styles of the Western avant-garde, many of which deliberately mocked the conformist ideals of China's socialist society. Particularly popular among young Chinese artists was *cynical realism*—a style that utilized academic and commercial painting techniques to draw attention to social and political conditions. Cynical realism reflects the sentiments of post-Tiananmen artists who, having abandoned the idealism of the 1980s, use roguish humor to register a sense of powerlessness. Cynical realists share the subversive tone of China's *political pop* painters, who seize on Western icons to glamorize the mundane aspects of contemporary Chinese life. Painters of political pop art are involved in a search for a new cultural rationale that might resolve the contradictions between ancient (Confucian) values and modern (communist) ideals, between Chinese holism and Western materialism, and between socialist realism and other, less conventional, modes of expression. One of China's most publicized artists, Wang Guangyi (b. 1956), united the conventions of old China—specifically, the propaganda posters of the Cultural Revolution—with the imagery of consumer-driven commercialism. His political pop art series, entitled *The Great Criticism* (Figure **38.20**), combines flat bright colors and broad, simplified shapes in a style reminiscent of the communist-approved social realist poster art

Science and Technology

1981 lasers are utilized for the study of matter

1983 the first commercial cellular (wireless) phones are produced by AT&T

1983 the first commercial use of MRI (Magnetic Resonance Imaging)

1986 development of high-temperature superconductors

1990 the internationally-linked computer network (the Internet) becomes accessible to personal computers

1990s advances in microprocessing make possible microcomputers, palm TVs, and smart bombs

Figure 38.21 YVES KLEIN, *Anthropometry ANT49*, 1960. Photo: © Harry Shunk, New York. © ADAGP, Paris and DACS, London 2005.

distinctive comment on twentieth-century technology with a series of machines he programmed to self-destruct amid a public spectacle of noise, fire, and smoke.

The American pioneer of *happenings*, Allan Kaprow (b. 1927), shifted performance from artist to audience. Kaprow called the "happening" a performance that occurs "in a given time and space." That space might be a city street, a beach, or a private home. During the 1960s, Kaprow wrote and orchestrated more than fifty happenings, most of which engaged dozens of ordinary people in the dual roles of spectator and performer. *Fluids* (1967), a happening staged in Pasadena, California, called for participants to construct a house of ice blocks and then witness the melting process that followed. As in most happenings, chance played a key role; the performance was itself the work of art. Performance pieces influence the way the information age processes the semiritualized events of postmodern life—political demonstrations, street riots, rock concerts, and more recently "raves" have become extensions of the total art enterprise. Clearly, however, performance pieces are ephemeral: the only lasting "product" is the photographic or videotaped record of the event.

Somewhat more permanent is *installation art*, which remakes or transforms a specific space. Room-sized installations, popular since the 1970s, invite the physical presence of the viewer into the work of art itself. One such piece, a "walk-in infinity chamber" consisted of mirrors studded with hundreds of miniature lights. Another was filled with menacing, fur-covered furniture, and yet another retooled the interior of an Airstream trailer with thousands of sparkling black and white beads. To such installations might be added recorded sound and even preconfigured odors.

The most monumental version of total art is the *earthwork* or earth sculpture, which, as introduced in chapter 37, takes the work of art out of the gallery or museum and into the natural environment. Using nature as both its subject matter and its medium, earthworks are usually

colossal, heroic, and temporary. Some, like Smithson's *Spiral Jetty* (see Figure 37.4), have ecological implications; others, however, are aesthetic transformations of large physical spaces or their landmarks. Such is the case with the works of the Bulgarian-American husband-and-wife team Christo and Jeanne-Claude (both b. 1935), whose site-specific projects are among the most inventive examples of total art. The Christos have magically transformed natural and human sites by embellishing or enveloping them with huge amounts of fabric. They have wrapped monumental public structures, such as the Pont Neuf in Paris and the Reichstag in Berlin, and they have reshaped nature, wrapping part of the coast of Australia, for instance, and surrounding eleven islands in Miami's Biscayne Bay with over six million square feet of pink woven polypropylene fabric. In 2005, they lined the 23-mile-long footpath of Manhattan's Central Park with 7,500 saffron-colored fabric flags—a 16-day-long spectacle called "The Gates." One of the Christos' earliest projects, *Running Fence* (Figure **38.22**), involved the construction of a nylon "fence" 24½ miles long and 18 feet high. The nylon panels were hung on cables and steel poles and ran through Sonoma and Marin Counties, California, to the Pacific Ocean. The fascinating history of this landmark piece, which cost the artists over three million dollars and mobilized the efforts of a large crew of workers, is documented in films, photographs, and books. The fence itself, meandering along the California hills like a modern-day version of the Great Wall of China, remained on site for only two weeks. Unlike Smithson, the Christos do not seek to remake the natural landscape; rather they modify it temporarily in order to dramatize the difference between the natural world and the increasingly artificial domain of postmodern society.

Total art is essentially conceptual, since it is driven by ideas rather than by purely visual or formal concerns. Perhaps the purest kind of *conceptual art*, however, is that which consists only of words. Since the 1960s, a variety of artists have created artworks that feature definitions, directions, or messages. Barbara Kruger's billboard-style posters (see Figure 36.12) combine photographic images and words that make cryptic comment on social and political issues. The superstar of conceptual art is the American sculptor Jenny Holzer (b. 1950). Holzer carves paradoxical and often subversive messages in stone or broadcasts them electronically on public billboards. She often transmits her slogans by way of light-emitting diodes, a favorite medium of commercial advertising. In language that is at once banal and acerbic, Holzer informs us that "Lack of charisma can be fatal," "Myths make reality more intelligible," "Humanism is obsolete," "Decency is a relative thing," and "Ambivalence can ruin your life." Holzer's

Figure 38.22 **CHRISTO AND JEANNE-CLAUDE**, *Running Fence*, Sonoma and Marin counties, California, 1972–1976. Nylon panels on cables and steel poles, height 18 ft., length 24½ miles. © Christo 1976. Photo: Jeanne-Claude, New York.

postmodern word-art wryly tests the authority of public information, particularly information as dispersed by contemporary electronic media.

Video Art

In the 1950s, the Korean artist and musician Nam June Paik (b. 1932) predicted that the television cathode ray would replace the canvas as the medium of the future. The now-acclaimed "father of video art" was not far from the mark, for art that employs one or another form of electronic

Science and Technology

1995 the Hubble Space Telescope confirms the existence of extra-solar planets and fifty billion galaxies

1996 Dolly, the cloned sheep, is born in Scotland

2000 scientists complete the mapping of the human genome

Israeli scientists pioneer the use of ultrasound waves to destroy tumors nonsurgically

2002 WiFi (wireless technology) connects computers to the Internet

2004 NASA scientists land a rover probe on Mars

Robotic aircraft acquire capability to drop smart bombs

technology has come to dominate the current art world. Video art had its beginnings in the 1960s, shaped by Paik himself. Influenced by Zen Buddhism and by the visionary work of John Cage, Paik began his career with performance pieces and electronic installations. Some were among the first interactive experiments in sound and image. With the help of an electronic engineer, he designed and built one of the first videosynthesizers—a device that makes it possible to alter the shape and color of a video image.

In the 1990s, Paik assembled television sets, circuit boards, and other electronic apparatus to produce the "Robot" series (see Figure 37.1). More monumental in scope and conception, however, are the artist's multiscreen television installations. *Megatron* (1995), for instance, consists of 215 monitors programmed with a rapid-fire assortment of animated and live-video images drawn from East and West. The Seoul Olympic Games and Korean drummers, rock concert clips, girlie-magazine nudes, and quick-cuts of Paik's favorite artists alternate with the national flags of various countries and other global logos (Figure **38.23**). The animated contour of a bird flying gracefully across a wall of screens brings magical unity to this ocular blitz, while a two-channel audio track adds booming syncopated sound to the visual rhythms. Paik's wall of video monitors dazzles viewers with a kaleidoscopic barrage of images whose fast-paced editing imitates mainstream television and film.

Figure 38.23 **NAM JUNE PAIK**, *Megatron*, 1995. 215 monitors, 8-channel color video and 2-channel sound, left side 11 ft. 10½ in. × 22 ft. 6 in. × 23½ in.; right side 10 ft. 8 in. × 10 ft. 8 in. × 23½ in. Guggenheim Soho. Courtesy the artist and Holly Solomon Gallery, New York.

In contrast with the frenzied dazzle of Paik's video projects, the art of Bill Viola (b. 1951) is profoundly subtle. Viola uses rear-projected video screens to deliver personal narratives in the form of large, slow-moving, mesmerizing images. Mortality, identity, and consciousness, Viola's central themes, draw inspiration from Zen Buddhism, Christian mysticism, and Sufi poetry. In *Stations* (a reference to the Stations of the Cross, Christ's journey to Calvary), a computer-controlled, five-channel video/sound installation projects the image of a male body (immersed in water) onto three vertical slabs of granite; the image is reflected onto mirrored slabs placed on the floor (Figure **38.24**). Viola wants the viewer to experience the piece "insofar as possible,

as a mental image" evoking the human journey from birth to death. Viola's art is contemplative and deeply embedded in the exploration of conceptual reality. It makes reference to the current "crisis of representation and identity" in which new media technologies leave viewers unsure as to whether an optical image is real or unreal. According to Viola, "representing information" will be the main issue in the arts of the future. Video and sound installations, which became a major form of late twentieth-century expression, are related to the film experience. Both immerse the viewer in the moving image; but, as with Viola's work, video art works to concentrate experience in a way that film—especially film as entertainment—does not usually achieve.

Figure 38.24 **BILL VIOLA**, *Stations* (detail), 1994. Video/sound installation with five granite slabs, five projections and five projection screens. The Museum of Modern Art, New York. Gift to the Bohen Foundation in honour of Richard F. Oldenburg. Photo: Charles Duprat.

Since the 1970s, video installations have moved in the direction of political theater. More elaborate in their staging and often interactive, they make use of holograms, laser beams, digital images, and computer-generated special effects, all of which may be projected onto screens and walls to the accompaniment of electronically recorded sounds. Some, like Mary Lucier's sound and video installation that recreates the disastrous effects of the 1997 flood in Grand Forks, North Dakota, are dramatic ruminations on personal and communal experience. Others are cast in the form of live theater. The leading American performance artist, Laurie Anderson (b. 1947), appropriates images from classic movies, newsreels, and other video resources and combines them with tape-recorded and live music. In one of her earliest performances, she played an electric violin with a neon-lit bow that produced both sound and computer-generated images. For artists like Anderson, the computer has become a "metamedium"—a medium that transcends and transforms all other forms.

Computers and the Visual Arts

Digital computers are transforming the manner in which art is made and experienced. Computer technology is now essential to the design and construction of architecture and art. In fiberglass sculpture, for instance, the computer makes possible the execution of otherwise unachievable three-dimensional curves. New software programs allow artists to draw and paint electronically. At the same time, the use of the computer to manipulate old images and generate new ones—a specialty known as *digital imaging*—has revolutionized the world of film, television, video, holography, and photography (Figure **38.25**). Digital imaging is of two varieties: one involves combining photographic originals to create new images with the aid of special computer programs; the other involves generating entirely new photorealistic material by purely digital means. In the second approach, the artist gives the computer a set of instructions about the "look" of an image, which is then electronically simulated. Among photographers, computer technology has inspired multilayered, futuristic artworks that could never have been achieved in the traditional darkroom.

Contemporary Japanese artists have been particularly successful in using computer technology to generate photographic and video projects. Yasumasa Morimura (b. 1945) transforms Western masterpieces into camp spoofs in which he impersonates one or more of the central characters. In *Portrait (Twins)*, Morimura turns Manet's *Olympia* (see Figure 30.18) into a drag queen decked out in a blond wig and rhinestone-trimmed slippers (Figure **38.26**). Using himself as the model for both the nude courtesan and the maid, he revisualizes a landmark in the history of art. By "updating" Manet's *Olympia* (itself an "update" of a painting by Titian),

Morimura also questions the authority of these historical icons, even as he makes sly reference to the postwar Japanese practice of copying Western culture. *Portrait* is a computer-manipulated color photograph produced from a studio setup—a combination of postmodern techniques borrowed from fashion advertising. Here, and in his more recent photographs in which he impersonates contemporary icons and film divas (Madonna, Marilyn Monroe, and Liza Minnelli) Morimura pointedly tests classic stereotypes of identity and gender.

Morimura's younger contemporary Mariko Mori (b. 1967) produces billboard-sized electronic installations, three-dimensional videos, and computer-generated photographs that combine pop culture with self-spoofing autobiographical motifs. She employs sophisticated technologies for futuristic installations that combine image, music, and perfume—engaging all of the senses at once. In *Pure Land*, (a reference to the Buddhist paradise of Japan's Pure Land sect), the artist appears as the Japanese goddess Kichijoten (see Figure 14.23), floating in extraplanetary space among an assembly of alien cartoon musicians—which come alive in digitally animated versions of the piece (Figure **38.27**).

The use of the computer in making art is no longer exclusive to artists, however. *Interactive art* programs, available both in the art gallery and on the home computer screen, invite the viewer to become a partner in the creative act. In *Piano* (1995) designed by the Japanese media artist Toshio Iwai (b. 1962), the spectator creates a musical "score" by manipulating a trackball that triggers star-shaped points of light that travel along a scroll until

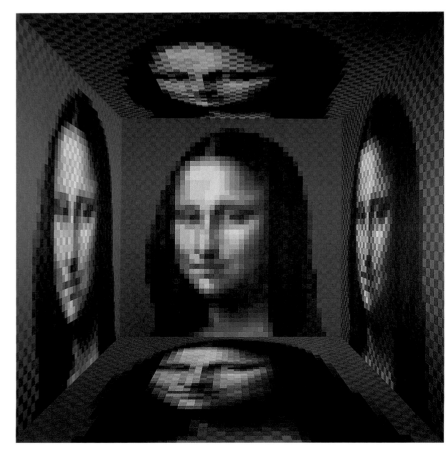

Figure 38.25 JEAN-PIERRE YVARAL *Mona Lisa Synthétisée*, 1989.
© ADAGP, Paris and DACS, London, 2005.

Figure 38.26 (above) **YASUMASA MORIMURA**, *Portrait (Twins)*, 1988. Color photograph, clear medium, 6 ft. 10½ in. × 9 ft. ´ 0 in. NW House, Tokyo. Courtesy Luhring Augustine, New York.

Figure 38.27 MARIKO MORI, *Pure Land*, 1997–1998. Photograph on glass, five panels, 10 ft. × 20 ft. × 8 ft. 5 in. Courtesy Deitch Projects, New York.

they "strike" a piano keyboard; both visual and aural patterns are generated by the spectator—within limits predetermined by Iwai. With *Electronic Eve* (1997), an interactive project conceived by Jenny Marketou (b. 1944), "image consumers" create their own multimedia environment by selecting (through direct touch on the computer screen) from a database of video sequences, still images, computer graphics, texts, and sounds. Other electronic installations invite the audience to turn words (the sounds of speech) into colored shapes and images. The World Wide Web provides a virtual theater in which one may assume an online identity—or more than one identity—in cyberspace.

Postmodernism's most intriguing fusion of media, often called *hypermedia*, is a powerful combination of high technology tools—computers, videotape, and photography—designed to generate a form of **virtual reality**. By means of optical discs, high-powered computers simulate artificial environments that are flashed onto a huge screen or onto the inside of a helmet. Like a giant video game, virtual reality combines visual illusion, sound, and spoken texts. A synthesis of all retrievable informational forms, interactive hypermedia offer an image-saturated playground for the mind.

The computer has put at everyone's disposal the entire history of art, as well as a vast assortment of electronic technology. Sophisticated telecommunication systems facilitate collaborative electronic artworks and electronic art galleries, while the Internet provides access to the contents of more than 5,000 museums around the world.

The Visual Arts and the Global Paradigm

The new spirit of global collectivity is readily apparent in the art of the information age. Such art reflects the stimulus of international tourism, the migration of artists from one part of the world to another, the impact of television and film, and the rapid accessibility and exchange of images (via digital and commercial media) from all over the world.

The Chinese-born Cai Guo-Qiang (b. 1957) moved to Manhattan in 1995, bringing with him the age-old traditions of his homeland. Trained in stage design at the Shanghai Drama Institute, Cai has produced a number of public works that rephrase the disquieting and traumatic aspects of contemporary life. Some of these explore the properties of gunpowder—an explosive used for centuries in Chinese fireworks. Cai's most ambitious work to date is a four-part installation called *Inopportune*. Stage One features a brilliant array of colored lights pulsing from long transparent rods that burst from nine identical Ford sedans suspended in mid-air along a 300-foot gallery in a sequence that unfurls like a Chinese scroll or a series of frozen film frames (Figure **38.28**). Stage Two, installed in an adjacent gallery, presents nine leaping, life-sized tigers pierced by hundreds of bamboo arrows—a reference to a popular thirteenth-century Chinese tale glorifying a hero who saves a village from a man-eating tiger. Stage Three startles the viewer with a ninety-second continuous film loop (projected on a huge screen): here, a phantom car (filled with fireworks and filmed by Cai) silently bursts into flames and floats in a dreamlike manner through Manhattan's bustling, nocturnal Times Square. The final part of the installation consists of a huge image of nine exploding cars, "drawn" by igniting gunpowder on the surface of the paper. Cai combines a global assortment of traditions, symbols, and images to capture the haunting violence of the urban scene. He claims that he uses the materials of destruction and terror for healing purposes—indeed, the Chinese characters for "gunpowder" translate literally as "fire medicine," once thought to cure the ailing body. But his powerful fantasies capture the convulsive realities of an age of terrorism.

Born to Nigerian parents in Manchester, England, Chris Ofili (b. 1968) makes artworks that capture the exoticism of the multicultural marketplace. He layers a wide variety of provocative magazine images onto canvases that he ornaments with sequins, push-pins, blobs of brightly colored lacquer, and elephant dung—symbols of good fortune in African culture. Usually mounted on varnished globs of dung, his pieces are celebratory amalgamations

Figure 38.28 CAI GUO-QIANG, *Inopportune*, Stage 1, 2005. Mixed media. Location: Massachusetts Museum of Contemporary Art Photo: Courtesy Cai Guo Qiang Studio

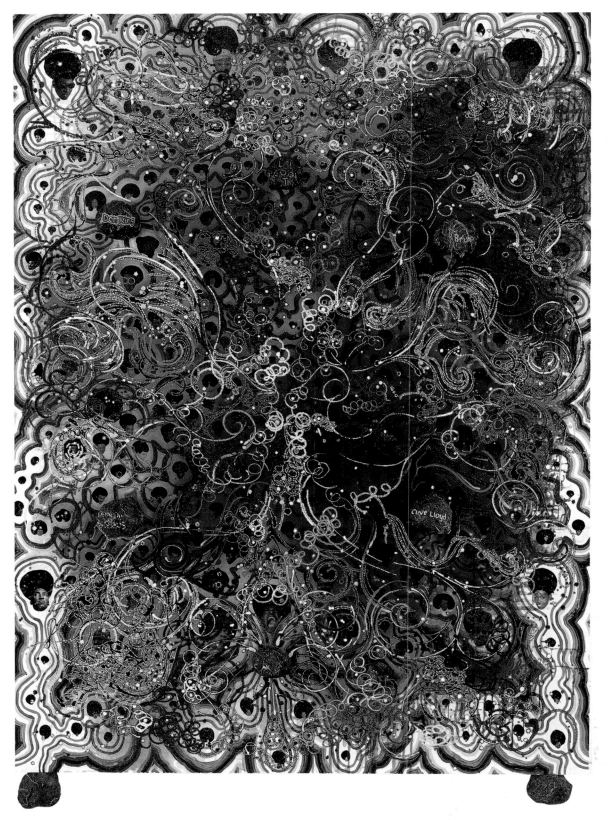

Figure 38.29 CHRIS OFILI, *Afrodizzia* (2nd version), 1996. Elephant dung, map pins, collage, resin and oil on canvas, 8 ft. × 6 ft. Courtesy Victoria Miro Gallery, London.

of the world's diverse "stuff"—from African legend and Christian lore to pornography and comic-book characters (Figure **38.29**). During his 1992 stay in Zimbabwe, for instance, Ofili learned the dot painting style of ancient African cave frescoes and the scarification designs of Nuba tribespeople. While Ofili assumes the multiple identities of African, Westerner, Roman Catholic, and urban artist,

his work powerfully conflates icons of the multiple (and hybrid) selves that populate the global arena.

The panoramic photographs of the German artist Andreas Gursky (b. 1957) are the products of his global travels. Focusing on contemporary life in Europe, Brazil, Mexico, Japan, Vietnam, and the United States, Gursky documents industrial interiors, rock concerts, prisons,

Figure 38.30 ANDREAS GURSKY, *Nha Trang, Vietnam*, 2004. C-print on Plexiglas, 9 ft. 8 in. × 6 ft. 9½ in. Matthew Marks Gallery, New York.

and the urban landscape. Precision of detail and grandeur of effect are usually achieved in one and the same image, digitally prepared on surfaces limited only by the dimensions of the largest photographic printing paper made by Kodak. *Nha Trang, Vietnam* shows a sea of orange-shirted female factory-workers weaving straw baskets and chairs (Figure **38.30**). The repetitive motifs interrupted by lines of electric lights work to create a compelling visual image that comments on uniformity, anonymity, and the omnipresence of working women in the global economy.

Architecture in the Information Age

Some contemporary critics link the birth of postmodernism to the architecture of the 1960s and, specifically, to the demise of the international style. The American Robert Venturi (b. 1925), who first introduced architectural postmodernism in his book *Complexity and Contradiction in Architecture* (1966), countered Mies van der Rohe's dictum "less is more" with the claim "less is a bore." Venturi rejected the anonymity and austerity of the glass and steel skyscraper (see Figure 35.15) and the concrete high rise (see Figure 32.26), along with the progressive utopianism of modernists who hoped to transform society through functional form. Instead, he opted for an architecture that emphasized visual complexity, individuality, and outright fun. In contrast to the machinelike purity of the international style structure, the postmodern building

COMPUTERS AND FILM

Digital technology has transformed the world of filmmaking. Special effects, achieved by way of the computer, not only alter familiar images, but juxtapose them in ways that distort both history and nature. Like the docufictions of Don Delillo (see chapter 37), cinema has devised the technical means of conveying what is not true. Robert Zemeckis' *Forrest Gump* (1994), for example, had its antihero shaking hands with the long-dead president John F. Kennedy. Digital technology facilitates the fabrication of imaginary images and realistically rendered processes that do not exist in reality, as for example James Cameron's liquid-metal cyborgs (*Terminator 2, Last Judgment*, 1991), whose shape-shifting abilities are generated by digital "morphing" techniques. The year 1995 marked the culmination of a four-year project that produced the first entirely computer-animated film (John Lasseter's *Toy Story*). Many more such films have followed, none of which is notable for its lasting artistic value. As vehicles of the hyperimages of our time, however, these films provoke attention to distinctions between reality and illusion (see Science Fiction Film, page 129). Computer technology can also be used to recreate the past with greater accuracy: Eric Rohmer (*Lady and the Duke*, 2001), uses period paintings of such remote locations as eighteenth-century Paris, into which the footage of separately filmed action (performed on an empty soundstage) is digitally inserted. Seismic changes in filmmaking since 1990 have made possible the development of nonstudio films with noncelebrity actors, which, in turn, has produced the currently flourishing independent (INDI) movie industry.

Figure 38.31 PEREZ ASSOCIATES WITH CHARLES MOORE, RON FILSON, URBAN INNOVATIONS, INC., Piazza d' talia, New Orleans, 1976–1979. © Norman McGrath, New York.

is a playful assortment of fragments "quoted" from architectural traditions as ill-mated as a fast-food stand and a Hellenistic temple. Postmodern architecture, like postmodern fiction, engages a colorful mix of fragments in a whimsical and often witty manner. It shares with *deconstructivist* literary theorists (see chapter 37) the will to dismantle and reassemble "the text" in a search for its multiple meanings. Just as there is (according to deconstructivism) no single text for the whole of our experience, so there is no unifying pattern or defining style in the design of any single piece of architecture.

One example of this postmodern aesthetic is the Piazza d'Italia in New Orleans, designed by Charles Moore (1925–1993). The plaza, which serves as an Italian cultural center, is a burlesque yet elegant combination of motifs borrowed from Pompeii, Palladio, and Italian baroque architecture (Figure **38.31**). Its brightly colored colonnaded portico—looking every bit like a gaudy stage set—is adorned with fountains, neon lights, and polished aluminum balustrades. Moore's parodic grab-bag appropriation of the Italian heritage culminates in an apron shaped like a map of Italy that floats in the central pool of the piazza.

Figure 38.32 I. M. PEI & ASSOCIATES, Louvre Pyramid, Paris, 1988. Photo: © R.M.N., Paris.

Postmodernism has engendered numerous architectural experiments in **geodesic** and modular design. One of the most inventive of these is the extraordinary glass pyramid that serves as the formal entrance to the Louvre Museum in Paris (Figure **38.32**). Built in 1988 by the Chinese-born American I. M. Pei (b. 1917), this monumental cage of stainless steel and Plexiglas opens up vast areas of interior space in the greenhouse style initiated by Paxton's Crystal Palace (see chapter 30). Pei has transcended national styles and periods by synthesizing the techniques of modern technology (including the glass-and-steel vocabulary of the international style) with the designs of seventeenth-century French landscape architects and the geometry of the Great Pyramid at Giza. His pyramid complex, despite its references to the historic past, is futuristic—a kind of space station for the arts.

As we enter the new millennium, many of the world's largest cities are enjoying a "building boom." A great era of museum construction and expansion appears to be in process. Museums have become sacred spaces, visited by millions not only to see great art, but to enjoy an experience unlike that of other leisure activities. Some of the new art venues compete in their futuristic impact with Frank Lloyd Wright's Guggenheim Museum (see Figures 35.17 and 18). The expanded Milwaukee Museum of Art, designed by the Spanish-born Santiago Calatrava (b. 1951), is a case in point. Dominating the shore of Lake Michigan like the skeleton of a large bleach-boned dinosaur, its signature element is a 90-foot-high glass enclosed reception hall covered by a moveable winglike sun screen (*brise-soleil*) made of 72 steel fins that control the temperature and light of the interior (Figure **38.33**). A 250-foot-long suspension bridge with angled cables links downtown Milwaukee to the lakefront and the museum. Calatrava,

Figure 38.33 SANTIAGO CALATRAVA, Milwaukee Art Museum, Milwaukee, Minnesota, 2003. Photograph © Joseph Sohm; Visions of America/Corbis.

who has designed some extraordinary hotels and bridges throughout the world, brings a new bravura to steel-and-glass building construction.

The architectural giant of our time, Frank Gehry (b. 1930), was born in Toronto, Canada, but lives and works in California. His early buildings reflect an interest in humble construction materials, such as plywood, corrugated zinc, stainless steel, and chainlink fencing, which he assembled in serial units. Gehry's structures, in which façades tilt, columns lean, and interior spaces are skewed, reflect his deliberate rejection of the classical design principles of symmetry and stability. More recently, in monumental projects that combine steel, titanium, glass, and limestone, he has developed a vocabulary of undulating forms and irregular shapes inspired by everyday objects: a fish, a guitar, a bouquet of flowers. Gehry's latest masterpiece is the Walt Disney Concert Hall in Los Angeles, California (Figure **38.34**). The 2,265-seat hall engages glass curtain-walls and a majestic multileveled lobby; but it is in the breathtaking design of the exterior, with its billowing, light-reflecting stainless steel plates, that the building achieves its singular magnificence. His concert hall, like his highly acclaimed Guggenheim Museum in Bilbao, Spain (1997), combines the spontaneous vitality of action painting with the heroic stability of minimalist sculpture. Gehry's creative process is intuitive: he designs "in his head," develops the contours on paper and in models, and then makes use of five aerospace engineers and a

Figure 38.34 (above) **FRANK GEHRY**, Walt Disney Concert Hall, Los Angeles, California, 2003. Photograph © Rufus F. Folkks/Corbis.

Figure 38.35 (left) **RICHARD SERRA**, (from front to back) *Torqued Ellipse I*, 1996; *Double Torqued Ellipse*, 1998–1999; *Double Torqued Ellipse II*; *Snake*, 1996. Guggenheim Museum, Bilbao. Photograph © FMGB Guggenheim Bilbao. Photographer: Erika Barahona Ede.

Philip Glass (b. 1937) received his early training in the fundamentals of Western musical composition. In the 1970s, however, after touring Asia and studying with the Indian sitar master Ravi Shankar (b. 1920), Glass began writing music that embraced the rhythmic structures of Indian *ragas*, progressive jazz, and rock and roll. The musical drama *Einstein on the Beach* (1976), which Glass produced in collaboration with the designer/director Robert Wilson (b. 1941), was the first opera performed at the Metropolitan Opera House in New York City to feature electronically amplified instruments. Like traditional opera, *Einstein on the Beach* combines instrumental and vocal music, as well as recitation, mime, and dance. But it departs radically from operatic tradition in its lack of a narrative story line and character development, as well as in its instrumentation. The opera, which is performed with no intermissions over a period of four-and-a-half hours, is not the story of Albert Einstein's life or work; rather, it is an extended poetic statement honoring the twentieth century's greatest scientist. The score consists of simple melodic lines that are layered and repeated in seemingly endless permutations. Mesmerizing and seductive, Glass' music recalls the texture of Gregorian chant, the sequenced repetitions of electronic tape loops, and the subtle rhythms of the Indian *raga*. Harmonic changes occur so slowly that one must, as Glass explains, learn to listen at "a different speed," a feat that closely resembles an act of meditation.

Historical themes have continued to inspire much of the music of Glass. In 1980, he composed the opera *Satyagraha*, which celebrates the achievements of India's pacifist hero Mohandas Gandhi (see chapter 36). Sung in Sanskrit and English, the opera uses a text drawn from the *Bhagavad Gita*, the sacred book of the Hindu religion. For the quincentennial commemoration of the Columbian voyage to the Americas, the composer wrote an imaginative modern-day analogue (*The Voyage*, 1992) that links the idea of great exploration to the theme of interplanetary travel.

Postmodern Opera

In the late twentieth century, opera found inspiration in current events such as international hijacking (John Adams' *Death of Klinghofer*), black nationalism (Anthony Davis' *X*), gay rights (Stewart Wallace's *Harvey Milk*), and the cult of celebrity—witness Ezra Laderman's *Marilyn* (Monroe), John Adams' *Nixon*, and Robert Xavier Rodriguez's *Frida* (Kahlo). Other composers turned to the classics of literature and art as subject matter for full-length operas: Carlyle Floyd's *Of Mice and Men* (1970) is based on John Steinbeck's novel of the same name; William Bolcom's *A View from the Bridge* (1999) is an adaptation of the Arthur Miller play; John Harbison's *Gatsby* (1999) was inspired by F. Scott Fitzgerald's novel *The Great Gatsby*; and Tennessee Williams' classic play *A Streetcar Named Desire* (1998) received operatic treatment by the American composer Andre Previn. Few of these

operas attained the compositional sophistication of the century's first typically postmodern opera: *The Ghosts of Versailles* (1992) composed by John Corigliano (b. 1938). Scored for orchestra and synthesizer and cast in the style of a comic opera, *Ghosts of Versailles* takes place in three different (and interlayered) worlds: the eighteenth-century court of Versailles, the scenario of a Mozartean opera, and the realm of the afterlife—a place peopled by the ghosts of Marie Antoinette and her court. The score commingles traditional and contemporary musical styles, alternating pseudo-Mozartean lyricism with modern dissonance in a bold and inventive (although often astonishingly disjunctive) manner. In the spirit of postmodernism, Corigliano made historical style itself the subject; his multivalent allegory tests the text against past texts by having one of his characters in the opera suddenly exclaim, "This is not opera; Wagner is opera."

Rock Music

The origins of the musical style called *rock* lay in the popular culture of the mid-1950s. The words "rocking" and "rolling," originally used to describe sexual activity, came to identify an uninhibited musical style that drew on a broad combination of popular American and African-American music, including country, swing, gospel, and rhythm and blues. Although no one musician is responsible for the birth of rock, the style gained popularity with such performers as Bill Haley, Little Richard, and Elvis Presley. In the hands of these flamboyant musicians, it came to be characterized by a high dynamic level of sound, fast and hard rhythms, a strong beat, and earthy, colloquial lyrics.

From its inception, rock music was an expression of a youth culture: the rock sound, associated with dancing, sexual freedom, and rebellion against restrictive parental and cultural norms, also mirrored the new consumerism of the postwar era. While 1950s rock and roll often featured superficial, "bubble-gum" lyrics, 1960s rock became more sophisticated—the aural counterpart of Western-style pop art. With the success of the Beatles—a British group of the 1960s—rock became an international phenomenon, uniting young people across the globe. The Beatles absorbed the music of Little Richard and also the rhythms and instrumentation of Indian classical music. They made imaginative use of electronic effects, such as feedback and splicing. Their compositions, which reflected the spirit of the Western counterculture, reached a creative peak in the album *Sergeant Pepper's Lonely Hearts Club Band* (1967). Although the electric guitar was in use well before the Beatles emerged, it was with this group that the instrument became the hallmark of rock music, and it remains the principal instrument of the rock musician.

During the 1960s, "establishment" America faced the protests of a youthful counterculture that was disenchanted with middle-class values, mindless consumerism, and bureaucratic authority. Counterculture "hippies"—the word derives from "hipster," an admirer of jazz and its subculture—exalted a neoromantic lifestyle that called for peaceful coexistence, a return to natural and communal habitation, more relaxed sexual standards, and experimentation with mind-altering drugs such as marijuana and lysergic acid diethylamide (LSD). The use of psychedelic drugs among members of the counterculture became associated with the emergence of a number of British and West Coast acid rock (or hard rock) groups, such as The Who and Jefferson Airplane. The music of these groups often featured ear-splitting, electronically amplified sound and sexually provocative lyrics. The decade produced a few superb virtuoso performers, like the guitarist Jimi Hendrix (1942–1970). The 1960s also spawned the folk-rock hero Bob Dylan (b. 1941), whose songs gave voice to the anger and despair of the American counterculture. Dylan's lyrics, filled with scathing references to modern materialism, hypocrisy, greed, and warfare—specifically, the American involvement in Vietnam—attacked the moral detachment of contemporary authority figures.

Music and the Global Paradigm

The global paradigm may be most apparent in contemporary music, in which Western traditions of harmony and form have been energized by the modes, rhythms, textures, and inflections of Asia, Africa, and the Caribbean. Inspired by ancient and non-Western oral and instrumental forms of improvisation, much of today's music relies less on the formal score and more on the ear. Some contemporary composers create musical tapestries that utilize conventional Western instruments along with ancient musical ones (such as the Chinese flute or the *balafon*, an African version of the xylophone), producing textures that may be further enriched by electronic means. These innovations are evident in the compositions of Tan Dun (b. 1957), a Chinese-born composer who has lived in the United States since 1986. Tan's works, ranging from string quartets and operas to multimedia pieces and film scores, represent a spirit of cultural pluralism that blends Chinese opera, folk songs, and instruments, with traditional Western techniques and traditions ranging from medieval chant and romantic harmonies to audacious aural experiments (in the style of John Cage) using the sounds of water, torn paper, and bird calls.

One of the most notable experiments in intercultural music is the Silk Road Project, which involves the exchange of Western musical traditions with those of the ancient Silk Road, the vast skein of trade routes that linked East Asia to Europe prior to 1500 C.E. (see chapter 7). Begun in 1998, this extended effort to connect East and West was the brainchild of the renowned Japanese-American cellist Yo-Yo Ma (b. 1955). The Silk Road, which Ma calls "the Internet of Antiquity," was a network of cultural exchange, the spirit of which has been revitalized by this project. Musicians and composers from across Central Asia, in consort with a group of American virtuoso musicians (selected by Ma), are currently producing exciting and often passionate music that integrates radically different compositional forms, instruments, and performance styles.

Cultural interdependence and the willful (and often electronically synthesized) fusion of different musical traditions have transformed contemporary music. The influence of Arabic chant, Indian ragas, and Latino rhythms is evident in jazz; rock and country blues give gospel music a new sound; Cuban brass punctuates contemporary rock; and shimmering Asian drones propel New Age music. The global character of contemporary music is also evident in popular genres that engage issue-driven lyrics. The Jamaican musician Bob Marley (1945–1981) brought to the international scene the socially conscious music known as *reggae*—an eclectic style that draws on a wide variety of black Jamaican musical forms, including African religious music and Christian revival songs. *Hip-hop*, which combines loud, percussive music (often electronically mixed and manipulated by disc jockeys), jarring lyrics, and breakdancing (an acrobatic dance style) has moved from its inner-city origins to assume an international scope. This "mutating hybrid" makes use of various musical traditions: modern (disco, salsa, reggae, rock) and ancient (African call and response). *Rap*—the vocal dimension of hip-hop—launches a fusillade of raw and socially provocative words chanted in rhymed couplets over an intense rhythmic beat.

While some critics lament that Western music has bifurcated into two cultures—art music and popular music—the fact is that these two traditions are becoming more alike, or, more precisely, they share various features of a global musical menu. One example of this phenomenon is the orchestral suite *Portraits in Blue* (1995) by the American jazz pianist Marcus Roberts (b. 1963). Composed in what Roberts calls "semi-classical form," the composition is a "personal listening mix" that conflates Beethoven, John Coltrane, Chopin, Little Richard, Billie Holiday, and George Gershwin. In the genre of free jazz, such musicians as John Zorn (b. 1953) borrow harmonic and rhythmic devices from the domains of bluegrass, klezmer (Jewish folk music), and punk rock. Such fusions of Eastern and Western, urban and folk, tribal and lyric styles, constitute the musical mosaic of the new millennium. Imaginative efforts to join music to theater, film, dance, and the visual arts move toward a new synthesis of word, image, and sound.

Dance in the Information Age

Composed in conjunction with *Einstein on the Beach*, the choreography of Lucinda Childs (b. 1940)—who also danced in the original production—followed a minimalist imperative. In line with the hypnotic rhythms of the piece, her choreography featured serial repetitions of ritualized gestures and robotlike motions. Childs reduced the credo of pure dance to a set of patterned movements that were geometric, recurrent, and—for some critics—unspeakably boring. The role of improvisation in dance—the legacy of Merce Cunningham—has had a more successful recent history. Contemporary companies such as the Sydney (Australia) Dance Company, Pilobolus, and Momix have produced exceptionally inventive repertories that embrace the realms of acrobatics, aerobics, gymnastics, vaudeville, and street dance. The new dance projects

---

♪ See Music Listening Selections at end of chapter.

CHAPTER 36

Appel, Alfred. *Jazz Modernism: From Ellington and Armstrong to Matisse and Joyce*. New Haven: Conn.: Yale University Press, 2004.

Broude, Norma, and Mary D. Garrard, eds. *The Power of Feminist Art: The American Movement of the 1970s, History and Impact*. New York: Abrams, 1996.

Giddens, Gary. *Visions of Jazz: The First Century*. New York: Oxford University Press, 1998.

Gioia, Ted. *The History of Jazz*. New York: Oxford University Press, 1999.

Isaacs, Harold R. *Power and Identity: Tribalism and World Politics*. New York: Harper Collins, 1979.

Lewis, Samella. *Art: African American*. Berkeley: University of California Press, 2003.

Long, Richard A. *The Black Tradition in American Dance*. New York: Rizzoli, 1989.

Lucie-Smith, Edward. *Race, Sex, and Gender: Issues in Contemporary Art*. New York: Abrams, 1994.

Powell, Richard J. *Black Art and Culture in the 20th Century*. New York: Thames and Hudson, 2002.

Saslow, James M. *Pictures and Passions: A History of Homosexuality in the Visual Arts*. New York: Viking Press, 1999.

Watson, Steven. *The Harlem Renaissance: Hub of African American Culture, 1920–1930*. New York: Pantheon, 1996.

CHAPTER 37

Dunning, William V. *The Roots of Postmodernism*. Englewood Cliffs, NJ: Prentice Hall, 1995.

Gablik, Suzi. *The Reenchantment of Art*. London: Thames and Hudson, 1992.

Harbison, O.B. *Disappearing Through the Skylight: Technology in the Twentieth Century*. New York: Penguin, 1989.

Hassan, Ihab. *The Postmodern Turn: Essays in Postmodern Theory and Culture*. Columbus, Ohio: Ohio State University Press, 1987.

Kaku, Michio. *Beyond Einstein: The Cosmic Quest for the Theory of the Universe*. New York: Doubleday, 1995.

Loveless, Richard L., ed. *The Computer Revolution and the Arts*. Tampa, Fla.: South Florida Press, 1989.

Maybury-Lewis, David. *Millennium: Tribal Wisdom and the Modern World*. New York: Viking, 1992.

Mazower, Mark. *Dark Continent: Europe's Twentieth Century*. New York: Vintage Books, 2000.

Shlain, Leonard. *The Alphabet Versus the Goddess: The Conflict between Word and Image*. New York: Penguin/Arkana, 1998.

Wilson, Stephen. *Information Arts: Intersections of Art, Science, and Technology*. Cambridge, Mass.: MIT Press, 2003.

CHAPTER 38

Anker, Jenny and D. Nelkin. *The Molecular Gaze: Art in the Genetic Age*. New York: Cold Spring Harbor Laboratory Press, 2004.

Carr, C. *On Edge: Performance at the End of the Twentieth Century*. Hanover, N.H.: Wesleyan University Press, 1993.

Cope, David. *New Directions in Music*. New York: Waveland Press, 2000.

Felshin, Nina, ed. *But Is It Art? The Spirit of Art as Activism*. Seattle: Bay Press, 1994.

Fineberg, John. *Strategies of Being: Art Since 1945*. Englewood Cliffs, N.J.: Prentice Hall, 1995.

Foster, Hall. *The Return of the Real: The Avant-Garde at the End of the Century*. Cambridge, Mass.: MIT Press, 1996.

Gere, Charlie. *Digital Culture*. London: Reaktion Books, 2003.

Jencks, Charles. *The Architecture of the Jumping Universe*. London: Academy Editions, 1995.

Lovejoy, Margot. *Postmodern Currents: Art and Artists in the Age of Electronic Media*. Upper Saddle River, N.J.: Prentice Hall, 1997.

Morse, Margaret. *Virtualities: Television, Media Art, and Cyberculture*. Bloomington, Ind.: Indiana University Press, 1998.

Rush, Michael, *New Media in Late 20th Century Art*. London: Thames and Hudson, 1999.

Shaw, Jeffrey and P. Weibel, eds. *Future Cinema: The Cinematic Imaginary after Film*. Cambridge, Mass.: MIT Press, 2003.

Taylor, Brandon. *Contemporary Art*. Upper Saddle River, N.J.: Prentice Hall, 2004.

CREDITS

CHAPTER 32

READING 6.1 (p. 4): Ezra Pound, "In a Station of the Metro" and "The Bathtub" from *Personae*, copyright 1926 by Ezra Pound. Reprinted by permission of New Directions Publishing Corporation.

READING 6.2 (p. 5) Robert Frost, "The Road Not Taken" from *The Poetry of Robert Frost*, edited by Edward Connery Lathem (Jonathan Cape, 1969), copyright 1944 by Robert Frost, © 1916, 1969 by Henry Holt & Company, LLC. Reprinted by permission of Henry Holt & Co., LLC.

CHAPTER 33

READING 6.3 (p. 27): From Sigmund Freud, *Civilization and Its Discontents*, translated by James Strachey (W.W. Norton, 1989), © 1961 by James Strachey, renewed 1989 by Alix Strachey. Reprinted by permission of W. W. Norton & Company Inc and The Random House Group Ltd.

READING 6.4 (p. 30): From Marcel Proust, *Swann's Way* in *Remembrance of Things Past*, translated by C.K. Scott Moncrieff (Chatto & Windus, 1981), translation © 1981 by Random House Inc. and Chatto & Windus. Reprinted by permission of the Estate of Marcel Proust and The Random House Group Ltd.

READING 6.5 (p. 32): From Franz Kafka, "The Metamorphosis" in *The Basic Kafka* (Washington Square Press/Schocken Books, 1979).

READING 6.6 (p. 34): E. E. Cummings, [she being Brand] from *Complete Poems, 1904-1962*, edited by George J. Firmage (Liveright Publishing, 1994), copyright 1926, 1954, © 1991 by the Trustees for the E. E. Cummings Trust, © 1985 by George James Firmage. Reprinted by permission of the publisher.

CHAPTER 34

READING 6.7 (p. 51): W. B. Yeats, "The Second Coming" from *Collected Poems* (Picador, 1990). Reprinted by permission of A. P. Watt Ltd on behalf of Michael B. Yeats.

READING 6.8 (p. 52): From Erich Maria Remarque, *All Quiet on the Western Front*, © 1929, 1930 by Little Brown & Company; © renewed 1957, 1958 by Erich Maria Remarque. Reprinted by permission of Pryor Cashman Sherman & Flynn LLP on behalf of the Estate of the late Erich Maria Remarque.

READING 6.9 (p. 61): Randall Jarrell, "The Death of the Ball Turret Gunner" from *The Complete Poems* (Farrar, Straus & Giroux, 1969), © 1969, renewed 1997 by Mary von S. Jarrell. Reprinted by permission of the publisher; Kato Shuson, three haiku from *Modern Japanese Literature: An Anthology*, edited by Donald Keene, © 1956 by Grove Press Inc. Reprinted by permission of Grove/Atlantic Inc.

READING 6.10 (p. 64): From Elie Wiesel, *Night*, translated by Stella Rodway, © 1960 by MacGibbon & Kee; © renewed 1988 by The Collins Publishing Group. Reprinted by permission of Farrar, Straus & Giroux Inc.

CHAPTER 35

READING 6.11 (p. 70): From Jean Paul Sartre, "Existentialism", translated by Bernard Frechtman (Philosophical Library, 1947), © Editions Gallimard, 1996. Reprinted by permission of Editions Gallimard and Philosophical Library.

READING 6.12 (p. 73): From Samuel Beckett, *Waiting for Godot*, © 1954 by Grove Press; © renewed 1982 by Samuel Beckett. Reprinted by permission of Grove/Atlantic Inc.

READING 6.13 (p. 75): T. S. Eliot, "The Love Song of J. Alfred Prufrock" from *Collected Poems 1909-1962* (Faber & Faber, 1963), © this edition by T. S. Eliot 1963. Reprinted by permission of the publisher.

READING 6.14 (p. 77): Dylan Thomas, "Do Not Go Gentle Into That Good Night" from *Collected Poems, 1934-1952* (Dent, 1989), © 1952 by Dylan Thomas. Reprinted by permission of David Higham Associates and New Directions Publishing Corporation.

READING 6.16 (p. 78): Iqbal, "Revolution" and "Europe and Syria" from *Poems from Iqbal*, translated by V. Kiernan (John Murray, 1955). Reprinted by permission of the publisher.

CHAPTER 36

READING 6.17 (p. 94): Pablo Neruda, "United Fruit Co." from *Five Decades: Poems 1925-1970*, translated by Ben Belitt, © 1974 by Ben Belitt. Reprinted by permission of Grove/Atlantic Inc.

READING 6.18 (p. 95): Langston Hughes, "Theme for English B" and "Dream Deferred" ('Harlem') from *Collected Poems* (Knopf, 1994), © 1994 by the Estate of Langston Hughes. Reprinted by permission of Alfred A. Knopf, a Division of Random House Inc; Gwendolyn Brooks, "The Mother" and "We Real Cool" from *Blacks* (Third World Press, 1991).

READING 6.19 (p. 97): From Richard Wright, "The Ethics of Living Jim Crow" in *Uncle Tom's Children* (Harper & Row, 1937), © 1937 by Richard Wright, © renewed 1965 by Ellen Wright. Reprinted by permission of HarperCollins Publishers Inc.

READING 6.20 (p. 99): Martin Luther King, from *Letter from Birmingham Jail*, © 1963 Martin Luther King Jr., renewed 1991 by Coretta Scott King. Reprinted by arrangement with The Heirs to the Estate of Martin Luther King, Jr., c/o Writers House Inc as agent for the proprietor.

READING 6.21 (p. 101): From Malcolm X, *Malcolm X Speaks* (Pathfinder Press, 1965), © 1965, 1989 by Betty Shabazz and Pathfinder Press. Reprinted by permission of the publisher. (p.103) Bloke Modisane, "it gets awful lonely" from *Poems from Black Africa*, edited by Langston Hughes (Indiana University Press, 1963).

READING 6.22 (p. 102): From Ralph Ellison, "The Prologue" in *Invisible Man*, © 1952 by Ralph Ellison. Reprinted by permission of Random House, Inc.

READING 6.23 (p. 103): Alice Walker, "Elethia" from *You Can't Keep a Good Woman Down: Short Stories*, © 1979 by Alice Walker. Reprinted by permission of Harcourt Brace & Company.

READING 6.24 (p. 110): From Virginia Woolf, "A Room of One's Own" (L & V Woolf, 1929), © 1929 by Harcourt Brace Jovanovich Inc., renewed 1957 by Leonard Woolf. Reprinted by permission of Harcourt Inc and the Society of Authors as the Literary Representative of the Estate of Virginia Woolf.

Index